DEMOCRATIZING HIGHER EDUCATION

Higher education systems around the world are undergoing fundamental change and reform due to external pressures—including internationalization of higher education, increased international competition for students, less reliance on public funding, and calls to create greater access opportunities for citizens. How are higher education systems evolving structurally as a result of these and other pressures? In light of these changes, how can higher education be a positive force for democratizing societies?

This book examines the emerging trends taking place in higher education systems around the world, focusing on the most salient political and social forces that underlie these trends. Each chapter provides a case study of a country, exploring its cultural and political history, the political and social developments that have affected its higher education system, and the result of these changes on the higher education system. In a fast-changing, knowledge-intensive, democratic society, *Democratizing Higher Education* explores how higher education systems can be developed to provide access, affordability, participation, and quality lifelong learning for all.

Patrick Blessinger is the founder and Executive Director of the International Higher Education Teaching and Learning Association (HETL) and a lecturer, author, and researcher in education.

John P. Anchan is Professor and Associate Dean of the Faculty of Education at the University of Winnipeg, Canada. He is President of the International Higher Education Teaching and Learning Association (HETL).

DEMOCRATIZING HIGHER EDUCATION

International Comparative Perspectives

Edited by Patrick Blessinger and John P. Anchan

Routledge
Taylor & Francis Group

NEW YORK AND LONDON

First published 2015
by Routledge
711 Third Avenue, New York, NY 10017

and by Routledge
2 Park Square, Milton Park, Abingdon, Oxon, OX14 4RN

Routledge is an imprint of the Taylor & Francis Group, an informa business

© 2015 Taylor & Francis

Library of Congress Cataloging in Publication Data
Democratizing higher education : international comparative perspectives / edited by Patrick Blessinger and John P. Anchan.
    pages cm
    Includes bibliographical references and index.
    1. Education, Higher—Aims and objectives—Cross-cultural studies.
    2. Democracy and education—Cross-cultural studies.   3. Educational equalization—Cross-cultural studies.   4. Higher education and state—Cross-cultural studies.   I. Blessinger, Patrick, editor of compilation.   II. Anchan, John P., editor of compilation.
    LC213.D45 2015
    378.01—dc23
                                                                    2014038932

ISBN: 978-1-138-02094-8 (hbk)
ISBN: 978-1-138-02095-5 (pbk)
ISBN: 978-1-315-77813-6 (ebk)

Typeset in Bembo
by Keystroke, Station Road, Codsall, Wolverhampton

Dedication

This book is dedicated to educators all over the world and to the members of the International Higher Education Teaching and Learning Association (HETL) whose passion for teaching, learning, research, and service are helping to transform the academy in many positive ways.

Vision, Mission, and Values Statement

The long-term vision of HETL is to improve educational outcomes in higher education by creating new knowledge and advancing the scholarship and practice of teaching and learning.

To bring that vision to reality, the present mission of HETL is to develop a global community of higher education professionals who come together to share their knowledge and expertise in teaching and learning.

To effectively fulfill that mission, HETL adheres to the values of academic integrity, collegiality, and diversity. As such, HETL supports academic and pedagogical pluralism, diversity of learning, as well as practices that promote sustainable learning and peace.

Membership, Conference, Publishing, and Research Information

For information about HETL, please see www.hetl.org

Patrick Blessinger
Founder & Executive Director
The HETL Association
patrickblessinger@gmail.com

John P. Anchan
President, 2013–2015
The HETL Association
j.anchan@uwinnipeg.ca

CONTENTS

FOREWORD

The editors of this informative book have provided readers with a stimulating introduction to its contents, so I will not offer a summary here. Instead, I will suggest some questions that should be kept in mind as reading progresses.

Are there conflicts between the two related purposes of education stated here? One is to develop the personal agency of the individuals being educated; the second is to promote the growth and stability of democracy globally by democratizing education. Few of us would argue against either of these aims. But there are worrisome signs. In the United States, for example, the traditional purpose of higher education, to produce better individuals—"better" defined in moral, civic, and intellectual terms—has been overshadowed by economic interests and purposes. Many young people think that the primary reason for obtaining a college degree is to get a well-paying job, and at the national level, we continually emphasize the need for better educated workers in order to maintain our country's economic superiority. If this is a world-wide trend—watch for it as you read—we may be impeding progress toward global democratization. On the one hand, we seek global cooperation through democratization; on the other, we seek economic superiority through successful competition. This is not so much a conflict between the two great aims as it is a neglect of the first; perhaps we are not giving enough attention to the fundamental moral purpose underlying the aim to develop personal agency.

Consider another closely related issue. The democratization of higher education implies greater accessibility, greater participation drawn from the full range of racial, ethnic, and economic classes. Some powerful critics, while harboring no bias against any cultural group, express a fear that the quality of education will suffer—is already suffering—as a result of admitting many students who are not qualified for college. Among other concerns, they point to a proliferation of courses that they believe are intellectually inferior. Many deplore the increasing decline of interest in the liberal arts as more and more students undertake higher education for economic reasons. Should this be a widespread concern? If so, can it be remedied? What is the role of K-12 education in reducing this worry?

The rapid increase in technology also raises questions for higher education. The chapter writers tell us a lot about innovative modes of instruction and assessment that employ technology. But, if we use technology extensively as a teaching tool, might we lose what many of us consider to be the foundation of education—a strong relationship of care and trust between teachers and students? The aim, for wise educators, should be to find balance.

The use of technology also gives rise to financial concerns. Institutions of higher education all over the world seem to be experiencing financial problems. Greater use of technology might reduce the cost of instruction, but the continual demand for new instrumentation and personnel to supervise and maintain it might increase costs. It is widely agreed that careful analysis and deliberation on the matter are necessary, but we should also be aware that a concentration on financial matters might distract us further from reflective dialogue on educational philosophy—in particular on the moral and civic purposes of higher education.

Although there are many problems to consider as we move to a more inclusive organization of higher education, readers of this book will be heartened by the growing dedication to the democratization of higher education. Better education not only increases the life-opportunities for many more individuals, but it should—when properly defined—also contribute to the quest for global cooperation and intercultural understanding. A well-educated citizenry should be well-informed and better able to exercise the critical thinking required in an increasingly complex world. This book points us in the right direction.

Nel Noddings
Lee Jacks Professor of Education, Emerita
Stanford University

PREFACE

Patrick Blessinger and John P. Anchan

The Book

Higher education systems around the world are undergoing fundamental change and reform due to common pressures, such as the internationalization of higher education, increased international competition for students, increased pressure to become more self-sustaining financially, and calls for greater access opportunities for all citizens. Within this call for widening participation, movements such as open education, open learning, and open educational resources may be viewed as part of the wider movement to democratize higher education (Kramer, 2014). The global demand for tertiary education is at an all-time high and will continue to expand. It is predicted that by 2025 there will be over 262 million tertiary students worldwide, a dramatic increase from the 97 million level in 2000 (UNESCO, 2009). Within this context, this book examines how higher education systems are changing structurally and how international sociopolitical struggles and governmental policy reforms are helping to shape emerging higher education systems around the world (Altbach, Gumport, & Berdahl, 2011; Burke, 2012; DeMillo, 2011; Kezar, 2014; Kovbasyuk & Blessinger, 2013; Palfreyman & Tapper, 2009; Polyzoi, Fullan, & Anchan, 2003; Trow & Burrage, 2010).

Purpose

The main purpose of this book is to provide higher education professionals with an overview of the emerging changes taking place in higher education systems around the world. The book will focus on the most salient forces that drive these changes. It provides a wide-ranging body of empirical evidence to show how sociopolitical forces have had a democratizing effect on higher education over the last century. For the purposes of this book, we intentionally use a broad definition of higher education as any formal education received beyond high school from an institution of higher education that is recognized as such, by the state or state sanctioned accreditation organization. Each chapter therefore focuses on a different higher education national or regional system around the world in an attempt to address the following questions: What are the broad forces/pressures impacting higher education? What are the major trends and structural changes occurring as a result of these forces/pressures? How can we best interpret this process of change and the developing trends from a sociopolitical lens?

Structure

The major premise of the book is that the main underlying forces and mechanisms driving change in higher education appear to be fundamentally sociopolitical in nature (e.g. government policy reforms, growing global demand for higher education). Within the last few years, we have also seen an explosion of new technologies (e.g. open educational resources, massive open online courses, online universities) and new economic models (e.g. market-driven proprietary universities) that have helped to open access to higher education to anyone in society who wants to avail her/himself of such services. Many scholars and academics could not have imagined, even a generation ago, how fast these new technologies and new economic models would be developed and how they have helped address the pent-up latent demand for higher education.

In addition to traditional public and private universities, we now have many online universities and community colleges and university distance education programs that allow whole new segments of society to attend higher education. In the US for instance, nearly half of all undergraduate higher education students are now enrolled in the community college system (Community College Research Center, n.d.). Thus, an exclusive focus on the research university would not sufficiently address the increasing diversity of the higher education space and a sole emphasis on technology or economics would not sufficiently explain the increasing expansion of higher education. Each chapter in this collection is presented as a case study of a representative country and includes empirical evidence to support the book's main thesis.

Aims

The book editors have analyzed the findings presented in the chapters to identify the major emerging themes occurring in higher education around the world and they discuss their findings in the introductory and concluding chapters. The authors provide their unique perspectives based on their own interpretations of the research they have conducted and based on their unique disciplinary lens to arrive at particular understandings of the emerging patterns occurring in higher education development in their respective countries. This book is therefore intentionally multi-disciplinary, interdisciplinary, and international as we try to develop a more integrated understanding of the process of change occurring in higher education around the world. It is one of the responsibilities of the volume editors to provide to the authors a common framework (i.e. the major questions to be addressed) within which to present their findings.

With respect to the common framework for the book, the chapter authors focus on the most salient features (e.g. accessibility, affordability, meaningfulness, quality, lifelong learning) germane to higher education in their countries. This book explores the linkages between higher education diversification, affordability, accessibility, participation, and quality and democracy. The case studies also explore imaginative scenarios and visions of future democratic possibilities (e.g. around lifelong learning and meaningful learning) for higher education. In attempting to address these questions and contexts, the chapters also examine other questions such as: Are different and competing educational models compatible? Can or should competing self-interests and models be reconciled or harmonized? How can new measures of academic achievement such as meaningful learning, creative learning, and authentic assessment be reflected in higher education?

Chapter Overviews

John Anchan reviews the historical development of higher education over the centuries, thus providing the broader context through which to view higher education. Anchan explains how everything we do as educators has international implications and that the world is no more just a collection of separate nations and our decisions impact on people living elsewhere. Anchan reminds us that we need to ask ourselves a fundamental question: What exactly do we expect from education?

Linda Watts raises the notion of education for critical thinking. Education is more than just training toward specific job skills; it is an endeavor to becoming an effective citizen by learning to reason, dialogue, and engage in critical thinking, which involves the development of a learner who can contribute to the building of a stronger democracy. Education is about creating spaces of discomfort that challenge students—goading them into critical thinking and meaningful praxis.

Arshad Ahmad and Lori Goff highlight the fact that education in Canada remains a provincial jurisdiction. The authors raise an important point on the evolution of higher education—from teaching to more research, liberal education to skills-based, and traditional to systems-based on emerging technologies reflecting new demands. However, the meaning of innovation differs between educators in liberal arts and training specialists in corporate or business models. The authors highlight the need for stronger professional development for teaching faculty.

As an introduction to the European context, María Luisa Pérez Cañado provides a good overview of the Bologna initiative. This is quite refreshing and helpful in tracing the trajectory and providing a frame of reference to the individual case studies throughout the book. Though specific to the European context, many of the concerns, strategies, and reactions are similar to some of the developments in other countries.

Portugal, like most other case studies, exhibits the same historical trajectory of higher education catering to the elite but gradually evolving to become more accessible and affordable. As Luísa Soares and Catarina Faria explicate, these processes are work in progress and will continue to develop in response to the demands placed upon them. Systemic changes are core to structural constraints and remain resilient to dramatic movements. Portugal is not immune to the same financial pressures that plague other countries.

As Craig Mahoney and Helena Lim note, the UK has seen some degree of devolution as centralized responsibilities for higher education are ported on to regions that assume the responsibility for the sustainability of the system. The UK has also evolved from an elitist and exclusivist privileged system to a more egalitarian system and the UK has been a pioneer in the concept of open education. The UK is also experiencing the global phenomenon of more mature students entering the post-secondary institutions. The UK reflects the ongoing discourse surrounding access and equity relative to the democratization of higher education at the global level.

Jørgen Nielsen and Lars Andreasen describe Scandinavian countries reassessing their educational models. Higher education in the Scandinavian countries has common historical trends, in that the development compares with the changes in the rest of the world. They all tend to have similar origins, common restraints, familiar constraints, and comparable evolutionary paths. There appears to be an inherent attempt to move from a socialist perspective to a meritocratic model. Nevertheless, considering the histories of these countries, a combination of these two approaches appears to be developing.

Lorraine Stefani discusses the history of New Zealand's education system. The history of New Zealand paints a very disconcerting, and yet familiar scene from the pages of history of aboriginal peoples in Canada and the US, for instance. The disparity, disconnect, and disillusionment are common strands that have a striking similarity to the concerns of autochthonous peoples in postcolonial narratives. This is especially poignant in analyzing education for democratization. Stability, access, excellence, sustainability, student attrition and retention rates, global economy, and educational attainment for the local residents all appear to be the same concerns plaguing the rest of the world. Stefani presents a number of promising possibilities to address inequalities—a true democratization theme.

Mandla Makhanya and Jeanette Botha present the complexities that emphasize the usual post-secondary challenges around the world but within the context of a post-apartheid country. The disparity and disconnect become more accentuated in a country that has suffered systemic historical grievances plagued by racism, inequality, and injustice. As the authors aptly note, a system "that was deeply divided and fragmented, isolated" had become an historical legacy that had to overcome an entrenched and diverse culture. Nevertheless, South Africa has moved on to face the challenges and embark on a restructuring of education and beyond.

Natalia Moscvina and Olga Kovbasyuk raise an interesting dilemma and, perhaps, a paradoxical truism as they explore the contradictions between an inherited, national, culturally relevant system versus a more global perspective to adopting an acceptable educational system that works for all. These tensions are ubiquitous to any nation and tend to be more problematic when the legacy of a country indicates disruptive histories. Yet, as they suggest, a contextual and situational approach to contemporary needs might be a reasonable compromise.

As Hei-hang Hayes Tang describes, the Hong Kong situation is quite unique, in that it has had to transition from a postcolonial nation to a modern state under China. With such a unique cultural and political heritage, Hong Kong has adopted various models of higher education institutions. As always and elsewhere, the ongoing tensions are quite familiar with the ideals of a higher calling in education versus the pressing needs of the individual and the State. Amidst this tension lies the notion of a democratic enterprise.

India is another postcolonial country with ancient history tied to entrenched systemic cultural nuances. As is the case with most postcolonial contexts, an enduring strain exists between the evolving society and the historical legacies. Arputharaj Devaraj highlights the need for change toward democratization—in essence, exploring the nature of an educational system tied to histories and cultural diversity, adapting to become a successful global player. With its federal influence over higher education and many variations of higher education models across the country, India has an entrepreneurial approach to the educational enterprise.

Enakshi Sengupta's case study again ties in with the postcolonial legacies of the developing countries. Not unlike the Indian context, Malaysia is another postcolonial country with diverse histories. In many developing countries, the emphasis has been education for employment. The common strand seems to be the triad—nationalization, economic growth, and citizenship. As with most other countries, Malaysia cannot ignore the realities of internationalization in a global economy. Once again, the system has to contend with similar concerns faced by other countries—access, equity, excellence, and sustainability.

In the penultimate chapter, Patrick Blessinger proposes a democratic theory of higher education that maintains that the ultimate purpose of higher education is to promote personal agency through the development of freedom and responsibility. This notion implies that opportunities to learn should be equal. Blessinger emphasizes that this aim can only be achieved by moving from a mindset of exclusivity, which tends to be oriented around power and privilege claims, and toward a mindset of inclusivity, which is oriented around fairness and self-determination claims. Thus, democratizing higher education involves a higher education system based on a vision of higher education that is inclusive, participatory, representative, transformative, meaningful, and rooted in practices of shared ethical values and an ethos of political, social, and economic justice.

Conclusion

This book represents an increasing interest in how higher education is changing, the trends and mechanisms underlying these changes, and what higher education may emerge into in the coming decades (i.e. future possibilities) given its current trajectory. However, there is no assumption that disparate educational systems will eventually converge around a single model—nor should they. The chapters investigate the extent to which democratic ideals such as diversity, inclusiveness, equality, and pluralism are reflected in higher education and how these underlying ideals are helping to shape the higher education landscape.

We hope that this compilation will be useful to faculty and students in schools of education who are interested in the future direction of higher education and to those who are preparing to become teaching faculty or administrators in institutions of higher education. This body of work may also provide other higher education policymakers and leaders (e.g. government, NGOs, accreditation bodies) who do not work directly within higher education institutions but whose decisions impact higher education, with insight into emerging trends in international higher education. As such, this collection is intended to serve as a meaningful resource to anyone who is interested in or cares about the future direction of higher education.

References

Altbach, P.G., Gumport, P.J., & Berdahl, R.O. (2011). *American Higher Education in the Twenty-First Century: Social, Political, and Economic Challenges.* Baltimore, MD: The Johns Hopkins University Press.

Burke, P.J. (2012). *The Right to Higher Education: Beyond Widening Participation.* Abingdon: Routledge.

DeMillo, R.A. (2011). *Abelard to Apple: The Fate of American Colleges and Universities.* Cambridge, MA: The MIT Press.

Kezar, A. (2014). *How Colleges Change: Understanding, Leading, and Enacting Change.* New York: Routledge.

Kovbasyuk, O. & Blessinger, P. (2013). *Meaning-Centered Education: International Perspectives and Explorations in Higher Education.* New York: Routledge.

Kramer, L. (2014, February 25). The Role, Development, Expansion, and Importance of Open Education Resources: An HETL Interview with Larry Kramer. *The International HETL Review.* Vol. 4, Article 2. Retrieved from www.hetl.org/interview-articles/the-role-development-expansion-and-importance-of-open-education-resources-an-hetl-interview-with-larry-kramer

Palfreyman, D. & Tapper, T. (2009). *Structuring Mass Higher Education: The Role of Elite Institutions.* New York: Routledge.

Polyzoi, E., Fullan, M., & Anchan, J.P. (2003). *Change Forces in Post-Communist Eastern Europe: Education in Transition.* New York: RoutledgeFalmer.

Trow, M. & Burrage, M. (2010). *Twentieth-Century Higher Education: Elite to Mass to Universal.* Baltimore, MD: The Johns Hopkins University Press.

UNESCO. (2009). *Global Education Digest 2007: Comparing Education Statistics Across the World.* Montreal: UNESCO Institute of Statistics.

1

AN INTRODUCTION TO DEMOCRATIZING HIGHER EDUCATION

John P. Anchan

Preamble

The term *Higher Education* may carry distinct meanings to different readers. This discourse (and the chapters in this book) will imply "education beyond the k-12" system. There are many works on the history of higher education—even writings about early Greek and Roman education such as Clarke's 2012 *Higher Education in the Ancient World*. The intent of this discussion is not to track or create a compendium of the development of higher education around the world. Available contributions provide excellent records describing the meanings, history, evolution, application, and current issues surrounding higher education. This exposition aims to contribute to the ongoing dialectic on contemporary issues relating to higher education in selected sample countries. While comparing systems across countries can create its own limitations and cautionary tales, a global village (*thank you*, Marshall McLuhan) challenges us to think beyond the traditional borders of nation states. We are global and indeed, everything we now do has some international consequence. With international migration, an increase in global travel, interconnected manufacturing and distribution/consumption systems, interrelated political systems, and shared natural resources and calamities, the world is no more a collection of nations. We are truly connected and our decisions will have an impact on people living elsewhere and what happens elsewhere affects us all.

The terms *post-secondary education*, *higher education*, *tertiary education*, and *third-level education* are sometimes used interchangeably but may carry slightly different meanings in different countries. In some countries, tertiary education, post-secondary education, or third-level education normally refers to any formal education beyond high school and may include higher education and further/ continuing education. In other countries, higher education is not included in further/continuing education or, in fact, may indicate any education that does not lead to a degree from an accredited institution. This discourse uses the UNESCO (1998) definition of higher education that includes, "all types of studies, training or training for research at the post-secondary level, provided by universities or other educational establishments that are approved as institutions of higher education by the competent State authorities" (n.p.).

A Quick Backdrop

Education has existed from pre-recorded history throughout ancient civilizations around the world in different forms. For example, the Chinese Confucianism existed in 124 BC and the Qing dynasty from 200 BC; similarly, the Japanese education in the early 6th century was mostly influenced by the Chinese system. The diverse countries on the African continent evolved within their own unique histories with oral histories giving way to written histories and concurrently, various forms of education systems developing across the large continent.[1] Egypt had its own system of education and so did the Middle East with its scribal schools. Ancient Israel had its Torah schools. The more popularly known ancient Greek education in the 5th century BC aimed at democratization. With the familiar Plato and other influential pioneers, education in Greece was more ideological and relatively less religious. By the 4th century BC, Rome had its elitist educational institutions in place. In India, from the 12–13th centuries, the ancient Vedic Temple schools were followed by the residential *Gurukula* system. Chinese Buddhist scholars in India had a great influence on the Indian system, which was then succeeded by the Pre-Mughal rulers with the Islamic *Madrassas*. Many of the early forms of educational initiatives can be closely linked to religious training (e.g. Catholicism, Islam, Buddhism, Hinduism, etc.). In most instances, these were predominantly elitist, private, and exclusive teacher-student learning endeavors. The interaction inherently involved the master transmitting knowledge to the students. The precursor to the current educational institutions as teaching and research bodies can be traced back to the archetypical learning situations. In fact, the research university's roots can be followed back to the founding of the University of Bologna in 1088. By the 19th and 20th centuries, the Humboldtian German model of higher education, with its emphasis on academic freedom, scientific inquiry and research, knowledge creation, and specialization, became the de facto model for most modern universities. The research university model has its historical roots in the German ideal of education for self-cultivation (Bildung). The parallel development of liberal arts colleges with their focus on exposure to multiple disciplines (e.g. the classics, humanities, math, and science) focused on the development of well-rounded students through the enlargement of general intellectual capacity. This model has it historical roots in the English ideal of liberal education. Whereas the research university model has traditionally focused on faculty research and producing students as specialists, the liberal arts college model emphasized faculty teaching and producing students as generalists.

The idea of Bildung was based on the notion of self-cultivation through the harmonization and transformation of the mind, heart, and personality, and the development of personal agency along with self-identity. In short, this idea entailed a process of becoming a more self-regulating and self-determining individual with life-long development and empowerment. The idea of Bildung was greatly influenced by the writings of Hegel, a contemporary of Humboldt (Bruford, 1975; Hegel, 1977). The English idea of liberal education is oriented around the cultivation of the individual but also focuses on education as personal empowerment through the development of broad intellectual capacity and transferable skills (Hoerner, 1970). In addition to this historical perspective, Kovbasyuk and Blessinger (2013) have reviewed the two major epistemological paradigms that dominated educational thought over the centuries.

The Research University

Until recent history, the research university and the liberal arts college have been the two dominant models of higher education. Broadly speaking, and as a result of their historical developments, research universities have been mainly faculty-centered institutions focusing on research and publishing, whereas liberal arts colleges have been mainly student-centered institutions emphasizing under-graduate teaching. However, in today's higher education landscape, a great deal of cross-pollination has occurred and there are elements of many traditions—ancient and modern—in higher education institutions from around the world. These interactions can be viewed as a positive development. The higher education landscape is now dotted with several different types of institutions (e.g. business colleges, community colleges, vocational colleges, non-research proprietary universities). It is interesting to note that in the USA, for instance, more students attend community colleges rather than research universities.

Yet, for much of society, higher education has been shrouded in mystery and governed by a labyrinth of rules and customs that have been handed down from previous generations of educational institutions. Despite many changes within higher education, these institutions around the world still follow arcane rituals, traditions, and rites of passage that reflect their historical legacies. For most of their 800-year history, European universities have been medieval and monastic in character, reflective of their early religious roots. These customs and rites (e.g. as a passage from youth to adulthood and as a passage from novice to expert) are so embedded in the university life that many historical artifacts still remain with us today (e.g. the donning of robes and hoods and the use of other regalia at graduation). For the general public, all this symbolism can mask the true inner workings of a higher education institution. In spite of these historical vestiges, today's higher education institutions are also very bureaucratic organizations and many have grown into massive multimillion and multibillion dollar enterprises that must operate in an increasingly competitive higher education landscape and within a complex nexus of government regulations and constituent interests. The changing demographics of the student population together with increased calls for reforms to modernize higher education institutions have put additional pressures on educators to institute such changes (DeMillo, 2011).

Higher Education and Globalization

The history of higher education is hardly limited to the growth and development of educational institutions. It is a complex and highly interrelated set of events and movements that connect to the cultural and political histories, social developments, civil rights, and the overall evolution of the nations themselves.[2] Thus, post-colonial legacies, diversity and equality, industrial revolution, the role of the church and state, and the individual trajectories of nation states define the nature of higher education in general. A corollary but important focus of discussion is the role of national and global competition in higher education that has resulted in what Marginson (2006) calls "positional goods" that allow major world players from mostly English-speaking countries to compete for research and teaching stature—which in turn affect student recruitment and the institutional prestige (see Altbach and Knight, 2007, for an excellent explication on this topic). The internationalization of higher education has grown dramatically and for various reasons. Increasingly, a number of sources publish world rankings of educational institutions, e.g. Times Higher Education World University Rankings, the QS World University Rankings, CWCU of Shanghai Ranking, and The Global Higher Education Rankings 2010. This obsession with world rankings of dramatically different institutions with diverse histories, differing challenges, and disparate resources has further raised questions on the metrics of such comparisons.

There is a rich source of academic record of the history of the American higher education—especially focusing on the development of American colleges and universities. These detailed discourses explore the development of higher education in relation to politics, post-colonial institutions, gender, immigration, religion, and Land Acts (Goodchild & Harold, 1997; Lucas, 2006; Thelin, 1976). Similarly, the Canadian context appears familiar and yet unique, with many variations across provinces, with education being a provincial jurisdiction (Dunning, 1997; Harrigan, 1986; Harris, 1976; Sheehan, 1985; Skolnik & Jones, 1991). In the past, there have been sincere attempts to analyze the evolution of higher education in Australia, Canada, Europe, and other parts of the world (Lee & Knight, 1996; de Wit, 1995).

Technology and Higher Education

This overview would be deficient without briefly mentioning by far the most important factor impacting the learning environment and the educational academies at all levels—emerging technologies. Like any technology, academic technologies are promising, in that they can enhance the learning environment. The latest buzzword has been the MOOC (Massive Open Online Course): a system that can provide the space and access to affordable learning. Despite the inundation of literature holding us hostage to the MOOC-lingo, the debate will eventually subside and one or more forms will become the favored delivery method. Though quite premature, MOOCs will undergo adaptations that can further assist in enhancing the learning process. Currently, blended or hybrid approaches can allow educators to experiment with what works for a given situation. Learning is contextual and hence one cannot suggest that any single system would work for all. These are not universal panacea for pedagogical practices, but rather cautious opportunities for adopting emerging technologies to enrich the learning processes. MOOCs and other such technologies will exist in various formats and provide multifarious learning opportunities. Importantly, these technologies will address the needs of a specific population of learners in defined situations. Nevertheless, in the hands of entrepreneurial advocates, a promising tool could turn into a constraining instrument. One such area is the management of institutions by administrators tasked with the sustainability of the establishment. An unfortunate trend has risen with increasingly more administrators (e.g. Bowen, 2013) beginning to adopt arguments for using MOOCs as a means to an end in cost-cutting measures—tending to present approaches under the guise of pragmatic solutions to fiscal challenges.

The MOOC conundrum is only one of many other such technological concerns worrying well-intentioned educators. With the dramatic development of the internet, along with rapid growth of the social networking service (SNS), the process of education itself has undergone a big shift. From individual SNS clients (Facebook, Skype, LinkedIn, YouTube, Google+, Twitter, etc.) to larger networks and cloud systems (Dropbox, Box, Mega, iCloud, Google Drive, SkyDrive, Tresorit, etc.), the landscape has experienced a radical change. Academic technologies, including eBooks, Learning Management Systems (LMS) (BlackBoard, BB Collaborate, D2L, Angel, Moodle, Sakai, etc.), along with telepresence and various emerging tablet and other mobile technologies (iOS devices—iPad, iPhone, iPods; Android devices; Windows mobile; BlackBerry QNX Neutrino, and Symbian systems), the academic enterprise has dramatically changed on-campus and online learning systems in both the developed and developing world. Along with the newer technologies arise unexpected but important issues such as intellectual property, confidentiality, security, stability, and sustainability.

This is by no means an attempt to list all the available technologies; it is a quick attempt to highlight the amazing changes that have engulfed us—changes we could not have imagined or predicted even a few years ago. Tablets, laptops, smartphones, and communication systems in classrooms have become ubiquitous and in some cases, even mandatory. While some are more positive and optimistic about technology's role in education (Palfrey & Gasser, 2008; Tapscott, 2009, 1998, 1996, 1993; Turkle, 2012, 1995, 1984), a growing cadre of critics (Bauerlein, 2009;

Carr, 2009, 2010; Cuban, 2001; Postman, 1993; Roszak, 1986; Stoll, 1995, etc.) are less enamored by such claims. Despite taking a moment to acknowledge the impact of these major influences on higher education, due to space it is beyond the scope of this discussion. After all, it is irrefutable that these are tools and the teachers using the tools will influence the quality of such experiences. Tools on their own can do nothing. The pedagogical practice influences the process and the outcome. As Eleanor Doan rightly said, "Good tools do not make a good teacher, but a good teacher makes good use of tools."

The Overarching Goals of Higher Education

One cannot talk about the role and changes in higher education without the goals and critiques of such ventures. One of the main themes of any education is *reform*. In fact, many aspiring learners and their families, especially in the developing countries, view higher education as a prerequisite for change. Literacy, in particular, and education, in general, remain the cornerstones of societal change. The education of women tends to confirm that it plays an important role in the overall betterment of a society. Education is considered as a tool for change. Factors such as mortality rates, health, human rights, democracy, employability, and the quality of life are all directly attributed to education. Larry Kramer, the current president of The William and Flora Hewlett Foundation, aptly connects higher education with educational reform:

> Education is the foundation on which everything else rests: our economy, our democracy, our cultural heritage, our future. To accomplish anything as a society, whether that be protecting the environment or addressing inequality, we need an educated, literate citizenry that can reason analytically, grasp scientific principles, and work collaboratively to solve the big problems that confront us.
>
> *Kramer, 2014*

For many educators, higher education implies quality, excellence, access, equity, growth, commitment, sustainability, and overall development. With such altruistic ideals and a heritage of noble intentions, the evolving nature of higher education and the increasing role of for-profit training institutions have raised the ire of many educators. On a more cautious note, critics have questioned the relationship of corporations with post-secondary institutions. Bok (2003) has raised a number of concerns about commercialization of higher education. As a critique of the current trend in universities, he emphasizes preserving the educational values and not succumbing to the corporate agenda. When profits become the "bottom line" and efficiency and measurable outcomes become buzz words, true educational values such as neutrality and "integrity of research" tend to be devalued and ignored.

The overall goal of education becomes the overarching question. David Noble (2011) has remained a strong critic of the current "digital diploma mills," in that the "automation" of higher education has become a hierarchical top-down, administrator-driven agenda with the intent to commoditize research and teaching. According to Noble, the "high tech remedies" are misconstrued and he questions the desperate attempts to solve diverse issues and challenges in contemporary higher education institutions. This is further complicated when we consider the increasing role of information and communication technology (ICT) in education. It is easy to see why many educators become disillusioned with the onerous Sisyphean task of reforming the entrenched education system.

Theoretical Framing

In exploring the sociopolitical struggles, tensions, and competing ideas and values, we have to consider the factors that have influenced the structure of higher education historically and to date. This discourse also explores a vision of education where people freely engage in life-long and life-wide learning, and where higher education works for all. People around the world continue to demand access to meaningful, high-quality education because they see higher education as one of the primary means to improve the quality of their lives. Higher education increases possibilities for greater political and social participation as well as greater self-determination and personal development. Policymakers in many countries also see higher education as a promising means to drive economic development and innovation. In order to achieve these aims a new vision of higher education is required where its purposes are manifold and where higher education is truly representative of the population it serves. This inevitably requires a change in mindset as well as a restructuring (i.e. changes in purposes, assumptions, and means) of education systems based on needed reforms that redress policies of previous decades that have favored and privileged some groups and discriminated against others. In this context, Chomsky (2002) reminds us that "[t]he university will be able to make its contribution to a free society only to the extent that it overcomes the temptation to conform unthinkingly to the prevailing ideology and to the existing patterns of power and privilege" (p. 181).

Although progress has been made in recent decades to open up higher education to more people, barriers to access and participation still exist and these concerns need to be addressed. The ongoing power struggles to achieve equal opportunity will undoubtedly continue as different segments of society continue to strive for fair and equal access to higher educational resources. As Burke (2012) notes, existing cultural values that favor one group over another are often established to serve the interests of historically privileged segments of society, which in turn are often reflected in institutional policies, practices, and attitudes. Therefore, the dialogue around widening participation must, among other issues, concern itself with addressing the under-representation of groups that have been historically excluded from accessing higher education. Within this context, the key question then becomes: How do we bring about greater inclusivity and a more democratic dialogical space for access and participation for all? In other words, how do we move from a space of exclusivity to a space of inclusivity so that higher education works for all?

The specific phenomenon of widening access and expanding participation has been written about by, among others, Trow and Burrage (2010), focusing mainly on the USA higher education system; Palfreyman and Tapper (2009), analyzing mostly research universities around the world; DeMillo (2011), exploring the historical development of higher education; Burke (2012), examining the underlying assumptions and perspectives shaping modern concepts and theories on widening participation policies and practice; Barnett (2012), investigating a range of possibilities for universities of the future; and Kezar (2014), explicating the mechanisms and models of change in higher education. These and other works add to our understanding of the evolving higher education systems around the world and their potential trajectories.

The work on this topic owes a great debt to the foundational research conducted by Trow, whose work focused mainly on the USA and UK higher education systems. He believed that his notion of elite-to-mass-to-universal higher education could be applied to any modern society. Recent developments in new educational models (e.g. community and technical colleges, online universities, distance education, open universities) have massified and diversified higher education to an astounding degree. In fact, using Trow's benchmark for universal access (50 percent of a nation's population participating in tertiary education in some manner), several nations can be said to now have achieved universal access for their citizens. However, Burke (2012) and Kirby (2009), among others, note that, in spite of remarkable gains in access in many countries, persistent patterns of under-representation continue within higher education—a phenomenon at odds with the basic democratic notion of equal access opportunity and inclusion.[3]

Palfreyman and Tapper (2009) state that the world is experiencing a major transition period in higher education and the nature of the relationships between higher education, government, and society is changing dramatically. Nevertheless, the idea of a common trajectory or the development of a single convergent model of global higher education is still uncertain. They state that:

> There is no assumption that the pressures for change set in motion the trend towards a converging model of higher education, but we do believe that in the present circumstances no understanding of "the idea of the university" remains sacrosanct.
>
> *Palfreyman & Tapper, 2009, p. ix*

In addition to the case studies and empirical data, this book draws upon a substantial body of work from areas of international higher education, changes in higher education, democracy and education, life-long learning, global learning, meaningful learning, and other relevant topics (e.g. Altbach, Gumport, & Berdahl, 2011; Blessinger & Kovbasyuk, 2012; Burke, 2012; Chomsky & Otero, 2003; Deardorff, de Witt, Heyl, & Adams, 2012; DeMillo, 2011; Kezar, 2014; Knapper & Cropley, 2000; Kovbasyuk & Blessinger, 2013; Palfreyman & Tapper, 2009; Polyzoi, Fullan, & Anchan, 2003; Trow, 1974; Trow & Burrage, 2010).

As illustrated by the case studies in this book, higher education has become massified (even universalized in some countries) just as primary and secondary education have become increasingly universalized over the course of its evolution in the 20th century. With primary and secondary education, the principle of universal education is now seen as a human right, fundamental to producing an educated citizenry—a necessity for the proper functioning of a modern democratic society. Although different than primary and secondary education in several respects, the notion of universalizing access to higher education is now viewed by many as a necessity for acquisition of life-long and life-wide learning opportunities.

One assumption in these writings is that higher education can be a positive force for democratizing societies within which it functions. Conversely, democratic sociopolitical transformations can also lead to changes in the structures of higher education systems. The aim is to discuss these bidirectional forces and impact because change occurs at all levels and in complex ways (see Polyzoi, Fullan, & Anchan, 2003). As previously mentioned, we look at higher education change mainly through a sociopolitical lens (i.e. social and political factors). Each chapter will present a country case study covering the following themes and questions:

Institutional Diversification: To what extent are different institutional types (e.g. private, public, proprietary, sectarian, research universities, liberal arts colleges, community colleges, vocational-technical colleges) represented in the country?

Higher Education Affordability: What are the different, major forms of higher education financing (e.g. higher education as a public investment—public financing versus higher education as a private investment—student financing) in the country? What are the implications of these different policies and economic models?

Accessibility to Higher Education: To what extent can citizens access higher education? Do all citizens have the opportunity to access higher education or is higher education only accessible to certain segments of society and, if so, who decides who has access and who does not?

Participation in Higher Education: To what extent are citizens participating in higher education? Equal opportunity of access does not automatically equate to equitable participation.

Quality of Higher Education: To what extent does the quality of teaching and learning exist in the country? Is quality assurance accomplished via peer-based accreditation agencies or government agencies or other models?

In addition, some segments of society (e.g. women, minorities) who represent well over 50 percent of the population in many countries, and to a large extent were historically denied access to higher education, are now gaining access in unprecedented numbers. However, much work still needs to be done across the world to break down the barriers of discrimination and lingering monopolistic practices and to ensure that everyone has fair and equal access to all forms of higher education. Ironically, it is against this backdrop that we have also witnessed a widening gap between the developed and developing countries with respect to access and growing stratification in higher education systems.

Given the advent of the globalized world and the transition to knowledge-based societies and economies within the last few decades, the development of a widespread and equitable system of higher education that works for all is becoming increasingly important and necessary as we move further into the 21st century. This means to raise the quality of life for everyone regardless of where they live. Restructuring alone is not the answer and technology alone is not the panacea. It entails real reforms that benefit everyone in society. Universal primary and secondary education, although vitally important, is not sufficient to meet the needs of modern societies. Rather, people must learn to become life-long and life-wide learners, which depends on access to education throughout their lives. This is necessary because, among other reasons, the currency of knowledge continues to decrease as knowledge changes.

In many ways, this diversification has not only fundamentally changed the way higher education functions and is structured, but also how it dramatically changes people's perceptions of and experience with higher education—from chancellors to presidents to provosts to deans to faculty to students as well as all other constituencies (e.g. policymakers, citizens). Since we live in an increasingly globalized, interconnected, and interdependent society, it is important to understand this phenomenon on a global scale and from an international comparative perspective.

Conclusions

In simple terms, one could surmise the grand question in this compilation to be: What is the purpose of education? As a book that explores the essence of democratization in higher education, the authors also hail from various backgrounds with differing emphases on the grand question. Indeed, there are no metanarratives in this discourse. These contributions are from scholars local to their countries and sensitive to their respective histories and cultures. Many of them have lived and experienced the nuances of higher education in relation to their own situation. An earlier work similar to this approach focused on schooling around the world (Mazurek & Winzer, 2006) and education in transition in post-communist Eastern Europe (Polyzoi, Fullan, & Anchan, 2003). The field of Comparative or International Education continues to be enriched by illuminating writers speaking from their own environmental "labs" without being affected by the "othering" aspect that many post-colonial critics have voiced.

It is interesting to see a common thread that connects the various case studies in terms of histories, challenges, resolutions, and development. While all of them agree on the basic fundamental principles of education, they may have individual perspectives on how these can and could be achieved. Amidst the technological changes, changing demographics, international migration, and dwindling resources, not unlike all other public and private enterprises, higher education institutions around the world will continue to be under enormous pressure to respond to societal demands, political pressures, and economic challenges. In the end, we need to ask the question: What exactly do we expect from education? How can we retain the sanctity of a liberal education along with the ancient noble ideals even as we make that experience enriching and rewarding? How can we make the educational enterprise sustainable? How can education provide the assurance of being able to respond to the changing needs of the learners in particular and the society in general? How can we balance between idealism and practicality? How can we make higher education, or any formal education, accessible to those who cannot really afford it? In essence, how can we democratize higher education? What kind of a world will we leave for our children and what does the future hold for higher education?

Notes

1 See Mokhtar (1981) for a compendium of the ancient civilizations and their influence in Africa.
2 For an excellent and exhaustive repository of the most contemporary collection of globalization, internationalization, and higher education, see the Center for International Higher Education at Boston College spearheaded by Philip G. Altbach— a pioneer in this area.
3 One could contend that mere access to educational institutions does not imply democratization. While the argument warrants debate, space precludes extending the discourse to the indagation of this critique.

References

Altbach, P.G. & Knight, J. (2007). The internationalization of higher education: Motivations and realities. *Journal of Studies in International Education*, Vol. 11, No. 3/4, 290–305. Also: Highly recommended resource: Center for International Higher Education. www.bc.edu/content/bc/research/cihe/about/pga/bookchaptersandarticles. html.

Altbach, P.G., Gumport, P.J., & Berdahl, R.O. (2011). *American higher education in the twenty-first century: Social, political, and economic challenges*. Baltimore, MD: The Johns Hopkins University Press.

Barnett, R. (Ed.) (2012). *The future university: Ideas and possibilities*. New York and Abingdon: Routledge.

Bauerlein, M. (2009). *The dumbest generation: How the digital age stupefies young Americans and jeopardizes our future – or, don't trust anyone under 30*. New York: Jeremy P. Tarcher/ Penguin.

Blessinger, P. & Kovbasyuk, O. (2012). Higher education needs to build global learning communities. *The Guardian*. Retrieved from www.theguardian.com/higher-education-network/blog/2012/may/23/global-virtual-learning-environments.

Bok, D. (2003). *Universities in the marketplace: The commercialization of higher education*. New York: Princeton University Press.

Bowen, W.G. (2013). *Higher education in the digital age*. Princeton, NJ: Princeton University Press.

Bruford, W.H. (1975). *The German tradition of self-cultivation: Bildung from Humboldt to Thomas Mann*. Cambridge: Cambridge University Press.

Burke, P.J. (2012). *The right to higher education: Beyond widening participation*. Abingdon: Routledge.

Carr, N. (2009). *The big switch: Rewiring the world, from Edison to Google*. New York: W.W. Norton & Company.

Carr, N. (2010). *The shallows: What the internet is doing to our brains*. New York: W.W. Norton & Company.

Chomsky, N. & Otero, C.P. (eds.) (2002). *Chomsky on democracy and education: Social theory, education and cultural change*. New York: Routledge.

Clarke, M.L. (2012). *Higher education in the ancient world*. Routledge Library Editions: Education. Abingdon: Routledge. Retrieved from http://books.google.ca/books?id=IX6tQElCXrQC.

Cuban, L. (2001). *Oversold and underused: Computers in the classroom*. Cambridge, MA: Harvard University Press.

de Wit, H. (ed.). (1995). *Strategies for the internationalisation of higher education. A comparative study of Australia, Canada, Europe and the United States of America*. A Report from the EAIE Secretariat, European Association for International Education, Amsterdam; Association of International Education Administrators, Carbondale, IL; Organization for Economic Cooperation and Development, Paris. ERIC Number: ED398804.

Deardorff, D.K., de Wit, H., Heyl, J.D., & Adams, T. (2012). *The SAGE handbook of international higher education*. Los Angeles, CA: SAGE Publications.

DeMillo, R.A. (2011). *Abelard to Apple: The fate of American colleges and universities*. Cambridge, MA: The MIT Press.

Dunning, P. (1997). *Education in Canada: An overview*. Ontario: Canadian Education Association.

Goodchild, L.F. & Harold S. (eds.) (1997). *The history of higher education*. Association for the Study of Higher Education. ERIC Number: ED449768.

Harrigan, P.J. (1986). A comparative perspective on recent trends in the history of education in Canada. *History of Education Quarterly*, Vol. 26, No. 1, 71–86.

Harris, R.S. (1976). *A history of higher education in Canada 1663-1960*. ERIC Number: ED153574.

Hegel, G.W.F. (1977). *Phenomenology of spirit*, trans. A.V. Miller. Oxford: Oxford University Press.

Hoerner, J.L. (1970). *An historical review of liberal education*. Coral Gables, FL: University of Miami.

Kezar, A. (2014). *How colleges change: Understanding, leading, and enacting change*. New York: Routledge.

Kirby, D. (2009). Widening access: Making the transition from mass to universal post-secondary education in Canada. *Journal of Applied Research on Learning*, Vol. 2, Special Issue, Article 3. Retrieved from www.ccl-cca.ca/pdfs/JARL/Jarl-Vol2Art3-Kirby_EN.pdf.

Knapper, C. & Crople, A.J. (2000). *Lifelong learning in higher education*. Sterling, VA: Stylus Publishing.

Kovbasyuk, O. & Blessinger, P. (2013). *Meaning-centered education: International perspectives and explorations in higher education*. New York: Routledge.

Kramer, L. (2014). The role, development, expansion, and importance of open education Resources: An HETL Interview with Larry Kramer. *International HETL Review*, Vol. 4. Retrieved from www.hetl.org/interview-articles/the-role-development-expansion-and-importance-of-open-education-resources-an-hetl-interview-with-larry-kramer/.

Lee, H. & Knight, P.T. (1996). *Transforming higher education*. Pennsylvania: The Society for Research into Higher Education & Open University Press.

Lucas, C.J. (2006). *American higher education: A history*. Second Edition. New York: Palgrave Macmillan.

Marginson, S. (2006). Dynamics of national and global competition in higher education. *Higher Education*, Vol. 52, 1–39.

Mazurek, K. & Winzer, M.A. (2006). *Schooling around the world: Debates, challenges, and practices*. New York: Pearson.

Mokhtar, G. (1981). Paris: United Nations Educational, Scientific and Cultural Organization. Retrieved from http://unesdoc.unesco.org/images/0018/001842/184265eo.pdf.

Noble, D.F. (2001). *Digital diploma mills: The automation of higher education*. New York: Monthly Review Press.

Palfrey, J. & Gasser, U. (2008). *Born digital: Understanding the first generation of digital natives*. New York: Basic Books.

Palfreyman, D. & Tapper, T. (2009). *Structuring mass higher education: The role of elite institutions*. New York: Routledge.

Polyzoi, E., Fullan, M., & Anchan, J.P. (2003). *Change forces in post-communist Eastern Europe: Education in transition*. New York: RoutledgeFalmer.

Postman, N. (1993). *Technopoly: The surrender of culture to technology*. New York: Vintage Books.

Roszak, T. (1986). *The cult of information: The folklore of computers and the true art of thinking*. New York: Pantheon Books.

Sheehan, N.M. (1985). History of higher education in Canada. *The Canadian Journal of Higher Education*, Vol. XV–1, pp. 25–38.

Skolnik, M.L. & Jones, G.A. (1991). A comparative analysis of arrangements for state coordination of higher education in Canada and the United States. *Journal of Higher Education*, Vol. 63, No. 2, 121–142.

Stoll, C. (1995). *Silicon snake oil: Second thoughts on the information highway*. New York: Double Day.

Tapscott, D. (1993). *Paradigm shift: The new promise of information technology*. New York: McGraw-Hill.

Tapscott, D. (1996). *Digital economy: Promise and peril in the age of networked intelligence*. New York: McGraw-Hill.

Tapscott, D. (1998). *Growing up digital: The rise of the net generation*. New York: McGraw-Hill.

Tapscott, D. (2009). *Grown up digital: How the net generation is changing your world*. New York: McGraw-Hill.

Thelin, J.R. (1976). *The cultivation of Ivey: A saga of the College of America*. Cambridge, MA: Shenkman Publishing Co.

Trow, M. (1974). Problems in the transition from elite to mass higher education. Published in *General Report on the Conference on Future Structures of Post-Secondary Education*, 55–101. Paris: OECD.

Trow, M. & Burrage, M. (2010). *Twentieth-century higher education: Elite to mass to universal.* Baltimore, MD: The Johns Hopkins University Press.

Turkle, S. (1984). *The second self: Computers and the human spirit.* New York: Simon & Schuster.

Turkle, S. (1995). *Life on the screen: Identity in the age of the internet.* New York: Simon & Schuster.

Turkle, S. (2012). *Alone together: Why we expect more from technology and less from each other.* New York: Basic Books.

UNESCO (1998). *World declaration on higher education for the twenty-first century: Vision and action.* Retrieved from www.unesco.org/education/educprog/wche/declaration_eng.htm.

2

DEMOCRATIZING HIGHER EDUCATION IN THE UNITED STATES

A Legacy of Democratic Learning

Linda S. Watts

Introduction: How Do We Act on Our Legacies in U.S. Higher Education?

Key advocates of progressive education from John Dewey to W.E.B. DuBois have asserted the responsibility to provide 'education for democracy.' Higher education must do more than season the thinker and qualify the worker; it must also support learners in realizing the ideals of a democratic society. That outcome requires an informed citizenry that understands and fulfills its obligations to self, other, and society. Through the same means that such education engages students—through its emphases on reason, dialogue, and critical engagement—it also equips and energizes them to become engaged citizens. According to this premise, the effective student emerges as an effective citizen.

Of course, this view of democratic learning is not exclusive to higher education. Educator Louise Rosenblatt advocated that school children be entrusted with the authority to inflect and interpret what they read. Her notions about creative readers (to match the more common notion of creative writers) were closely tied to her conviction that democratic society hinged on an informed electorate. If the people are to decide, they must continually inform views and update understandings. To practice citizenship actively, one must have the autonomy to construct—not merely construe—meaning. By promoting personal choice and valuing unique perspective in a learner, teachers and schools acknowledged the collective need for independent thought. Diversity of perspectives also helps a population to realize the benefits of democracy, as opposed to settling for a forced (or enforced) consensus.

Similarly, educational reformer Alexander Meiklejohn (best known for his Experimental College at the University of Wisconsin and his School of Social

Studies in San Francisco) argued that higher education must guide students in the mature exercise of their responsibilities as citizens in a democratic society. Only through intellect could individuals shape their environments to reflect right deeds by individuals and right relations among people. He emphasized the need for thoughtful action if the ideals of democracy were to be realized, and he saw higher education as an agent for cultivating such intelligence. For Meiklejohn, the college curriculum in a democracy pivoted around liberal education. In fact, he defined democracy as "a society whose citizens are liberally educated" (Meiklejohn, 1943, quoted in Harris, 1970, p. 115).

The impulse toward 'education for democracy' involves character education, at least insofar as it seeks to extol virtues and inculcate values. Proponents of democratizing U.S. higher education highlight within their visions of the academy a set of values including truth, tolerance, equality, honesty, humility, rigor, fairness, respect, integrity, freedom, justice, sensitivity, compassion, privacy, diversity, participation, and human rights. (See Morrill, 1981; Trow, 1976; Smith, 1970; Amundson, 1991.) Values-based education, or civic learning, proceeds from the notion that while a society's laws can deny a citizen efficacy, even the best legislation cannot guarantee that citizens will prize and practice rights afforded them in a democracy.

If higher education is charged with more than information transmission or credential conferral, it becomes imperative to scrutinize this relationship between education and civic agency. How can higher education honor, model, protect, and promote democratic ideals of opportunity, equality, and social justice? For the purposes of this overview, the focus remains on questions at the center of the history of U.S. higher education. In addressing each, I discuss several promising developments that might have enduring implications for democratic higher education. The first ("Whom do we teach, whom do we reach?") considers issues of participation and persistence in higher education. The second ("What do we teach?") weighs competing notions about essential learning in democratized U.S. higher education. The third ("How do we teach?") examines the impact changes in pedagogy have on democratizing U.S. higher education. The fourth ("Who learns, and with what lasting result?") probes the effort to assess the impact of student learning, particularly in terms of democratic process. The fifth ("What questions remain?") acknowledges that the goal of democratizing higher education is still an ideal rather than a reality, and so poses questions that might fate that process for success. The concept of inclusive practice predominates within this discussion, for only those granted standing may directly contribute to, or benefit from, democratized higher education. Furthermore, the emphasis here remains on undergraduate education, for without it advanced degrees remain impossible.

What is at stake in prioritizing democratic learning within U.S. higher education? Without civic-mindedness, learners may become cynical about education, engaging in it as little more than a means to an end (a mere credential rather than an enriching experience and enlivening awareness). They may also find it difficult to find common cause with peers, thinking instead that their predicaments are individual in both nature and remedy. Finally, they may abrogate their responsibilities and forfeit their rights as national, cultural, and global citizens.

In this regard, higher education, at its best, serves to discomfort students with the status quo and their complicity in it. Author James Baldwin cast the dilemma as an educational paradox: "that precisely at the point when you begin to develop a conscience, you must find yourself at war with your society. It is your responsibility to change society if you think of yourself as an educated person" (Baldwin, 1985, p. 331).

Whom Do We Teach, Whom Do We Reach?

U.S. higher education has undergone dramatic change, especially in terms of intended audience. Although in Fall 2010 U.S. postsecondary enrollments were robust at 21,016,000 (with 15,143,000 enrolled in public institutions, and 5,873,000 attending private institutions), it has not always been the case. The first U.S. college, an institution subsequently known as Harvard, was established in the Massachusetts Bay Colony in 1636. The original student population consisted chiefly of sons of the elite, many of whom sought a classical education to support their entry to the clergy. During the colonial period, other institutions came into operation, including the College of William and Mary (1693) along with the campuses that would later become Yale University (1701), University of Pennsylvania (1740), Princeton University (1746), Columbia University (1754), Brown University (1764), and Dartmouth College (1769).

As these early U.S. institutions opened their doors, they did not open them very widely. Only males from wealthy families had the means to pursue education, and there was only limited room for them to attend. Neither women nor persons of color were welcome to participate in higher education.

Following the American Revolution, the notion took shape that each state would need to provide free schooling to youth. Foundational documents such as the Constitution call for a universal system of public education, such that it might promote the democratic values of the emerging nation. These democratic ideals were not routinely extended to all Americans, however, as the founders had concerned themselves first and foremost with property-holding white males. This friction between discourse and the lived world, between democratic principles and practices of exclusion, became an enduring tension within the history of U.S. higher education.

It would not be until the nineteenth century that women, African Americans, Native Americans, and other culturally diverse students were permitted to pursue U.S. higher education. Even then, many continued to be rebuffed or channeled into preparatory programs thought suitable for what were perceived as their distinctive needs, such as teachers' colleges and vocational institutes. Rarely were such learners accorded the same status as their white male counterparts.

Since that time, several historical developments have rendered access to higher education more equitable for students across such categories as gender, race, class, ethnicity, veteran status, or difference/disability. Among the most noteworthy of such shifts in practice within U.S. higher education are: (1) the establishment of land grant schools, (2) racial desegregation of schools, (3) coeducation, (4) the formation of a comprehensive community colleges system, (5) educational policies attentive to the needs of veterans, students with learning differences or disabilities, and foster children, and (6) legislation designed to make higher education more affordable through scholarships, grants, and financial aid.

Although there were attempts during the first half of the nineteenth century to widen access to higher education through establishment of 'worker's colleges' such as the People's College (New York) and The Agricultural College (Michigan), these efforts remained limited and isolated. During the second half of the nineteenth century, the federal government allocated properties in the Northwest Territory for siting of universities (Morrill Acts of 1862 and 1890), and these institutions came to be known as land-grant schools. These schools helped make higher education more physically accessible for those residing beyond the eastern coast. Land-grant colleges also welcomed a wider spectrum of students, some of whom had been denied higher education, including students from agricultural and/or working-class families.

The second Morrill Act (1890) provided support for founding 17 'historically black colleges and universities' (HBCUs). Land-grant colleges, along with these HBCUs (such as Hampton and Tuskegee), began to make room for students of different racial and ethnic origins in higher education. Subsequent legislation (Hatch Act of 1887; Smith-Lever Act of 1914) promoted both engineering and agricultural research/outreach at state universities throughout the United States, further diversifying the student population in higher education.

Despite these measures to extend and enhance higher education for U.S. students, entire populations still were systematically denied access to education. Long after the 15th Amendment, racial discrimination constrained the availability of education to African Americans. It took the Civil Rights Movement, particularly the movement to desegregate the nation's schools, to topple the practices that held many back from higher education. Not until landmark legal cases, such as *Brown v. Board of Education* (1954), did the practice of segregated education and the claim of 'separate but equal' facilities for education fall to challenges. Popular protests eventually led to legislation such as the Civil Rights Act (1964), which helped eradicate educational segregation in America. Black undergraduate enrollments have soared from 943,400 in 1976 to 2,698,900 in 2011 (U.S. Department of Education, NCES, Table 263).

Like racial desegregation, coeducation, or mixed-sex education, in U.S. higher education was also the product of struggle. In much the same way that separate institutions of higher education were established for African American students, a variety of women's colleges were founded during the latter portion of the nineteenth century in the United States. Examples include Vassar College (1861), Wells College (1868), and Radcliffe College (1879). In addition, some institutions, such as Spelman College (1861), were established specifically as African American women's colleges. During the twentieth century, other women's colleges, such as Skidmore College (1903) and Sarah Lawrence College (1926), followed. Since these opportunities became available, women have begun to outnumber their male counterparts in undergraduate study, with 10,246,100 female enrollments as compared to 7,817,000 males in 2011–2012 (U.S. Department of Education, NCES, Table 263).

The 1960s marked a time of brisk growth for two-year undergraduate institutions in the United States. In part, this was due to the Higher Education Facilities Act of 1963, which made available capital funds for many community colleges. During the 1970s, the United States consolidated a network, including many junior colleges and technical institutes, to form a comprehensive system. In this way, students gained flexibility for moving among such institutions. Although transfer programs represent only some of the curricular pathways at community colleges, such programs helped many students realize a four-year degree. Such learners began to benefit from dual enrollment at, and articulation agreements with, four-year institutions. Such arrangements enhanced the clarity in planning for, and efficiency in earning credits toward, four-year degrees initiated at two-year campuses. This transparency proved especially helpful to a growing population of non-traditional students, including both those returning to undergraduate study after time away, and those who deferred college until later in life. Since many community colleges offer open (non-competitive) enrollment, they increase access to students who might not otherwise be admitted to baccalaureate programs. Because community college education is generally more affordable than enrollment at four-year institutions, it also aided students seeking less costly routes to undergraduate degrees. In 2011–2012, the average undergraduate tuition and required fees at two-year institutions averaged $2,647, as compared to $7,701 at four-year institutions (U.S. Department of Education, NCES, Table 381).

During the period following World War II, the Servicemen's Readjustment Act of 1944 (popularly dubbed the 'GI Bill,' because the abbreviation 'GI' was widely used to describe the U.S. military population), helped close the educational cost gap for millions of Americans returning after military service. Through this provision, tuition and other expenses for veterans attending college would also be covered in consideration for their service. Because youth of color and persons of modest means have always been disproportionately represented in the U.S. military, the GI Bill offered a significant number of returning veterans access to higher education.

Like the GI Bill, the findings of the Truman Commission of 1946, a group charged by President Harry Truman to explore the problem of access in higher education, concentrated on funding students rather than institutions of higher learning. They issued a report entitled 'Higher Education for Democracy,' which helped make college financially feasible for a greater number and variety of students. In 1964, the Higher Education Act sought to extend similar educational benefits to the general population. This measure provided loans and grants directly to students (rather than to institutions they attended). The Higher Education Act, and its 1972 amendment, which created the Basic Educational Opportunity Grants (BEOG, or better known as 'Pell Grants'), offered support to students irrespective of the college chosen. These moves to provide grants, loans, and scholarships have improved accessibility of U.S. higher education. Total fall enrollment in degree-granting institutions rose from 10,985,600 in 1976 to 20,994,100 in 2011 (U.S. Department of Education, NCES, Table 263).

One of the most persistent barriers to U.S. higher education involves students with learning differences or disabilities. Long after women, students of color, and veterans were welcomed, different and disabled learners were discouraged from pursuing higher education. Even those who graduated from high school were seldom guided toward applying to colleges. Those who did might not be reviewed fairly for admission based on the difficulties they had experienced in securing learning accommodations needed to demonstrate their potential for advanced study. With passage of the Individuals with Disabilities Education Act (1990) and the Americans with Disabilities Act (1990), such students began to receive more equitable access to, and treatment within, higher education.

In addition, populations of historically underserved and underrepresented students in the United States, such as youth who age out of the foster care system, have faced a nearly insurmountable hurdle to higher education. The United States has begun to address the access and achievement gap with the Foster Care Independence Act of 1999, which assists foster children in attending college. Still being debated are provisions to make higher education more available and affordable for youth born in the United States to illegal residents and immigrants without documentation.

Although the earliest U.S. colleges were dedicated to educating only the most fortunate, the role of higher education has shifted markedly since then. Growth in both the number and variety of institutions made it possible for more students to attend. In fact, by the twentieth century, most American professions regarded university education as the necessary foundation to enter the field. Once the province of only the affluent, graduation with an undergraduate degree became the goal of an increasing percentage of American youth. For many, it became a given in visualizing their pathways to personal and financial independence. In fact, the percentage of those aged 25 or over who have attained at least a bachelor's degree has grown from 2.7 in 1910 to 30.9 in 2012 (U.S. Department of Education, NCES, Table 8).

Cost remains a barrier to higher education for many prospective students. Average undergraduate in-state tuition and fees at four-year institutions rose from $4,540 in 1969–1970 to $13,819 in 2011–2012 (U.S. Department of Education, NCES, Table 381). Critics of U.S. higher education pose difficult questions about what William Bowen terms the "cost disease" in higher education (Bowen, 2013, p. 1). Although a larger number, wider range, and fuller spectrum of students may gain admission to U.S. higher education, the rising expense of attendance renders college cost prohibitive. This burden threatens not only student access to higher education, but also the popular perception of its value. In the face of rising costs, alternative funding models hold promise in making higher education available to a higher percentage of qualified students. For example, proposals such as the State of Oregon's 'Pay Forward, Pay Back' pilot program, where students do not have to pay tuition fees up front (rather they undertake to pay back by contributing to the state a relatively small portion of their future income), may help make the dream of a college degree a financial reality for more individuals.

What the land-grant institutions began in terms of access to higher education, the digital environment now seeks to continue. At present, debates surround the potential for electronic connectivity to function as the next great equalizer in higher education. Distance learning, online degrees, hybrid courses, and massive open on-line courses (MOOCs) all attempt to bring opportunities for advanced study to an ever-widening population of learners (Davidson, 2012). In fact, the Massachusetts Institute of Technology (MIT)—itself established as a land-grant school—joined forces with Harvard University in 2012, announcing that they would be providing free online instruction world-wide. This news became public during an observance of the 150th anniversary of the Morrill Land Grant Act (Staley, 2013, Introduction, para. 1). It should be noted, however, that such enrollments are not recognized toward MIT or Harvard degrees, and many learners still find themselves barred from entry by the digital divide.

What Do We Teach?

Arguments about essential learning in higher education are hardly new. Most U.S. undergraduate institutions feature some version of general education, a program of study that exposes learners to a wide range of subjects and perspectives. In this respect, general education is designed to help students become intellectually well-rounded (rather than experts in only a specialty). Undergraduate general education is closely related to the model of liberal education, in which students develop broad understandings and versatile abilities.

At least since the nineteenth century, U.S. higher education has struggled to find the balance between general education and professional education, broad knowledge and narrow expertise. This friction persists at the nation's colleges, where students typically take coursework that combines specific career needs with those courses that cultivate habits of mind beneficial to all.

During the twentieth century, three major shifts characterized transformation of the undergraduate curriculum: (1) interdisciplinary inquiry, (2) multiculturalism, and (3) the use of elective courses. Each of these trends brought with it perils, possibilities, and the occasional controversy.

Interdisciplinary education in America came to prominence due to several factors. For one thing, as it became more common for students to add minors and second majors to their undergraduate degrees, they began to think and work in ways that crossed traditional boundaries between academic disciplines. Further, as students of the counterculture era called for higher education to be made more socially relevant, educators explored more holistic approaches to timely topics. The more problem-based college courses became, the clearer it became that no one specialty could suffice. Hunger cannot be eradicated by dieticians alone, nor homelessness by architects solely. Effective responses to issues of such complexity and consequence require cross- and trans-disciplinary partnerships. In addition, contemporary social movements began to inspire new curricula in U.S. higher education, from Women's Studies to Latino/Latina Studies. In these ways, students felt more empowered through their learning to respond to societal upheaval and injustice. Bachelor's degrees conferred in multi-interdisciplinary studies (exclusive of liberal arts or general studies) rose from 6,324 in 1970 to 42,228 in 2011 (U.S. Department of Education, NCES, Table 313).

In what might be described as a backlash, detractors published critiques of the revised curriculum in U.S. higher education. Some, like Allan Bloom (1987), E.D. Hirsch (1987), and Dinesh D'Souza (1998), lamented the state of education in the classical tradition and speculated that contemporary students were no longer culturally literate. Each seemed to fear that an expanded curriculum meant a diluted one. Other critics, such as Roger Kimball (1990) and David Horowitz (2009), posited that the changes to the curriculum in U.S. higher education were tantamount to indoctrination, foisting a leftwing, doctrinaire stance on young, impressionable minds. Such skirmishes over what content is central and what learning is essential in U.S. higher education came to be known as the "culture wars" (Hunter, 1991, book title).

While these battles have hardly subsided, there is little question that U.S. higher education now reflects a worldview that is wider and more inclusive than the Western tradition that had characterized the nation's previous undergraduate curriculum. In fact, many institutions build a diversity or intercultural awareness requirement into their baccalaureate degrees. Not only do required courses include a more culturally diverse perspective, elective courses are often available to explore the full spectrum of human experience.

Finally, the birth of the elective course is, in itself, an important development within the history of higher education. Where it was once supposed that students did not possess the powers of discernment to select appropriate courses for study, it is now almost universally the case that American undergraduates have allocated within their course of study at least one or more courses chosen to reflect their personal interests and goals.

These shifts in academic content helped an increasingly more plural student population in higher education find coursework that challenged them to explore the interstices of disciplinary study, encounter and reckon multiple perspectives across cultures, and customize aspects of their course schedules. In this way, U.S. higher education became more hospitable and supportive to its rapidly expanding and heterogeneous pool of undergraduates.

How Do We Teach?

Just as American educators transformed their notions about necessary undergraduate content, so did they begin to reconsider instructional methods and practices. The origins of this reexamination were similar to those fueling the rethinking of academic content. A more culturally diverse student population stimulated faculty to address themselves to divergent learning styles. In what may well be a related development, students and faculty grew dissatisfied with the format of the lecture, organized as it was around monologue in the classroom. During the second half of the twentieth century, college and university teachers experimented with more interactive models of instruction. Although lectures did not disappear, they began to recede as the dominant mode of teaching in America's colleges, especially in upper-division classes. Educators began to incorporate more active learning strategies in their classroom practice. Within this realm, professors serve more as the 'guide on the side' than the 'sage on the stage.' These interactive learning techniques served several purposes. First, they were more engaging to students than the passive act of session-long listening exercises. Second, they helped students take more responsibility and initiative in their learning by asking questions and contributing insights. Third, they gave students practical opportunities to apply, test, and refine their knowledge through hands-on lessons. The transformation might be described as a shift from "What do you know?" (such as might be measured by a multiple-choice test) to "What can you do with what you know?" (which might be manifested in projects, papers, and portfolios).

In the twenty-first century, U.S. higher education has arrived at a richer understanding of the benefits of interactive learning for all students. Some specific experiences have been found to promote academic success, student retention, higher-order thinking skills, student engagement, and cumulative learning. George D. Kuh termed these experiences "high-impact educational practices" (HIPS) (Kuh, 2008, book title). Among these practices are first-year seminars and experiences, common intellectual experiences, learning communities, writing-intensive courses, collaborative assignments and projects, undergraduate research, diversity/global learning, service learning and community-based learning, internships, and capstone courses and projects. Taken together, these features of higher education lead to student efficacy, autonomy, persistence, and satisfaction. Further, the active nature of such work proves compatible with the notion of democratizing higher education, as students become agents of learning and producers of knowledge.

Who Learns, and With What Lasting Result?

One of the areas of most dynamic growth within U.S. higher education is assessment—the effort to document impact of educational practices on learning, both while students are enrolled and after they conclude their studies. While educators have always endeavored to be reflective, in recent years that process has started to extend beyond what is taught to reckon what is learned (Angelo, 1995, pp. 7–9). Assessment can occur at any level at which learning may be documented—assignment, course, course sequence, year of study, major, and degree. Recent turns in educational discourse may be described as marking a shift from an instructor-centered paradigm (teaching) to a student-centered paradigm (learning), consistent with a more democratic learning environment.

Best practices in higher education assessment, however, do more than answer the demands of internal reauthorization or external reporting. They attune students and faculty to the implications of their educational choices and the lasting results of their shared work. As the student population in U.S. higher education grew and diversified, educators found themselves challenged to think more fluidly and flexibly about how to direct their pedagogy to the benefit of all students.

As the focus within higher education shifts from teaching to learning, something of an assessment movement has taken shape in the United States. Through such efforts, the nation's educators make more transparent to students, and to the public, their expectations for student performance and their criteria for academic excellence. Such transparency can help more students pursue, achieve, and demonstrate college success, thereby further democratizing higher education.

While institutions of higher education may boast a variety of prominent statements about their core activities (mission, values statement, and the like), these documents are typically aspirational. Assessment—whether of a course, program, or school—calls for educators to do more than state ideals and vow to strive toward them. Today's assessment strategies demand that higher education sets out clear and measureable goals and objectives, collect data regarding action toward those goals and objectives, and use those findings to inform and reform future practice.

This turn in higher education assessment often calls for faculty and academic staff to undertake professional development to support their work in crafting learning goals for courses, writing and applying rubrics for assignments, reading and responding to degree portfolios, and devising action plans to continue improvements to the curriculum and build its impact on student learning. As it makes benchmarks and success indicators in higher education more visible and legible to students, assessment of student learning also favors democratization of higher education. Students are better able to discern and meet (or exceed) expectations for their performance as learners.

What Questions Remain?

The process of democratizing education is continuous, never perfected or completed. In this sense, it is like the asymptote in mathematics, an axis always to be approached even if it can never be fully intersected. Institutional practices alone are not sufficient to ensure democratic education, but they nonetheless warrant first interrogation. The shape of an institution of higher education—everything from the way a college structures its units, governs its constituencies, defines its values, stewards its resources, centers its curriculum, delivers instruction, recognizes and rewards its faculty, dedicates its other services, identifies and supports its students, and imagines its optimal future—can widen or foreclose possibilities for democratic life. In this sense, the campus is a text to be studied closely for its premises and presuppositions. Whether overtly or subtly, institutional frameworks define the environment of higher education and may also, at least in part, determine the horizon of expectations for both academic and civic learning. As Henry A. Giroux and Susan Searls Giroux put it in *Take Back Higher Education: Race, Youth, and the Crisis of Democracy in the Post-Civil Rights Era*, "Higher education, in this reading, becomes a site of ongoing struggle to preserve and extend the conditions in which autonomy of judgment and freedom of action are informed by the democratic imperatives of equality, liberty, and justice" (Giroux and Giroux, 2004, p. 12).

It is, of course, easier to identify impediments to democratizing higher education than to remove them. Not all learners thrive under the same conditions, require the same services, or advance in the same manner or rate. On this basis, it is no simple matter to arrive at best practices for higher education. At times, the interests of student constituencies do not simply differ, they clash. If conflict is the inevitable result of lives spent in one another's company, how might institutions of higher education model productive ways for meeting such challenges equitably? Even if it were possible to reach agreement about best practices, there remains the work of implementing those ideas across divergent institutions of higher education. How, then, does each align recommended practice with these lived-world realities? In renewing U.S. higher education, how do we attend to the goal of democratizing it?

Groups of organizers have begun to unite behind initiatives designed to address the challenges facing higher education today. One such body is the Democratizing Education Network (DEN), established in 2009. The group's charter, which speaks to many of the central crises facing higher education, reads as follows:

1) Full Public Funding for Public Higher Education
2) Free Access to Higher Education and Abolition of Tuition
3) Affirmative Action to End Institutionalized Racism and Sexism
4) Full Recognition of the Rights of Students and Workers to Organize
5) Democratic Self-Government of Higher Education
6) Service to the Public Welfare, Not Corporate Profits
7) Free Speech and Academic Freedom
8) Debt Forgiveness of Student Loans
9) Civic Education for a Democratic Society
10) Education, not war. Schools, not jails.

DEN/Democracy Square, 2009, charter text

Wherever one stands on these issues, few would deny that the future of U.S. higher education hinges on the willingness to pose tough questions, both of itself and society.

In arriving at a preliminary protocol of such questions, I draw from two sources originally designed for investigating literary works: Stephen Greenblatt's piece on "Culture," in *Critical Terms for Literary Study* (Lentricchia and McLaughlin, 1989, pp. 225–232) and Tim Gillespie's guide, "On Interrogating Texts," from *Doing Literary Criticism* (2010). In this context, the questions reprinted below from Gillespie, may, with slight modifications, be posed of a range of different texts as they bear on democratic education, most notably (1) the campus and its narratives, (2) the curriculum and its canons, and (3) the teachers and their pedagogies:

- Whose story is this? Who is telling it? Who's observing? Who's being observed?
- Who speaks? Who is silent or silenced? What points of views are presented? What points of view are not? Is the text fair?
- Whose experiences are represented in this text and whose are not?
- Who is named? Who is not?
- Who gets the lead role? Who are secondary characters? Who remains invisible or unknown?
- Who is rounded or multidimensional? Who is flat or one-dimensional? Who is a stereotype or a cartoon?
- Who acts? Who is acted on? Who has power? Who does not? Who is independent? Who is dependent?
- Who fights for honor? Who triumphs? Who fails? Who suffers? Whose fate is unknown?
- What values and beliefs are explicit in the text? Embedded? Taken for granted? What questions about itself does the text not raise?
- Who stands to gain and who stands to lose from these values and beliefs?
- What view of the world is privileged by the text? What view is diminished? Ignored?
- What has been left out of the text? What are the gaps and silences? How does the text thereby construct a version of reality?
- What social, political, or cultural work does this text do?
- Who benefits from the text? Who loses? Who is being empowered and who is being disempowered?
- If we wanted to read as a resistant reader or against the grain of the text, even just to play devil's advocate, what counterarguments, counterexamples, or alternative stories might we offer?
- Who is the intended reader? What does the reader need to bring to the text to understand and embrace it?
- For whom is this text a full presentation of the world? For whom is it only partial?

- In terms of people who have been traditionally underrepresented or oppressed, how does this text treat issues of race, gender, sexual orientation, socioeconomic class, cultural difference, age, religion, political viewpoint, etc.?
- How might different readers read this text—or feel diminished or silenced by it?
- How and why does this text lead to certain readings—political or nonpolitical—by different readers in the class?
- How does our current historical, social, and political context alter the text's messages and meanings?
- Would the text be different if told in another time, another place or culture, or from a different point of view?

Gillespie, 2010, pp. 236–237

Although this series of questions was intended for use in the study of individual literary texts, many of the same queries guide and inform a rigorous review of higher education as it regards democratic learning. These questions must be asked sincerely, deeply, widely, and often.

Conclusion: How Do We Reframe our Legacies in U.S. Higher Education?

Educational reformers from Paulo Freire to bell hooks have challenged their readers to envision "education as the practice of freedom" (hooks, 1989, p. 62). In the current climate, with its renewed interest in participatory democracy, youth stand poised to join vital discussions. It is timely, then, that teachers have available to them compelling strategies for engaging students in civil and content-rich discourse about matters of consequence. Rather than regarding democracy exclusively as an ideal or a concept, we might help students to envision democracy as a set of practices, negotiations, and choices conducted continuously in daily living. The curricular content comes to life through its links to independent decision-making and thoughtful action.

In his book, *The Dissenters*, oral historian John Gwaltney describes principled dissent as the act of standing up and speaking out for a point of view, however unpopular, on the basis of a belief or deeply held value. The concept is a unifying thread through much of American history, literature, and artistic expression. Gwaltney writes:

> The courage to maintain unpopular views is a vital resource in any society striving for plural democracy. Principled dissent, though a troublesome treasure, is the most vital of social fluids. Without it the free marketplace of opinions is an arid sham . . . a decent respect for difference of opinion is crucial for any society that really means to avoid the deadly extremes of total anarchy and the tyranny of the majority.
>
> *Gwaltney, 1986, p. xviii*

Our capacity to maintain a society in which dissent occurs, and to glean from those views insights into the most urgent forms of social change, fuels a democratic society. Thoughtful protest and active listening are mainstays within a democratic society. By exploring the concept of principled dissent, students can consider questions such as those articulated by Ralph Young in *Dissent in America*:

> What is dissent? Is dissent unpatriotic or deeply patriotic? Is dissent reserved for those with moral grievances whose chief desire is to persuade the United States to live up to its ideals and to ensure that the nation is truly a land where 'all men are created equal,' or can dissent be used for more selfish purposes? Are both Susan B. Anthony and Timothy McVeigh equally dissenters? Does dissent ever become treason? Does dissent ultimately change society by offering new ideas, new perspectives, or does dissent merely confirm the status quo by providing a relatively harmless way of letting off steam?
>
> *Young, 2006, p. xxii*

Citizens need help cultivating the skills necessary to encounter differences respectfully. They also benefit from opportunities to develop effective ways to speak out, articulating the basis for dissent and the principle(s) underlying such a stance.

If we seek to nurture an informed, tolerant, and committed citizenry, our colleges must model the vitality and vibrancy of that lifelong learning. The efficacy of such education can be measured according to the extent to which students emerge from colleges and universities functioning as stewards of an inclusive and plural society. At times, this work is manifest in the willingness to speak truth to power. In the words of legendary folk musician and activist Pete Seeger (1919–2014), "Be wary of great leaders. Hope that there are many, many small leaders" (Talbott, 2014, Introduction, para. 3).

References

Amundson, K. (1991). *Teaching Values and Ethics. American Association of School Administrators Critical Issues.* Report 24. Arlington, VA: American Association of School Administrators.

Angelo, T. (1995, November). Reassessing (and Defining) Assessment. *The AAHE Bulletin,* 48(2), pp. 7–9.

Baldwin, J. (1985). *The Price of the Ticket: Collected Nonfiction.* New York: St. Martin's/ Marek.

Bloom, A. (1987). *The Closing of the American Mind.* New York: Simon & Schuster.

Bowen, W. (2013). *Higher Education in the Digital Age.* Princeton, NJ: Princeton University Press.

Davidson, C. (2012). *Now You See It: How Technology and Brain Science Will Transform Schools and Business for the 21st Century.* New York: Penguin.

Democratizing Education Network (DEN). Democracy Square, http://democracy square.org/.

D'Souza, D. (1998). *Illiberal Education: The Politics of Race and Sex on Campus.* New York: Free Press.

Gillespie, T. (2010). *Doing Literary Criticism: Helping Students Engage with Challenging Texts.* York, ME: Stenhouse Publishers.

Giroux, H. and Giroux, S. (2004). *Take Back Higher Education: Race, Youth, and the Crisis of Democracy in the Post-Civil Rights Era.* New York: Palgrave.

Gwaltney, J. (1986). *The Dissenters: Voices from Contemporary America.* New York: Random House.

Harris, M. (1970). *Five Counterrevolutionists in Higher Education.* Corvallis, OR: Oregon State University Press.

Hirsch, E.D. (1987). *Cultural Literary: What Every American Needs to Know.* Boston, MA: Houghton Mifflin.

hooks, bell. (1989). *Talking Back: Thinking Feminist, Thinking Black.* Boston, MA: South End Press.

Horowitz, D. (2009). *One-Party Classroom: How Radical Professors at America's Top Colleges Indoctrinate Students and Undermine Our Democracy.* New York: Crown.

Hunter, J. (1991). *Culture Wars: The Struggle to Define America.* New York: Basic Books.

Kimball, R. (1990). *Tenured Radicals: How Politics Have Corrupted Our Higher Education.* New York: Harper and Row.

Kuh, G. (2008). *High-Impact Educational Practices: What They Are, Who Has Access to Them, and Why They Matter.* Washington, DC: AAC&U.

Lentricchia, F. and McLaughlin, T. (1989). *Critical Terms for Literary Study.* Chicago, IL: University of Chicago Press.

Morrill, R. (1981). *Teaching Values in College.* San Francisco, CA: Jossey-Bass.

Rosenblatt, L. (1978). *The Reader, The Text, The Poem: The Transactional Theory of the Literary Work.* Carbondale, IL: Southern Illinois University Press.

Smith, T.V. (1970). Middle-Sized Values. In G. K. Smith, ed., *1945–1970: Twenty-Five Years.* San Francisco, CA: Jossey-Bass, pp. 19–33.

Staley, D. (2013, January). Democratizing American Higher Education: The Legacy of the Morrill Land Grant Act. *Origins: Current Events in Historical Perspective,* http://origins. osu.edu.

Talbott, C. (2014, January 28). "Folk singer, activist Pete Seeger dies in New York." *MSN News,* http:music.msn.com/music.

Trow, M. (1976). Higher Education and Moral Development. *AAUP Bulletin,* 62(1), pp. 20–27.

U.S. Department of Education, NCES (National Center for Educational Statistics), Digest of Educational Statistics, http://nces.ed.gov.

Young, R. (2006). *Dissent in America: The Voices that Shaped a Nation.* New York: Pearson Education.

3

DEMOCRATIZING HIGHER EDUCATION IN CANADA

Quality and Educational Development

Arshad Ahmad and Lori Goff

Connecting Quality and Educational Development to the Democratization of Higher Education

The new millennium may be remembered to have unleashed social, political, economic and technological forces that have ushered significant disruptions to prevailing educational systems and norms around the world. We applaud our colleagues and editors of this book to clearly identify major trends and structural changes that are responding to the disruptions globally.

We offer a Canadian perspective on how these forces have created a trajectory of change that is leaning towards a new narrative in higher education underlined by enhancing the quality of the student experience. The enhancement efforts are multidimensional and we only focus on two. First, using a system-wide perspective we explore quality-related issues, such as assurance frameworks, cultural factors, etc. Second, we provide a historical perspective on educational developmental practices locally and nationally that continues to shape teacher training, inform institutional priorities and ultimately impact on the student experience.

The forces, disruptions and changes that implicate quality frameworks and educational development are clearly part of another trajectory that is the democratization of higher education—the title of this book. While democratization itself is a complex idea that could be related to educational choice and pathways, institutional structures, governance and decision-making, etc., we associate it mainly with growth, access, massification and ultimately the globalization of

The authors thank Beth Levinson, Zafar Syed and Rebecca Lee, McMaster University, for contributions to contextualize the topic more broadly.

higher education. This definition of growth is partly based on the fundamental idea that higher education is vital to human development. Democratization in this sense also competes with other factors such as an aging population that competes for health care funding, or the infrastructure needs of society and so on, which the Canadian system considers in allocating its public and private resources towards higher education.

Regarding growth, Canadian universities have in fact experienced significant change, doubling their enrollment since 1980 (AUCC, 2011). Due in part to federal and provincial policy that has supported the expansion of access to higher education, this enrollment increase is also driven by a market demand for skilled labor capable of succeeding in a competitive knowledge-based economy. Universities continue to face pressure to increase enrollment in STEM fields (Science, Technology, Engineering and Mathematics) in order to stave off the impending skills shortage that Canada may face by 2016 according to the Canadian Chamber of Commerce (Morgan, 2014).

This chapter is likely to raise more questions than provide answers to the disruptions and the forces of change. This uncertainty is especially prevalent with respect to technology, which continues to increase and multiply the global mobility of knowledge, e-commerce and e-learning. We have already transitioned into a digital age built on speed and change. Technical infrastructure is in fact shrinking the world, transforming the workplace that includes a strongly collaborative and innovative environment (Tapscott, 2009) as we mark ours as a knowledge-based global economy in the 21st century. In this changing landscape, societies are increasingly looking to educational systems to address economic, social, political and environmental exigencies.

Is Canada prepared to lead or respond to these forces of change and disruption? We begin with a look at Canadian higher education and some of the pressures that are leading indicators of change.

The Canadian Higher Education System

Education in Canada is a sector that falls between control of the provincial and federal governments. This structure has historically caused considerable tension between the two governing bodies (Fisher et al., 2006) although we do not explore jurisdictional frictions in any detail in this chapter. Higher education is, however, a provincial responsibility that oversees education policy. It is important to note that Canada is the only industrialized country without a national office or department of education (Shanahan & Jones, 2007). According to the Council of Ministers of Education Canada (CMEC), higher education in Canada is comprised of 163 recognized public and private universities and 183 recognized public colleges and institutions as well as a number of institutions that offer selected programs under provincial approval. Higher education institutions are underwritten primarily through provincial operating funds. Add to this federal, provincial/territorial and municipal research grants, student fees, bequests and fundraising (CMEC). The Canada Research Chairs (CRC) and the Canadian Foundation for Innovation (CFI) have also added significant research money into higher education institutions (Wormald, 2013).

As mentioned earlier, higher education institutions in Canada have experienced a remarkable increase in enrolment over the past 30 years. This increase has another democratic element in that participation is from a diverse and growing student population, whose profile has evolved into something remarkably different. The Association of Universities and Colleges of Canada (AUCC) reports that while there were 338,000 full-time students enrolled in 1980, those numbers increased to 755,000 by 2010 (AUCC, 2011). Canada currently has the highest percentage of working-age adults who have obtained post-secondary qualifications (51 percent) when compared with other OECD countries with an average of 32 percent as of 2011 (OECD, 2013).

There are several reasons contributing to the increasing and diverse participation of Canadians in higher education. Canada is an attractive destination for international students given that Canada's growth remained constant or stronger than that of other OECD countries (AUCC, 2011). These students bring with them a wide-ranging set of needs and expectations to the classroom. The 2011 Canadian Census showed that approximately one in five Canadians reported a mother tongue other than English or French (Kymlicka, 2010; Shakya et al., 2013). Many of the new immigrants to Canada are themselves educated and create demand for higher education for their children (AUCC, 2011).

Perhaps the most significant factor contributing to the democratization of higher education in Canada comes from pressure from the private sector for a skilled and educated labor force. As Canada shifts from a resource-based to a service sector economy, the demand for post-secondary education has continued to increase (AUCC, 2011). The Canadian University Survey Consortium shows that as far back as 1998, students responded that getting a job is the most important reason for attending university.

As discussed previously, Canada faces a skilled labor market shortage. The Canadian national government has responded to this pressure recently by extending its Pathways to Education Canada 2013 Economic Plan. Since 2001, this program has worked as a partnership with the private sector, along with provincial governments to offer financial aid to economically under-represented and at-risk student populations (Canada's Economic Action Plan, 2013). According to the Canadian Undergraduate Survey Consortium (2004) about 30 percent of all undergraduates had received scholarships or financial aid as of 2007–2008. Institutions have increased their scholarships and bursaries from an average of $150 million in 1990 to approximately $1.6 billion in 2010–2011.

In the face of these successes in providing access to higher education among those students who previously did not participate in it, there remain a number of barriers that continue to challenge Canada in this respect. With respect to access, only 8 percent of Aboriginal people aged 25 to 64 in Canada have a university degree compared to 23 percent of non-Aboriginals (AUCC, 2014). Regarding funding, federal and provincial funds are often tied to research, making it challenging to get resources into the hands of those students who need it most. Annual Canadian tuitions average $22,475 while the OECD countries average is $13,528. Canada has the lowest level of public funding (57. percent) while other OECD countries average 68 percent (OECD, 2013). Additionally, the distance to universities for those students who live in rural localities remains a barrier, as most institutions of higher education are in urban areas. Rural students must incur the costs of travel and living expenses that their urban peers do not face (Kirby, 2008). Many students who have work responsibilities face inflexible admissions and class scheduling that can make participation unfeasible.

As the Canadian economy shifts to service, Canadian employers have invested half as much as their American counterparts into training programs. While the 21st century is commonly characterized as the information technology age, there is a significant portion of the Canadian population that has limited access to it. The digital divide between the technological have and have-nots poses a significant barrier to participation in higher education. Rural and lower socio-economic strata students are less likely to have computers in the home. Additionally, these students live in communities with unstable or limited Internet connectivity. While many of these students do possess computer skills, they use the computer much less frequently than their urban, middle class peers (Looker & Thiessen, 2003), although this is changing.

In order for Canadian higher education to remain relevant in the face of the challenges they face in the 21st century, there are calls for institutional restructuring and differentiation. The diverse student population today must emerge from higher education institutions as nimble thinkers who are capable problem solvers. Students must have the capacity to conceptualize new truths in their fast changing world of access to information technology. They must have the ability to adapt alongside an ever-evolving economy in which new technology renders fields obsolete at a pace much faster than ever before. Organizations must accommodate the thinking of a diverse collection of students who view the world from a number of different lenses and bring with them a variety of backgrounds, experiences and needs. At the same time, as noted by Tapscott (2009), today's students around the world are becoming more alike in their attitudes, behaviors and norms due to the technical infrastructure that brings them together. These demands exist alongside pressure on universities to focus their attention away from students in order to attract research capital. In the absence of a central policy, Canadian universities must endeavor to come together at the institutional, provincial and federal level to face these challenges.

Quality in Higher Education

The increasing emphasis on research intensity has slowly transformed teaching-focused universities of the 1960s to the research-focused institutions of today. As a consequence, undergraduate teaching assignments for full-time tenured or tenure-track faculty have decreased to allow for more focus on producing research results and applying for research funding (Clark et al., 2009). At the same time, because average class sizes have increased, universities have been compensating by hiring temporary and part-time faculty. This financially driven strategy is at odds with goals that aim to provide undergraduate education by teacher-researchers. This gradual shift from education-centered to research-centered institutions has caused many to worry about the quality of education students are receiving.

The mission statements of comprehensive universities across Canada assert their equal dedication to innovation and excellence in teaching and learning, research and scholarship. They aim to seek truth, disseminate knowledge and instill lifelong learning capabilities among their students. The faculty perspective, based on an early study of the most important purposes of a university, include: to impact knowledge and new ideas, to help develop critical thinking and to prepare students for a career (Alexitch & Page, 1997). By reflecting on this gap between perspectives of purpose and the pressure to focus more directly on research, the need for change becomes apparent. Before this study, Lindquist (1978) has identified a wide gap between what an institution thinks it should be doing and what it is doing, which creates opportunities to spark change. These gaps are sometimes identified by those internal to the university to champion change initiatives within. The gaps are also increasingly identified by students, by corporations who hire graduates, by government, or by other external stakeholders who exert pressure to implement new policies that necessitate change to improve quality. Many universities have recognized that these systematic factors implicate the need for quality assurance by instituting and maintaining a quality culture.

The concerns for university quality have been shaped by many influences. Political influences, with respect to federal and provincial funding and mandates, have led to decreased financial support and universal aid, and increased student enrolments, emphasis on accountability, support of privatization and support of marketable research (Shanahan & Jones, 2007). In the face of reduced funding, universities are encouraged to adopt corporatization strategies in order to stay competitive and to attract more students (Altbach, 2010; Cox, 2003; Hedges, 2009). Competition for students and between students puts pressure on the system for higher grades and more flexibility, thereby causing grade inflation and decreased value of credentials (Côté & Allahar, 2007). Credentialism occurs as a result of public beliefs that success is based on obtaining higher credentials, thus increasing the demand for higher education and creating the trends towards massification discussed earlier where an increasingly higher percentage of the population competes to access higher education.

Goff (2013) provided a detailed account of the political and economic trends along with other media, international, technology and social trends that have dynamically interacted with each other to create a demand for quality assurance in higher education within Canada. Together, many of these influences have imposed pressures to compare and contrast the variety of qualifications granted by academic institutions and impact student mobility, credit transfer, graduate study preparation and professional capacity.

Focus on quality is the collective formalization of quality through quality assurance systems (Harvey, 2007) and has led to the quality revolution we have experienced since the 1990s (Newton, 2010). In the absence of a national education system in Canada, the provinces and territories are given authority to establish their own laws, policies and procedures to govern operations of universities. There has been a collaborative system of response at the departmental level to address needs of quality assurance. The province of Ontario plays a central leading role in this movement. For example, the Council of Ontario Universities recently endorsed the Quality Assurance Framework (Ontario Universities Council on Quality Assurance, 2010) to assure the quality of education in universities across the province. The Quality Assurance Framework requires that departments articulate intended learning outcomes for the programs they offer to students. Their program learning outcomes need to be consistent with the university's mission, values, goals and strengths, and they need to at least meet the minimum threshold degree-level expectations endorsed by the university. Departments are encouraged to think critically about how the instructional strategies, assessments and evaluations that are used throughout the program help students to develop both disciplinary content knowledge and requisite skills. Ontario's Quality Assurance Framework is based on the principle of continuous improvement and involves multiple stakeholders, including students, as part of a cyclical and holistic program review and enhancement process.

Many Canadian universities are beginning to focus more attention on program-level curriculum development. A model and guide for facilitating curriculum development in higher education was constructed and put into practice (Wolf, 2007; Wolf, Hill & Evers, 2006) at the University of Guelph and is viewed as an exemplar in Canadian teaching and learning support centers. They promote a faculty-driven, data-informed and educational developer-supported approach to developing curriculum that guides a department through curriculum visioning exercises.

Developing and Supporting a Quality Culture

The faculty-driven and educational developer-supported approaches suggested earlier (O'Neill, 2010; Roy, Borin & Kustra, 2007; Wolf, 2007) may work effectively when curriculum change is initiated internally at a departmental level and spear-headed by change innovators within the department. But large-scale change often requires an external impetus, such as a new policy or quality assurance system, such as the Quality Assurance Framework that was implemented within universities in the province of Ontario.

The revolution and collective formalization of quality has had some noticeable benefits: it has given us a vocabulary to begin to talk about whether student learning has been affected (Ewell, 2010) and has legitimized the discussion of teaching (Harvey, 2007), making it acceptable to talk about teaching quality and innovation publicly. Perhaps it is the development of a quality culture—a culture that sees quality as "transformation" and capable of adding value through enhancement, growth and learning—that will have the most impact on improving the quality of teaching and learning within universities. A strong quality culture is more likely to emerge when examples of quality are recognized and rewarded among the instructors and when everyone is involved collaboratively in innovative quality improvement initiatives. Thus, an important step in the development of a quality culture might be to bring more participants to the table to make decisions on how specific programs within the higher education system can be enhanced and aligned with changing landscapes and contexts within Canada. By bringing together a diverse range of students, excellent and innovative instructors, and leaders of quality assurance systems, we can encourage further democratization of Canada's higher education system as we continue to involve greater participation of stakeholders in enhancing teaching and learning within our colleges and universities.

Preparing educators through collaborations of this nature makes a significant contribution to the shift to a quality culture. To encourage collaborative efforts that seek to imbue a quality culture, each province with its own educational ministry and framework creates its own conditions that influence professional development and training. Notwithstanding differences in these conditions, there are no formal provincial or national policies for training educators in Canada. As mentioned previously, education in Canada is largely a provincial jurisdiction, with a range of programs and strategies that are diverse and hard to report in any systematic way. The approach in Canada, therefore, is context specific. There is evidence that when educational, professional and learning development programs are done well, they become effective for a particular context, the locus of which is typically institutional. However, little can be said regarding any kind of national framework. Inherent in provincial quality assurance initiatives are implications for teaching and learning that can serve to guide the role of the educational developer as well as Teaching & Learning Centers on campus.

The Expanding Roles of Educational Developers

A necessary component of the quality culture implicates the role of the Educational Developer. Kolomitro (2013) provides a good historical account of educational development in Canada. She points to McGill's Centre for Learning and Development, opened in the late 1960s, which spurred other large universities in central Canada to launch similar teaching and learning centers at around the same time. According to Wilcox (1997), who interviewed Educational Developers for a monograph on the history of educational development in Canada, initial efforts focused on institutional concerns with the quality and evaluation practices of teaching. The term "educational development" in Canada was established in June 2003, with the formation of the Educational Developers Caucus (EDC)—a community of practice, or, more formally, a constituency of Canada's national Society for Teaching and Learning in Higher Education (STLHE).

In addition to advocacy through the efforts of a community of practice, some universities in Ontario, such as Guelph and Windsor, offer SEDA (Staff and Educational Development Association) accredited courses. Centers also offer a range of additional services including consultations, workshops, faculty orientations, formal courses of study, certificate programs and support for the Scholarship of Teaching and Learning initiatives, conferences and a wide range of teaching awards. Educational Developers are also known to offer Instructional Skills Workshops (ISW) in nearly all colleges and universities in the province of British Columbia as well as through many teaching and learning centers Canada-wide.

More recently, the roles of teaching and learning centers are shifting from providing development activities to interested faculty to providing evidence for effective practice. For example, McMaster University is transitioning its center to an institute for innovation based on research in teaching and engaging faculty in high-level scholarship of teaching and learning initiatives. Canadian institutions are continuing to appoint senior vice-presidents in teaching and learning that engage in strategic mandates of the university at large, which help to implement a narrative focused on student-centered learning. This is a dramatically different environment from what was once reported in the Smith (1991) report, which made national headlines declaring, "Teaching is seriously undervalued at Canadian universities and nothing less than a total re-commitment to it is required" (p. 63). This report was widely circulated and also called for teacher training to be made mandatory for all new full-time faculty members.

Changing Educational Paradigms, Quality and Educational Development

Today, reports are unlikely to produce significant changes in quality-related and faculty-development initiatives. The focus on outcomes-based education and the changing role of the instructor as facilitator within this context has encouraged a growing realization that teaching should not simply be about knowledge dissemination. Educational developers are on the frontlines advocating an expanded role for effective teaching. Beyond the dissemination of content, these roles increasingly focus on the design of learning activities that encourage students to synthesize the intellectual development theories of Perry (1970) and Baxter-Magolda

(1992); deep approaches to learning (Biggs & Tang, 2007; Marton & Säljö, 1976a, 1976b) and cultivating motivation in learning (Csikszentmihalyi, 1997).

Many others who have had a profound influence on educational practice worldwide have advocated changing the paradigm from a teaching to a more learning-focused approach (e.g. Barr & Tagg, 1995; Entwistle et al., 2000; Ramsden, 1979; Trigwell & Shale, 2004). Shuell argued almost three decades ago that to achieve intended learning outcomes, the instructor's

> fundamental task is to get students to engage in learning activities that are likely to result in their achieving these outcomes . . . It is helpful to remember that what the student does is actually more important in determining what is learned than what the teacher does.
>
> *1986, p. 429*

While traditional lecturing may be appropriate for rote and recall learning, Shuell agreed that deeper and more complex learning requires more needs to be fostered by other methods of teaching that go beyond transmission and dissemination of information.

In Canada, while many Educational Developers and University Centers of Teaching are increasingly asked to address real problems in student learning and develop more effective courses, programs, learning resources, policies and procedures that support student learning, some have asked whether more effective institutional approaches would require faculty to be better prepared as teachers when they enter higher education and also during their ongoing professional development. Some, however, question whether national training frameworks are desirable.

At a recent Faculty Engagement in Educational Development Summit at McMaster University that brought together representatives of 20 Ontario universities (FEED, 2013), there was considerable debate for a province-wide framework for development and training instead of the current institutional approaches. Some are uncomfortable with the term "training," interpreted as teacher-centered and rooted in their own roles; roles that assume a deficit or remedial model of development, implying teachers "need fixing" (McAlpine, 2006, p. 123), where developmental interventions are the fix. Perhaps the acquisition of professional expertise is better served in situated contexts (Skeff, Stratos & Mount, 2007) and away from a focus on development towards more of a focus on learning (Webster-Wright, 2009). However, according to Knapper (2013), whether systems with national policies better prepare teachers is a moot point. One may suspect that they probably do, but empirical evidence, says Knapper, is limited and almost all of the studies, including Gibbs and Coffey (2004), have methodological flaws.

Regardless of how faculty adopt new approaches to student-centered teaching, several Canadian not-for-profit organizations—such as the Society for Teaching and Learning in Higher Education (STLHE), Academics Without

Borders Canada (AWBC), The Canadian Society for the Study of Higher Education (CSSHE) and more recently, Teaching Learning Canada (TLC)—strive to provide a 21st-century solution to 21st-century pressures. They continue to encourage institutions of higher education to create more authentic problem-based and experiential learning activities for students using evidence-based practices that can be used by teachers from all disciplines. There is also a feeling of optimism, at least among the Presidents within the AUCC, that we are advancing 21st-century higher education that meets the current challenges.

Despite the encouraging signs of a focus on quality and educational development, Knapper (2013) reminds us that significant changes remain to be made. He considers the preparation of faculty for their teaching role as limited in scope, reach and impact. He goes on to say that most faculty members never have any systematic preparation and only a minority avail themselves of continuing professional development opportunities. Knapper's account, which assesses the impact of training on teacher effectiveness, is worth exploring as he describes Canada's situation in comparison with those in Britain, Nordic countries and Australasia. Although he includes some very impressive Canadian examples that prepare faculty for a career in teaching, Knapper regards these as exceptions with the majority of training programs

> that (exist) are often piecemeal, largely un-assessed, and often comprise a single course or an assembly of workshops that teachers select according to their interests, supplemented in some cases by completion of a teaching portfolio. Canadian practice more closely reflects the situation in the U.S., where formal preparation for teaching is limited.
>
> *Knapper, 2013, p. 61*

There is arguably silence surrounding a-theoretical approaches to teaching. It is worth asking why the majority of teachers are willing to remain mostly unaware of learning theories and the considerable empirical literature on student learning. Teachers may not feel a need to equip themselves with a theoretical grounding for a variety of reasons. However, ironically teachers are quick to appreciate this fundamental need within their own disciplines and certainly in professional fields such as architecture, engineering, law, business and medicine.

Similarly, Barber, Donnelly and Rizvi (2013) make the compelling argument that complacency in our traditional higher education institutions is not sustainable. They maintain that the forces of globalization and massive diversification in the range of providers, methods and technologies will transform universities, and that the revolution is already underway. The challenges of implementing new pedagogies, learning models and technologies in higher education highlight how inter-connected they are, where complexity is the new reality. Even if a small percentage of the profound changes being predicted come true, they are likely to influence the education of teachers in positive ways.

The good news is the concerted attempts among several Canadian universities and colleges to focus on student engagement through active participation with subject matter as a means towards meeting their educational needs. New approaches that include flipped learning (Talbert, 2014), mobile apps and tablet computing, open courseware and massive open online courses (MOOCs) all have attracted a sustained interest from the national media on improving the quality of post-secondary teaching and learning. Attis, Koproske and Miller (2012) describe the MOOC phenomena with elite universities leading the pack. They consider the biggest short-term impact of MOOCs will be to legitimize online and hybrid learning, moving these from the periphery to the center of attention in higher education. They go on to report that the biggest long-term impact will be pedagogical in terms of adaptive learning assessment, demonstration of competency and interactions carefully calibrated to student needs.

Overall, these are interesting times that bode well for a qualitatively richer experience for Canadian students and for increasing participation among teachers who are increasingly willing partners to co-design innovative learning experiences.

References

Alexitch, L. & Page, S. (1997). Faculty members' attitudes and perceptions about the quality of university education: An initial exploration. *Canadian Journal of Education*, 22(1), 82–88.

Altbach, P.G. (2010). The realities of mass higher education in a globalized world. In D.B. Johnstone (Ed.) *Higher education in a global society* (pp. 25–41). Northampton, MA: Edward Elgar Publishing.

Attis, D., Koproske, C. & Miller, C. (2012). Understanding the MOOC trend: The adoption and impact of massive open online courses. Washington, DC: The University Leadership Council, The Advisory Board Company.

AUCC (2011). Trends in Higher Education: Volume 1– Enrolment. Ottawa, ON: The Association of Universities and Colleges of Canada.

AUCC (2014). Aboriginal education. Retrieved April 18, 2014, from: www.aucc.ca/policy-issues/aboriginal-education/.

Barber, M., Donnelly, K. & Rizvi, S. (2013). AN AVALANCHE IS COMING. Higher education and the revolution ahead. Essay. Institute for Public Policy Research, UK.

Barr, R.B. & Tagg, J. (1995, Nov/Dec). From teaching to learning – A new paradigm for undergraduate education. *Change*, 13–25.

Baxter-Magolda, M.B. (1992). *Knowing and reasoning in college: Gender-related patterns in students' intellectual development*. San Francisco, CA: Jossey-Bass.

Biggs, J.B. & Tang, C. (2007). *Teaching for quality learning at university* (3rd ed.). Buckingham, UK: SRHE and Open University Press.

Canada's Economic Action Plan (2013). Pathways to Education. Retrieved from: http://actionplan.gc.ca/en/initiative/pathways-education-canada.

Canadian Undergraduate Survey Consortium (2004). Survey of first-year university students. Winnipeg, MB: Prairie Research Associates.

Clark, I.D., Moran, G., Skolnik, M.L. & Trick, D. (2009). *Academic transformation: The forces reshaping higher education in Ontario*. Montreal and Kingston: McGill-Queen's University Press.

Côté, J.E. & Allahar, A.L. (2007). *Ivory tower blues: A university system in crisis.* Toronto, ON: University of Toronto Press.

Cox, A.M. (2003). None of your business: The rise of the University of Phoenix and for-profit education—and why it will fail us all. In B. Johnson, P. Kavanagh & K. Mattson (Eds.) *Steal this university: The rise of the corporate university and the academic labor movement* (pp. 15–32). New York: Routledge.

Csikszentmihalyi, M. (1997). Flow and education. *NAMTA Journal*, 22(2), 2–35.

Entwistle, N., Skinner, D., Entwistle, D. & Orr, S. (2000). Conceptions and beliefs about good teaching: An integration of contrasting research areas. *Higher Education Research & Development*, 19(1), 5–26. doi: 10.1080/07294360050020444.

Ewell, P. (2010). Twenty years of quality assurance in higher education: What's happened and what's different? *Quality in Higher Education*, 16(2), 173–175.

FEED (2013). Faculty Engagement in Educational Development Summit. Retrieved from: http://dailynews.mcmaster.ca/article/feed-summit-offers-new-perspectives-on-teaching-and-learning/.

Fisher, D., Rubenson, K., Bernatchez, J., Clift, R., Jones, G., Lee, J., MacIvor, M., Merdith, J., Shanahan, T. & Trottier, C. (2006). *Canadian federal policy and postsecondary education.* Vancouver, BC: University of British Columbia, Faculty of Education.

Gibbs, G. & Coffey, M. (2004). The impact of training of university teachers on their teaching skills, their approach to teaching and the approach to learning of their students. *Active Learning in Higher Education*, 5, 87–100.

Goff, L. (2013). Quality assurance requirements in Ontario universities: How did we get here? In M. Kompf and P. Denicola (Eds.) *Critical issues in higher education: The next generation* (pp. 97–114). Rotterdam, The Netherlands: Sense.

Harvey, L. (2007). Quality culture, quality assurance and impact. In L. Bollaert, S. Brus, B. Curvale, L. Harvey, E. Helle, H. Toft Jensen, J. Komljenovic, A. Orphaides & A. Sursock (Eds.) *Embedding quality culture in higher education: A selection of papers from the 1st European forum for quality assurance* (pp. 81–84). Retrieved from: www.eua.be/typo3conf/ext/bzb_securelink/pushFile.php?cuid=2377&file=fileadmin/user_upload/files/Publications/EUA_QA_Forum_publication.pdf.

Hedges, C. (2009). *Empire of illusion: The end of literacy and the triumph of spectacle.* Toronto, ON: Knopf.

Kirby, D. (2008, May). Higher education in Canada: New millennium, new students, new directions. In *5th General Conference on the Idea of Education, Budapest, Hungary.*

Kolomitro, K. (2013). Educational developers and their use of learning theories: Understandings and practices. Dissertation. Graduate Department of Curriculum, Teaching and Learning, Ontario Institute for Studies in Education, University of Toronto.

Knapper, C.K. (2013). The impact of training on teacher effectiveness: Canadian practices and policies. In E. Simon & G. Pleschová (Eds.) *Teacher development in higher education: Existing programs, program impact, and future trends* (pp. 53–68). New York and London: Routledge.

Kymlicka, W. (2010). *The current state of multiculturalism in Canada and research themes on Canadian multiculturalism 2008–2010.* Ottawa, ON: Minister of Public Works and Government Services Canada.

Lindquist, J. (1978). *Strategies for change.* Berkeley, CA: Pacific Soundings Press.

Looker, E.D. & Thiessen, V. (2003). *The digital divide in Canadian schools: Factors affecting student access to and use of information technology.* Ottawa, ON: Research Data Centres, Statistics Canada.

McAlpine, L. (2006). Coming of age in a time of super-complexity (with apologies to both Mead and Barnett). *International Journal for Academic Development*, 11(2), 123–127.

Marton, F. & Säljö, R. (1976a). On qualitative differences in learning I. Outcome and process. *British Journal of Educational Psychology*, 46(1), 4–11. doi: 10.1111/j.2044-8279.1976.tb02980.x.

Marton, F. & Säljö, R. (1976b). On qualitative differences in learning II. Outcome as a function of the learner's conception of the task. *British Journal of Educational Psychology*, 46(2), 115–127. doi: 10.1111/j.2044-8279.1976.tb02304.x.

Morgan, G. (2014, April 6). Rising to the challenge of Canada's skills shortage. *The Globe and Mail*. Retrieved from: www.theglobeandmail.com/report-on-business/economy/rising-to-the-challenge-of-canadas-skills-shortage/article17850271/.

Newton, J. (2010). A tale of two 'qualitys': Reflections on the quality revolution in higher education. *Quality in Higher Education*, 16(1), 51–53. doi: 10.1080/13538321003679499.

OECD (2013). Country note—Canada. education at a glance 2013: OECD indicators. Retrieved from: www.oecd.org/edu/Canada_EAG2013%20Country%20Note.pdf.

O'Neill, G. (2010). Initiating curriculum revision: Exploring the practices of educational developers. *International Journal for Academic Development*, 15(1), 61–71.

Ontario Universities Council on Quality Assurance (2010). *Quality Assurance Framework*. Retrieved from: www.cou.on.ca/Related-Sites/The-Ontario-Universities-Council-on-Quality-Assura/Policies/PDFs/Quality-Assurance-Framework-and-Guide-Nov—2010.aspx.

Perry, W.G. (1970). *Forms of intellectual and ethical development in the college years: A scheme*. San Francisco, CA: Jossey-Bass.

Ramsden, P. (1979). Student learning and perceptions of the academic environment. *Higher Education*, 8, 411–427.

Roy, D., Borin, P. & Kustra, E. (2007). Assisting curriculum change through departmental initiatives. *New Directions for Teaching and Learning*, 112, 21–32. doi: 10.1002/tl.295.

Shakya, Y.B., Wilson, R., Zahoorunissa, Z., Dahy, S.M.A.A., Almeida, A., White, C., Galabuzi, G.E., Landolt, P., Siddiqui, S., Koch, A., Joly, M.-P. & Alley, S. (2013). *Where are the good jobs? Ten case stories of 'working rough, living poor'*. Toronto, ON: Access Alliance Multicultural Health and Community Services.

Shanahan, T. & Jones, G.A. (2007). Shifting roles and approaches: Government coordination of post-secondary education in Canada, 1995–2006, *Higher Education Research & Development*, 26(1), 31–43. doi: 10.1080/07294360601166794.

Shuell, T.J. (1986). Cognitive conceptions of learning. *Review of Educational Research*, 56(4), 411–436. doi: 10.3102/00346543056004411.

Skeff, K.M., Stratos, G.A. & Mount, J.F.S. (2007). Faculty development in medicine: A field in evolution. *Teaching and Teacher Education: An International Journal of Research and Studies*, 23(3), 280–285.

Smith, S.L. (1991). Report of the Commission of Inquiry on Canadian University Education. Ottawa, ON: Association of Universities and Colleges of Canada.

Talbert, R. (2014, April 1). Toward a common definition of "flipped learning". *The Chronicle of Higher Education*. Retrieved from: http://chronicle.com/blognetwork/castingoutnines/2014/04/01/toward-a-common-definition-of-flipped-learning/.

Tapscott, D. (2009). *Grown up digital: How the net generation is changing your world*. New York: McGraw-Hill.

Trigwell, K. & Shale, S. (2004). Student learning and the scholarship of university teaching. *Studies in Higher Education*, 29(4), 523–536.

Webster-Wright, A. (2009). Reframing professional development through understanding authentic professional learning. *Review of Educational Research*, 79(2), 702–739.

Wilcox, S. (1997). Learning from our past: The history of educational development in Canadian universities. Occasional Papers in Higher Education Number 8. Occasional Paper Series. Canada; Manitoba.

Wolf, P. (2007). A model for facilitating curriculum development in higher education: A faculty-driven, data-informed, and educational developer-supported approach. *New Directions for Teaching and Learning*, 112, 15–20. doi: 10.1002/tl.294.

Wolf, P., Hill, A. & Evers, F. (2006). *A handbook for curriculum assessment*. Guelph, ON: University of Guelph Publications.

Wormald, M. (2013). Emergence of Canadian Research University. *College Quarterly*, 16(3). Retrieved from www.collegequarterly.ca/2013-vol16-num03-summer/wormald.html.

4

DEMOCRATIZATION IN EUROPEAN HIGHER EDUCATION

The Past, Present, and Future of the Bologna Process

María Luisa Pérez Cañado

Introduction

The 21st century has witnessed profound reforms in the higher education (HE) scene. A series of forces—among them, globalization, technology, and competition (Green et al., 2002)—have reconfigured HE worldwide and called for immediate response in tertiary education systems. In Ma's (2008: 65) words, "Higher education in the world has experienced a drastic change in the last few decades."

The impact of these forces has been intensely felt in the European continent, where momentous changes have been operated in higher education. A specific policy framework has been created to guide action and channel such change: the European Higher Education Area (EHEA). The latter is the overarching aim of the so-called Bologna Process, a European convergence process initiated with the Bologna Declaration in 1999 which seeks to achieve more broadly comparable, compatible, and transparent HE systems, not dissociated from social change. "The Bologna Process has been driving forward the most important reforms in higher education in the modern era" (Eurydice, 2010: 3) and has promoted "key policy concepts" (Veiga, 2014: 91) which are deeply rooted in democratization.

This chapter will canvass the past, present, and future of the Bologna Process in order to determine whether it has truly democratized European HE over the course of the past 15 years. In doing so, it will address a series of *wh- questions* which will analyze the EHEA through the lens of the "policy cycle"[1] (Veiga, 2014: 91). To begin with, it will trace the past history of European HE reform by describing *how* the Bologna Process has emerged and developed. Here, the "context of influence" of European convergence will be analyzed by examining the main forces which have impacted European HE and how the continent has faced up to them by setting in motion an ambitious and coordinated project to help Europe become the most competitive and dynamic knowledge-based economy in the world (Lisbon Strategy 2000). The "context of text production" which has bolstered the plan will be examined by summarizing the chief policy documents which have pushed forward the Bologna Process and where the social dimension acquires an increasingly sharp relief.

Has the theory laid out in these documents successfully trickled down to on-the-ground practice? This is what the second chief section of the chapter will target, by describing *what* the results have been in the actual "context of practice" of the Bologna Process. It will establish where we stand at present vis-à-vis core variables related to the process of democratization (such as diversification, affordability, accessibility, participation, or quality assurance) in order to determine the extent to which European HE is providing meaningful, high quality, lifelong learning for all.

The third and final part of the chapter will perform a foresight exercise by addressing the question of *where* we are headed in this arena. The possible future of the Bologna Process will be foregrounded by mapping out three potential scenarios for European HE through which the social dimension continues to run. The ultimate aim of this historical overview is to paint a retrospective and prospective picture of the landscape of European HE in terms of the most salient political and social developments which have affected it from the outset of the 21st century and to identify the chief trends which will continue to impact it as the century advances.

The Past: History and Evolution of the Bologna Process

The Bologna Process burgeons largely as a reactive response to the main forces which began to reshape HE worldwide towards the end of the 20th century. These forces are, according to Green et al. (2002: 7), globalization, technology, and competition.

Although globalization is nothing new in the context of tertiary education (Healey, 2008)—universities have always been global in attracting students from across the world and in exchanging ideas internationally—it acquires a new dimension in the 21st century. According to Iglesias de Ussel et al. (2009), globalization is precipitating five main transformations in post-secondary education: *universalization* (gross enrolment ratios at university have reached an all-time high), *feminization* (female students vastly outnumber their male counterparts), *specialization* (the number of second- and third-cycle courses has notably escalated), *privatization* (research universities and institutes are increasingly private), and *geographic mobility* (there has been an intensification of the number of international students studying at university).

This process of globalization in tertiary education is leading to increased competition across national boundaries. Higher education institutions (HEIs) now compete for students across borders, teachers require an excellent preparation, and students need to acquire the knowledge and skills to tackle new challenges. Prestige and quality are essential, with general assessment measures and agencies being set in place to guarantee the excellence of the education provided.

Technology also heightens competition, as all three forces interact with each other (Green et al., 2002). According to these authors (2002: 7), technology is "the single greatest force for change in higher education" and it is exerting a notable effect on tertiary education through distributed learning. The latter allows students to study at their own pace, increases access to education, paves the way towards lifelong learning, and favors the development of teaching partnerships across institutions and countries. The impact of technology is also being particularly felt on pedagogical aspects, bringing innovation to the foreground and enhancing creativity and participation in the learning process.

Against this backdrop or "context of influence," the Bologna Process is envisaged to "effectively respond to the challenges of globalisation" (European Ministers Responsible for Higher Education (EMRHE), 2007: 1) and to increase "the international competitiveness of the European system of higher education" (European Ministers of Education (EME), 1999: 2). In Veiga's words (2014: 96), the Bologna Process "responded to globalisation and economic competitiveness pressures by launching the Lisbon Strategy with the aim of creating the most competitive knowledge-based economy in the world."

It has been pushed forward via a set of official texts and policy documents at the European level and specific legislation at the national level; what Veiga (2014: 92) terms the "context of text production." From the initial Sorbonne Declaration (1998), where four countries (France, Italy, the UK, and Germany) agreed on the homogenization of the European HE system, to the Bucharest Communiqué (EMRHE, 2012), endorsed by 47 European countries, significant steps have been taken to bolster the European convergence process and to reinforce the social dimension of European HE. Formal ministerial communiqués and declarations are issued every two years, where stocktaking is carried out, core lines of action are identified, and social concerns have been gathering momentum. Indeed, although issues related to democratization have been one of the overarching themes of the Bologna Process, they are not explicitly mentioned in the initial Bologna Declaration (EME, 1999), signed by 29 different countries. This document sets forth a number of important objectives necessary to consolidate the EHEA in order to adapt to the demands of a rapidly changing society and the advances in scientific knowledge. These goals include the establishment of comparable degree systems based on two main cycles—undergraduate and graduate—and on a European credit transfer system (ECTS) whose aim is to promote mobility for students, teachers, researchers, and administrative staff. European cooperation and quality assurance are pinpointed as central to achieve the main aims of the EHEA.

The commitment to these issues is reaffirmed two years later in the Prague Communiqué (European Ministers in Charge of Higher Education (EMCHE), 2001), which now has 33 signatories. For the first time, the idea that "education is a public good and is and will remain a public responsibility" (2001: 1) is explicitly stated. There is also repeated emphasis on the need "to take account of the social dimension in the Bologna Process" (2001: 3). Special relevance is attached to lifelong learning in education, quality assessment standards, and to enhancing not only the competitiveness, but also the attractiveness of HE in Europe. The research dimension in HE is highlighted, together with the benefits of the European credit transfer system to promote mobility, and the importance of having curricula include those competencies which are relevant to the labor market and which students consequently need to acquire.

It is, however, in the Berlin Communiqué (EMRHE, 2003) that the social dimension gathers momentum. The participating Ministers reaffirm its importance within the Bologna Process. Specific objectives are set for the first time, including "strengthening social cohesion and reducing social and gender inequalities both at national and at European level" (2003: 1) or ensuring that students "can successfully complete their studies within an appropriate period of time without obstacles related to their social and economic background" (2003: 5). Concomitantly, concrete measures are suggested to remove all obstacles to mobility (e.g. stepping up portability of national loans and grants) and to promote LLL (lifelong learning) (e.g. recognition of prior learning and the provision of flexible learning paths). This Communiqué, together with the Graz Declaration (European University Association (EUA), 2003), are also notable for the shift they operate to the practical plane. Both vouch for the consolidation of the European credit transfer and accumulation system and for the definition of learning outcomes, competencies, and lifelong learning. Quality assurance, the free and automatic provision of the Diploma Supplement, the promotion of mobility and integrated curricula, the link between the EHEA and the European Research Area (ERA), and ongoing stocktaking are particularly prominent at this stage.

The Glasgow Declaration (EUA, 2005) and the Bergen Communiqué (EMRHE, 2005), with 45 signatories, take the implementation of the EHEA to a further level of concretion. It is time to commit to the elaboration of national frameworks which embody the rationale and underpinnings of the EHEA. There is a conscious effort on the part of universities to articulate the structural change involved in the Bologna Process in terms of specific methodological adjustments. These involve introducing innovative teaching approaches, promoting student-centered learning, specifying learning outcomes in curricular design, bearing in mind potential employers' needs, promoting lifelong learning, and implementing the European credit transfer system. In order to improve the EHEA–ERA synergy, a third cycle—doctoral level—is introduced for the first time, something which had already been advanced in the Graz Declaration (EUA, 2003). The "social dimension" (Bergen Communiqué, EMRHE, 2005: 4) is overtly alluded to for the first time, along with accessibility, and there is a formal commitment to make "quality higher education equally accessible to all" and to help students "especially from socially disadvantaged groups, in financial and economic aspects" (2005: 4). Internationalization of the reform processes occurring in Europe is also underscored, together with the importance of opening them to other parts of the world.

Democratization continues to take root in the Lisbon Declaration (EUA, 2007) and London Communiqué (EMRHE, 2007), where it is now firmly entrenched. "Democratic principles" are mentioned as one of the pillars on which the EHEA is based (2007: 1) and the social dimension is included as one of the priorities for 2009. Fostering social cohesion, reducing inequalities, and reflecting the diversity of the European population that completes HE are all underscored. Stocktaking is particularly prominent at this point and adequate progress is documented vis-à-vis the increase in mobility; the consolidation of the three-tiered degree system; the implementation of national qualifications frameworks; quality assurance, especially through the creation of the European Quality Assurance Register (EQAR); or the enhanced visibility of the EHEA in a global context. Further data collection is called for on mobility, the social dimension, and the internationalization of the EHEA.

Stocktaking continues to be one of the central goals of both the Budapest-Vienna Declaration (EUA, 2010) and the Leuven Communiqué (EMRHE, 2009), whose signatories now amount to 46, and the Bucharest Communiqué (EMRHE, 2012), endorsed by 47 countries. The priorities set out for the 2020 horizon in the two latest official communiqués are practically identical and it is interesting to note that they are almost exclusively linked to the social dimension. Key concepts such as equity, access, participation, or underrepresented groups surface powerfully in both documents. They acknowledge for the first time the "damaging social effects" (2012: 1) of the economic and financial crisis which Europe is undergoing, but commit to securing the "highest possible level of public funding for higher education" (2012: 11). The achievements and consolidation of the EHEA are documented in both communiqués: the Bologna Process is now a reality and its reforms have "changed the face of higher education across Europe" (2012: 1). However, there is also overt acknowledgement of the fact that all the objectives set out in the Bologna Declaration have not been achieved and that further commitment and efforts are necessary for their full and proper implementation. Stocktaking and benchmarking are fundamental in this sense and improved and enhanced data collection, grounded on empirical evidence, are called for.

The priorities on which this stocktaking should focus are almost exclusively aligned with the social dimension in both official documents. A first goal is to provide "higher education for all" (2012: 1). This entails widening access to HE and overall participation, particularly of underrepresented groups; providing equal opportunities to quality education; raising completion rates and ensuring timely progression; and reflecting the diversity of Europe's populations. A second important objective affects mobility: by 2020, at least 20 percent of those graduating in the EHEA should have benefitted from a study period abroad

(Leuven Communiqué, EMRHE, 2009). There is increased commitment to financial support on this score in the Bucharest Communiqué (EMRHE, 2012) through the adoption of the "Mobility for Better Learning Strategy". Lifelong learning is also targeted as an integral part of European HE systems, by fostering flexible learning paths and favoring part-time studies and work-based routes. Finally, student-centered learning also figures high on the latest European agenda, through the promotion of innovative teaching methodologies and more individually tailored education paths. The next Ministerial conference will review progress on these priorities in Yerevan (Armenia) in 2015.

Thus, it can be gleaned from this historical overview of the Bologna Process that considerable strides have been made in its development in response to demands of an increasingly globalized, competitive, and technological society (the "context of influence"). A series of official biannual declarations and communiqués (the "context of text production") have provided a solid top-down push to the creation of the EHEA, whose foundations are now held to be "firmly in place" (Eurydice, 2010: 3). As the latest Eurydice Report (2012: 3) has put it, "The Bologna Process is a European success story of which we should be proud." As it has unravelled, the social dimension has acquired an increasingly sharp relief. From not being mentioned at all in the Bologna Declaration (1999) and only timidly appearing in the Prague Communiqué (EMCHE, 2001), social concerns have gone on to permeate the bulk of the latest Leuven (EMRHE, 2009) and Bucharest (EMRHE, 2012) communiqués. Commitment to core concepts such as accessibility, participation, equity, diversity, quality, mobility, lifelong learning, or student-centeredness is increasingly prevalent in the official European documents driving forward the EHEA. However, have these theoretically endorsed constructs actually filtered down to on-the-ground practice? The following section will provide empirical data on whether they have remained rhetoric or become a reality.

The Present: From Policy to Practice

Stocktaking has underpinned the Bologna Process from its very origins. "Continuous evaluation," as Veiga (2014: 100) terms it, has steered official documents and impinged on decision-making in each Ministerial Conference. Eurydice (2010, 2012), Eurostat (2011a, 2011b, 2012), Eurostudent (2008, 2011), the European University Association (EUA) (1999, 2008, 2011a, 2011b), or the EQUNET Project (working for equitable access to HE in Europe) have all been "data collectors" (Eurydice, 2012: 16) in the Bologna Process, on whose findings we draw to chronicle this next section on the "context of practice" of the EHEA.

The key terms in the official European documents which allow us to paint a comprehensive picture of democratization in European HE at present are *diversification, affordability, accessibility, participation,* and *quality.* They have all become cornerstones in the implementation of the Bologna Process and are closely intertwined. Although there is a considerable (and understandable) heterogeneity across the 47 EHEA countries on these issues, certain general trends can be discerned vis-à-vis where Europe currently stands in providing meaningful, high-quality learning for all. The most conspicuous ones are now identified within each of the afore-mentioned headings.

Diversification

The first issue under scrutiny—diversification—is already a pivotal one. In Reichert's (2009: 8) words, "Institutional diversity or differentiation is one of the most intensely debated topics of higher education policy and research." In response to the new and increased demands associated with the emergence of knowledge societies, European HEIs now have to be prepared to assume new roles and tasks which transcend the traditional functions of teaching and research. Among these novel dimensions of HE activities, Reichert (2009: 8) documents increased access, business innovation, knowledge transfer, and continuing professional development.

In order to step up to these new challenges, European HE systems "have become greatly diversified" (Jacob & Reimer, 2011: 223), and this differentiation has been intensified by the harmonization objectives of the Bologna Process, now being "widespread in higher education systems across Europe" (Jacob & Reimer, 2011: 224). The creation of the EHEA has had an impact on three main types of binary distinctions pertaining to institutional diversification:

- *Vertical vs. horizontal differentiation*: In order to meet the growing demand for HE in Europe, there has been a diversification of degree levels (vertical differentiation) and programs, courses, and fields of study (horizontal differentiation). The former has led to the creation of second-tier institutions, such as Polytechnics in the UK and *Fachhochschulen* in Germany, with new bachelor's and master's degrees being set up. The latter, in turn, has stemmed in a diversification of types of programs (e.g. academic vs. professional). This ties in directly with the following dichotomy.
- *Academic vs. professionally oriented HEIs*: These two different types of HEIs can be found across Europe, although, partly due to the Bologna Process, differences between them seem to be diminishing or ceasing to exist altogether (Eurydice, 2012).
- *Public vs. private HEIs*: Both types abound in the vast majority of the EHEA countries. Only Finland, Denmark, Italy, Andorra, Belgium, and Greece have all-public HEIs.

Affordability

In line with the foregoing, European HEIs are predominantly funded by public sources (Eurydice, 2012). Indeed, private expenditure per HE student is eight times higher in the US than in the EU, where, as Veugelers (2011: 9) documents, "most of the financing of higher education is public funding, where the State is seen as the provider of education services as public goods with low tuition fees." It is interesting to note that, despite the severe impact of the economic crisis on European HE—which resulted in a 2.2 percent decline of public expenditure in tertiary education in 2008–2009, as well as considerable budget cuts in HE in countries such as Iceland, Ireland, and Greece—these reductions were not embraced as a uniform response across the continent.

The EHEA median spending in HE is 1.15 percent of the GDP and, in terms of national expenditure, the median is 2.76 percent of the budget. In turn, the median value for annual total expenditure in tertiary education per full-time equivalent (FTE) student is 8,087€ (Eurydice, 2012). On all three indicators, the values are highest for Scandinavian countries (Sweden, Denmark, and Norway).

This trend also transpires for fees and financial support. Student fees are commonly charged across the EHEA: 14 higher education systems require their students to pay fees, vs. seven who do not charge them (especially in Nordic countries). The majority of the countries involved in the Bologna Process use a combination of three chief criteria to determine the eligibility of students to pay fees: financial considerations, academic performance, and part- or full-time status. In turn, student support is articulated in terms of grants (13 systems have them as the chief source of student support, particularly in Central and Eastern Europe), loans (which operate in conjunction with grants in four member states), and tax benefits for parents (in seven countries, they are combined with grants and in nine with both grants and loans). It is positive to ascertain that the median level of investment in student support has increased from 12.9 percent to 14.1 percent in the past decade, although it appears to have plateaued or even slightly regressed from 2002 onwards. Again, the highest share of financial aid to students can be found in the Scandinavian countries (it is as high as 44 percent in Norway), which invest above 25 percent of their HE budget in student support. Thus, it is not surprising to observe that countries like Sweden come across as the most affordable in the world in terms of HE, due to low education costs, generous grants, and high take-up of loans (Usher & Cervenan, 2005). Finland, Denmark, Sweden, and the Netherlands (Veugelers, 2011) also fare well in this arena.

Accessibility

Both affordability and differentiation clearly impact students' accessibility to HE, thereby attesting to the interplay of all the factors under examination. Affordability works towards the removal of obstacles related to students' social and economic background, one of the main missions of the EHEA regularly reaffirmed by European Ministers since 2001. In turn, according to Jacob and Reimer (2011), differentiation has also impinged on students' access to HE on two main fronts: the creation of lower-tier institutions has stepped up enrolment levels in tertiary education of students from underprivileged backgrounds and poorer students are still underrepresented in the more prestigious HEIs. This already points to one of the three main aspects on which equity of access is held to be reliant—socioeconomic background—with the other two being gender and age. Let us now examine all three in order to determine how equitable European HE currently is in terms of accessibility.

Access to higher education is defined by Usher and Medow (2010: 1) as "the ability of people from all backgrounds to access higher education on a reasonably equal basis." It has increasingly become pivotal due to the ageing challenge, to provide the skills required for future sustainable growth, and to reduce the risk of social exclusion (Veugelers, 2011: 2). Equitable access to HE is considered to be "the foundation of the modern knowledge economy, and without it, the bright futures of many youth around the world would be dimmed" (Usher & Cervenan, 2005: 2).

Although a wide divergence can be detected in the equity of HE systems (Camilleri, 2010), equitable access has been growing, albeit slowly, in the EHEA. According to Eurydice (2012), enrolments in European HE have increased between 1999 and 2009, and Usher and Cervenan (2005: 2) document the "massification" of HE, which has "provided opportunities to an ever-widening group of youth across OECD countries." This, however, has not been done in a uniform manner. Finland and the Netherlands are instances of success stories in terms of accessibility and gender parity scores, as opposed to Germany, Belgium, and Austria, which are at the bottom of the European cline in terms of accessibility measures. Western European countries are, on the whole, characterized by greater flexibility in terms of entry qualifications than their remaining EHEA counterparts (Eurydice, 2012).

This is particularly relevant given the significant barriers to access which have been identified for older students and those from an unfavorable socioeconomic background and which include insufficient pre-training, lack of financing, and poor job prospects (Veugelers, 2011). In terms of age, approximately 49 percent of the 16- to 34-year-olds in Europe can expect to participate in HE (Camilleri, 2010). The typical age of entry to HE across Europe currently ranges from 19 to 21 and the most common entry route is through secondary school (86 percent of entrants are secondary stage graduates). Older age groups (25+) still rarely embark on HE (less than 2 percent, according to Eurostat, 2009). Thus, access to HE still largely appears to be dependent on successful participation in earlier stages of education.

Gender-wise, women accessing HE outnumbered their male counterparts in the first decade of the Bologna Process (Eurydice, 2012). However, this varies according to fields of study: women tend to dominate the education field, veterinary science, health, and welfare, vs. men, who still prevail in computing, engineering, and transport services.

Finally, vis-à-vis socioeconomic background, differences are still pronounced. Students of a lower socioeconomic provenance, as measured by their parents' occupational and educational status, continue to have considerably less access to

HE in most European countries. They are less likely to attend HE to choose different courses of study, or to have a mobility experience, and are more prone to work during their studies (Camilleri, 2010: 103). This, however, varies across countries, with Finland, the Netherlands, Sweden, and Ireland presenting considerably lower underrepresentation due to socioeconomic background, vs. the Eastern European countries and Germany, where inequity on this front is particularly marked. Countries with low socioeconomic inequity show relatively high proportions of access to HE via alternative routes, from which non-traditional learners have been found to benefit (Eurydice, 2012). They include adult education, recognition of prior learning and knowledge/skills acquired outside formal learning contexts, or following specific preparatory programs. Consequently, the majority of EHEA countries have stepped up the creation of these non-traditional access routes and, at present, 22 HE systems have already established at least one alternative access route to HE. In 11 of them, alternative access routes represent between 2 percent and 15 percent of all admissions at present. Thanks to measures such as these, the proportion of students from lower socioeconomic backgrounds accessing HE in Europe has increased in absolute terms over the past decade. However, this access is still not equitable, as it would take "100 years for such students to reach the same participation rate as those from high socioeconomic backgrounds" (Camilleri, 2010: 103). Considerable headway, thus, still needs to be made on this front.

Participation

Do these students from lower socioeconomic backgrounds and higher ages remain in and successfully complete HE in Europe? This is one of the headline targets of the Europe 2020 Strategy, which seeks to increase the share of the population aged 30 to 34 to have completed HE from 32 percent to 40 percent, and to reduce drop-out rates to 10 percent. The diverse performance indicators (completion and graduation rates) unequivocally point to a steady and sustained growth of EU graduates over the last years, with an average annual growth rate of 2.8 percent from 2002 to 2007 (Veugelers, 2011). The median completion rate stands at 72 percent. In turn, the median net graduation rate increased between the academic years 2003–2004 and 2008–2009 from 30 percent to 36.2 percent (Eurydice, 2012). Completion data available for 22 EHEA countries evinces that three out of four HE entrants complete their studies with graduation, with the introduction of the ECTS and the two-cycle structure greatly having contributed to this situation. As with entry rates, this panorama varies greatly across countries, however. Nordic countries (e.g. Denmark, Finland, Sweden), together with the Netherlands and the UK, generally perform above EU average, evincing the highest completion rates (already well above the targeted 40 percent for 2020), in contrast to Mediterranean and Eastern European countries (like Italy or the Czech Republic), which are currently below the 20 percent threshold (Eurostat, 2009).

Similarly to entry data, four main factors impinge on graduation and completion rates: age, gender, social background, and migrant status. Figures for age and gender practically mirror those obtained for accessibility. Attainment levels are clearly higher for younger age groups. The median for the 25 to 34 age group is 33.2 percent, 26.5 percent for the 34 to 44 segment, and 21.5 percent for learners aged 45 to 64. The percentage of older age groups obtaining a HE degree is on the increase (Eurydice, 2012), but the overall participation of adults remains low (Camilleri, 2010). In terms of gender balance, over the last decade, men are less likely to attain HE than women and the percentage of female students in HE has increased between 2000–2001 and 2008–2009. However, women are still underrepresented among doctoral graduates.

Influence of parental education on HE attainment, as was the case with accessibility, continues to be intensely felt (even more so than having a migrant background). As the Eurydice report (2012: 79) has underscored, "Overall, the analysis of HE participation and attainment indicates that the goal of providing equal chances for all in the EHEA has not yet been achieved." The relative chances for students with highly educated parents to attain higher education in the EHEA are between two and five times higher than for students whose parents have a medium educational level. However, on the upside, this influence appears to be diminishing. The chance of the educationally most underprivileged to graduate from HE has increased over time (Camilleri, 2010). Interestingly, at present, if anything it is the level of attainment of students with a HE background that is not increasing at the same pace. As Reichert (2009: 155) documents, European HE systems "have displayed difficulty with the idea, definition and support of their elites, caught in the tension between the need to expand higher education to larger parts of society and the continuing need to develop some elite forms of provision."

Low participation rates in HE have also been consistently documented for first-generation migrant students, understood as "individuals for whom the country of birth is not the reference country" (Eurydice, 2012: 75). In almost all European countries, participation rates for migrants are lower than for non-migrants. Access problems and early school drop-out are some of the most forceful reasons ascribed to this circumstance, particularly in countries such as Greece, Italy, or Spain.

In the light of this data, the majority of the EHEA countries have set in place policies to address underrepresentation, provide equal opportunities for all to participate in HE, and increase the level of completion of tertiary studies. They include:

- increasing fees and financial support;
- introducing new HE programs, short-cycle, and professionally oriented programs;
- fostering greater flexibility in learning paths;

- providing guidance and counseling services to guarantee informed choices regarding further career development; and
- targeting specific underrepresented groups (e.g. students with disabilities, low educational background, migrant status, or specific gender and ages) via concrete measures.

Only a few countries (e.g. Austria, Ireland, Finland, and Norway) have set actual quantitative targets to be reached and only about half of the Bologna countries systematically monitor participation (Eurydice, 2010), but HEIs are increasingly being financially incentivized to improve completion rates. Indeed, in this sense, public budget allocations depend in part on student completion rates (e.g. in all the Scandinavian countries) and they are equally considered one of the central criteria of external quality assurance procedures (e.g. in Poland, Luxembourg, and Latvia).

Quality

It is precisely to quality assurance that we now turn. The latter has been one of the most notable features of the EHEA and a top priority on the European agenda since the launch of the Bologna Process. Impressive changes have been documented in the landscape of HE quality assurance since the Bologna Process began, although, as in other areas, there is still room for improvement: "While it is a moot question whether quality in higher education has improved during the past Bologna decade, there is no doubt whatsoever that quality assessment has seen dramatic developments" (Eurydice, 2010: 24). Three main indicators have been used to measure advances in this area: the stage of external quality assurance, the level of student participation in external quality assurance, and the level of international participation.

Since the outset of the Bologna Process, 22 countries have established agencies for quality assurance, with roughly half of these being set up from 2005 onwards. Eleven EHEA countries do not have quality assurance agencies (these are often nations with a small HE sector, such as Andorra or Liechtenstein), although quality assurance has not been neglected; it has merely been approached in a different manner. The vast majority of quality assurance systems (24) now focus on both institutions and programs. In the early stages, the onus was typically on program evaluation, which then generally evolved to an institutional focus, albeit not eschewing continuing attention to program assessment. Scorecard category indicators have been established to trace the stage of development of external quality assurance systems (from green to red zones). The outcomes evince that no EHEA countries are in the red zone (absence of adequate quality assurance system) and the remainder spread out over the remaining four categories. The majority are found in the green zones (18 in the dark green and six in the light green areas), with comprehensive quality assurance systems firmly in place (although some elements might be missing in the light green zone). Seventeen are situated in the yellow zone, which indicates that all the core quality assurance aspects are covered, but national agencies have not yet been evaluated against the European standards and guidelines. Finally, only six are in the orange zone, with quality assurance agencies not having been evaluated and all the key quality assurance issues not yet having been covered (Eurydice, 2012).

The area of student participation in external quality assurance still evinces considerable room for progress, as only 11 countries allow full student participation in all aspects of quality assurance systems. Finally, vis-à-vis the level of international participation, there is still a notable reluctance to defer responsibility for external quality assurance beyond national boundaries, despite the establishment of the EQAR as a major milestone in 2007. Only 14 countries allow their HEIs to be freely evaluated by national agencies other than their own. Thus, although the outcomes confirm the impressive changes which have been operated in the quality assurance area since the inception of the Bologna Process, there is still progress to be made in fully consolidating it.

The Future: Where is Democratization in the Bologna Process Headed?

The reconfiguration of European HE in the 2020 horizon is addressed by Magalhães (2014), who, in a foresight exercise carried out through prospective studies of present trends, envisages three possible scenarios for the future of the EHEA. The first of them, which he terms *Centralia* or *City of the Sun*, would be characterized by a strong presence of state coordination in HE and by an equally potent European integration and harmonization. Universities would be large organizations with enormous campuses and primarily public funding. Lifelong learning would run through European HE and differences would be found on two main levels: prestige (with the most prestigious institutions being found in Northern and Western Europe) and research (with R&D functions being developed mostly privately). Education systems would be largely reliant on upper European levels of administration and there would be a system of mandatory European accreditation.

A greater de-centralization would characterize the second possible scenario: *Octavia* or the *Spider-Web City* (Magalhães, 2014: 114). Here, although a rift would still be detected between Northern and Western European universities (more research-based) and Southern and Eastern European institutions (more focused on teaching), the system of governance would be more complex than in the previous picture, as power and authority would be de-centralized to a great extent and thus shared among supranational, national, and local actors. There would be greater diversity in terms of types of HE organizations, types and duration of programs, size of institutions (which would not be standardized, with the most successful being the smaller ones), and funding (with both public and private sources). Quality control would thus be more problematic due to this enhanced variety and flexibility.

At the other end of the cline, in the *Vitis Vinifera* or *City of Traders* scenario, the afore-mentioned diversity is extreme. In this "disperse and diverse" (Magalhães, 2014: 116) hypothetical context, Europe has not become the most competitive, knowledge-driven economy in the world, and it has been superseded by the US and Japan. Institutional autonomy is key and coordination of higher education and research are regulated by the market. Indeed, education is essentially seen as a kind of merchandise and HEIs are mostly private, with funding varying from institution to institution. Difficulties would thus be detected in promoting uniform standards of assessment and comparison, and quality control would hardly make sense.

As these three scenarios are "projections of present trends" (Magalhães, 2014: 117), all three are possible in the near future and not mutually exclusive. It behooves us to continue to keep an eye on and take stock of the way in which the Bologna Process unravels over the next half decade and to "become actively involved in the debate and to participate in the reconfiguration processes under way" (Magalhães, 2014: 122).

Conclusion

This constant stocktaking has, in fact, been the general trend since the launch of the Bologna Process, as has been ascertained in the present chapter. The creation of the EHEA has been a reactive and proactive response in harmony with the broader social and political forces which are reconfiguring HE on both sides of the Atlantic. They constitute the "context of influence" under which the Bologna Process has unfolded, whose past, present, and future have been canvassed in this chapter.

What are the broader take-aways of this historical overview vis-à-vis democratization? To begin with, in the official documents which have pushed forward the Bologna Process (the "context of text production"), a notable drive can be detected towards the democratization of European HE, through an increase in accessibility, participation, and quality. Considerable efforts have thus been made and specific quantitative targets have been set in the diverse declarations and communiqués to continue advancing in this area. And it is largely consensual that the afore-mentioned concepts *have* filtered down to the practical plane, albeit in heterogeneous ways (given the considerable number of countries within the EHEA) and more conspicuously in some areas than in others. European HE is now more diversified (in terms of degree levels, programs, and academic vs. professional orientation); public funding has not been scaled back despite the economic crisis and student support is on the increase (particularly in Scandinavian countries); equitable access is slowly on the rise, as is participation, with important policies being set in place to continue bolstering both; and advances in quality assurance have been particularly notable. The strapline for the democratization of European HE could thus be "slowly, but surely."

Considerable headway has thus been made, but European authorities acknowledge that this is "no time to take our foot off the pedal" (Eurydice, 2010: 3). This is what has continuously characterized the Bologna Process: it has driven forward specific measures to address the chief cornerstones of the social dimension, taken stock of how they have played out, and been responsive to those findings by effecting the necessary readjustments to keep them on track. The road has been paved; only time (and the 2020 horizon) will tell whether democratization continues to be on the upsurge within such an ambitious, far-reaching, and data-driven action plan as that fueled by the Bologna Process in the European continent.

Note

1 According to Veiga (2014), the "policy cycle" examines the different contexts of policy implementation: that which influences the emergence of a specific policy ("context of influence"); the way in which it is articulated via official texts and policy documents ("context of text production"); or its translation to and interpretation in the practical plane ("context of practice").

References

Camilleri, A. F. (2010). Conclusions and recommendations. In A. F. Camilleri & K. Mühleck (Eds.), *Evolving diversity. An overview of equitable access to higher education in Europe* (pp. 95–111). Brussels: The EQUNET Consortium.

EMCHE (European Ministers in Charge of Higher Education). (2001). *Towards the European Higher Education Area. Communiqué of the Meeting of European Ministers in charge of Higher Education in Prague on May 19th 2001.* www.eua.be/fileadmin/user_upload/files/EUA1_documents/OFFDOC_BP_Prague_communique.1068714711751.pdf (April 15, 2014).

EME (European Ministers of Education). (1999). *The Bologna Declaration.* www.bologna-bergen2005.no/Docs/00-Main_doc/990719BOLOGNA_DECLARATION.PDF (April 15, 2014).

EMRHE (European Ministers Responsible for Higher Education). (2003). *Realising the European Higher Education Area. Communiqué of the Conference of Ministers responsible for Higher Education in Berlin on 19th September 2003.* www.eua.be/fileadmin/user_upload/files/EUA1_documents/OFFDOC_BP_Berlin_communique_final.1066741468366.pdf (April 15, 2014).

EMRHE (European Ministers Responsible for Higher Education). (2005). *Achieving the goals. Communiqué of the Conference of European Ministers responsible for Higher Education. Bergen, 19–20 May 2005.* www.bologna-bergen2005.no/Docs/00-Main_doc/050520_Bergen_Communique.pdf (April 15, 2014).

EMRHE (European Ministers Responsible for Higher Education). (2007). *London Communiqué. Towards the European Higher Education Area: responding to challenges in a globalised world.* www.cicic.ca/docs/bologna/2007LondonCommunique.en.pdf (April 15, 2014).

EMRHE (European Ministers Responsible for Higher Education). (2009). *Leuven Communiqué. The Bologna Process 2020 – The European Higher Education Area in the new decade.* www.ond.vlaanderen.be/hogeronderwijs/bologna/conference/documents/leuven_ louvain-la-neuve_communiqu percentC3 percentA9_april_2009.pdf (April 15, 2014).

EMRHE (European Ministers Responsible for Higher Education). (2012). *Making the most of our potential: Consolidating the European Higher Education Area.* Bucharest *Communiqué.* www.ehea.info/Uploads/percent281percent29/Bucharestpercent20 Communiquepercent202012percent281percent29.pdf (April 15, 2014).

EUA (European University Association). (1999). *Project report: Trends in learning structures in higher education.* www.eua.be/eua/jsp/en/upload/OFFDOC_BP_trend_I.10687 15136182.pdf (April 15, 2014).

EUA (European University Association). (2003). *Graz Declaration – Forward from Berlin: The role of universities.* www.eua.be/fileadmin/user_upload/files/EUA1_documents/ COM_PUB_Graz_publication_final.1069326105539.pdf (June 29, 2010).

EUA (European University Association). (2005). *Glasgow Declaration – Strong universities for a strong Europe.* www.eua.be/fileadmin/user_upload/files/EUA1_documents/ Glasgow_Declaration.1114612714258.pdf (April 15, 2014).

EUA (European University Association). (2007). *Lisbon Declaration – Europe's universities beyond 2010: diversity with a common purpose.* www.eua.be/fileadmin/user_upload/files/ Lisbon_Convention/Lisbon_Declaration.pdf (April 15, 2014).

EUA (European University Association). (2008). *European universities' charter on lifelong learning.* Brussels: EUA.

EUA (European University Association). (2010). *Budapest-Vienna Declaration on the European Higher Education Area.* www.ond.vlaanderen.be/hogeronderwijs/bologna/ 2010_conference/documents/Budapest-Vienna_Declaration.pdf (April 15, 2014).

EUA (European University Association). (2011a). *Impact of the economic crisis on European universities. Update: first semester 2011.* www.eua.be/Libraries/Governance_Autonomy_ Funding/Economic_monitoring_June2011.sflb.as (April 15, 2014).

EUA (European University Association). (2011b). *EUA's monitoring of the impact of the economic crisis on public funding for universities in Europe.* www.eua.be/eua-work-and-policy-area/governance-autonomyand-funding/public-funding-observatory.aspx (April 15, 2014).

Eurostat. (2009). *Europe in figures. Eurostat yearbook 2009.* Luxembourg: Office for Official Publications of the European Communities. http://epp.eurostat.ec. europa.eu/cache/ITY_OFFPUB/KS-CD-09-001/EN/KS-CD-09-001-EN.PDF (November 18, 2014).

Eurostat. (2011a). *EU labour force survey database. User guide.* http://circa.europa.eu/irc/ dsis/employment/info/data/eu_lfs/lfs_main/LFS_MAIN/LFSuserguide/EULFS_ Database_UserGuide_2011.pdf (April 15, 2014).

Eurostat. (2011b). *Indicators of immigrant integration. A pilot study. Eurostat methodologies and working papers.* Luxembourg: Publications Office of the European Union.

Eurostat. (2012). *Educational attainment, outcomes and returns of education.* http://epp.eurostat. ec.europa.eu/cache/ITY_SDDS/EN/edat_esms.htm (April 15, 2014).

Eurostudent. (2008). *Social and economic conditions of student life in Europe.* www.eurostudent. eu/download_files/documents/Synopsis_of_Indicators_EIII.pdf (April 15, 2014).

Eurostudent. (2011). *Social and economic conditions of student life in Europe.* www.eurostudent. eu/results/reports (April 15, 2014).

Eurydice. (2010). *Focus on Higher Education in Europe. The impact of the Bologna Process.* Brussels: Education, Audiovisual and Culture Executive Agency.

Eurydice. (2012). *The European Higher Education Area in 2012: Bologna Process Implementation Report.* Brussels: Education, Audiovisual and Culture Executive Agency.

Green, M., Eckel, P., & Barblan, A. (2002). *The brave new (and smaller) world of higher education: A transatlantic view.* www.eua.be/fileadmin/user_upload/files/EUA1_documents/brave-new-world.1069322743534.pdf (April 15, 2014).

Healey, N. M. (2008). Is higher education *really* 'internationalising'? *Higher Education, 55,* 333–355.

Iglesias de Ussel, J., de Miguel, J. M., & Trinidad, A. (2009). *Sistemas y políticas de educación superior.* Madrid: Consejo Económico y Social.

Jacob, M. & Reimer, D. (2011). Differentiation in higher education and its consequences for social inequality: introduction to a special issue. *Higher Education, 61*(3), 223–227.

Ma, W. (2008). The University of California at Berkeley: An emerging global research university. *Higher Education Policy, 21,* 65–81.

Magalhães, A. M. (2014). Scenarios, dilemmas, and pathways to European Higher Education. In A. Teodoro & M. Guilherme (Eds.), *European and Latin American Higher Education between mirrors. Conceptual frameworks and policies of equity and social cohesion* (pp. 109–124). Rotterdam: Sense Publishers.

Reichert, S. (2009). *Institutional diversity in European higher education. Tensions and challenges for policy makers and institutional leaders.* Brussels: European University Association.

Usher, A. & Cervenan, A. (2005). *Global higher education rankings 2005.* Toronto, ON: Educational Policy Institute.

Usher, A. & Medow, J. (2010). *Global higher education rankings 2010. Affordability and accessibility in comparative perspective.* Toronto, ON: Higher Education Strategy Associates.

Veiga, A. (2014). Researching the Bologna Process through the lens of the policy cycle. In A. Teodoro & M. Guilherme (Eds.), *European and Latin American Higher Education between mirrors. Conceptual frameworks and policies of equity and social cohesion* (pp. 91–108). Rotterdam: Sense Publishers.

Veugelers, R. (2011). *A policy agenda for improving access to higher education in the EU.* Brussels: European Expert Network on Economics of Education.

5

SOUTH EUROPE HIGHER EDUCATION

Portugal and Its Peripheral Regions

Luísa Soares and Catarina Faria

Introduction

Education is, and should be, a public, irreplaceable and indispensable asset. The universal right to education is one of the most significant achievements resulting from the modernization of societies. Access to education and the right to learn are necessary for the talent development of people, the advancement of countries and the well-being of societies. The access to education is seen as a key factor in the realization of civil and political rights.

Portugal is part of the European community situated in the south of Europe, next to Spain. Two Autonomous Regions also belong to this country: the Azores and Madeira islands, both of which boast one University each. Lisbon is the capital city of Portugal. It is a cosmopolitan city with several Universities. Porto and Coimbra are also two main cities of Portugal, both of which also have great Universities. The establishment of the University was an important milestone in the development of education in Portugal, which followed the general education movement in Europe in the thirteenth century. Since that time, higher education institutions have been regarded as privileged means of promoting development and strengthening of national identity and self-determination. At that period of time, all Universities were public and few in numbers. During the dictatorship, Portugal was delayed with respect to the school open to all children and young people, and higher education reflected, of course, this late development. The University was reserved for social and economic elites as a privileged instrument of social reproduction. When the dictatorship ended in 1974, some private Universities were created, which increased the available courses allowing a greater number of students to enter the higher education system. Free and compulsory education was instituted. Beginning with the requirement of six academic years, in 1986 was implemented nine years of compulsory school and in 2005 this became 12 years. Also, another factor that contributed to democratization was that the University degree was considered as a way to have professional and personal success, which motivated young people to enter the University.

These changes that occurred with the implementation of democracy have brought to the public debate expressions such as *democratization, disqualification of diplomas* and *lifelong learning*. For a long time, the democratization of education was associated with levels of education like pre-school, primary and secondary, but over time the discussion has been expanded to higher education.

The term *democratization* can be analyzed from a social and political perspective or as a process. Arguing democratization from the social and political perspective is to argue that there is equal access to higher education. In Portugal, the democratization of access to higher education became increasingly diversified of educational opportunities and opened the possibility of a new public access to this level of education (Pascueiro, 2009).

In 1970, Portuguese higher education was comprised of just four public Universities, with about 50,000 students. Since 1970, a number of new Universities, Institutes and Polytechnic institutes have been created and there are currently 41 institutions of higher education in Portugal. In the academic year 2010/2011 the total number of courses being offered was 4,222, 54 percent of which were at master's level. Doctoral courses constituted approximately 24 percent of all national provision. Therefore, more technological specialization courses, as well as after hours (work) courses, post-graduate training and doctoral courses have been created. With regards to the area of study, the most common courses are the business sciences (46 percent) followed by social sciences and law (26 percent), (Conselho Nacional de Educação (National Council of Education), 2012).

According to the OECD (Organisation for Economic Co-operation and Development), the growth process in the Portuguese higher education system, in recent decades, has been remarkable. Comparing the number of students between the years 1975 and 2001, Portugal has one of the highest growth rates of participation among the European Union countries, with an approximate value of 6 percent growth per year. Although the percentage of students attending higher education is increasing, participation rates can by no means be regarded as high (OECD, 2007).

In 2004, 11 percent of Portuguese people aged between 18–39 years were attending higher education; this is very similar to the European average (11.1 percent, European Commission, Eurydice & Eurostat, 2007). The increased demand from students for higher education may have demographic, economic and structural causes. Besides increasing the number of teachers in the various levels of education, the enhanced ability of schools to receive students and the expansion of the minimum number of years that is required to attend school appear to be very important factors in increasing access to higher education.

Moreover, an increase of the value of birth and the number of school-age children, as well as a decline in the number of students who left school at different levels of education, may have contributed to this increase of students in higher education. Finally, the growth in the number of students in higher education was also possible through the increase of public and private higher education institutions.

In the 1980s and 1990s, there was a strong increase in private institutions of higher education, primarily as a result of the inability of public Universities to respond to the growing demand for higher education. The lack of investment in creating new vacancies and public higher education institutions allowed the growth of private Universities in Portugal. This happened due to excess demand associated with population growth resulting in thousands of students who failed to enter into public Universities. In 1995, 37 percent of students in higher education attended private institutions. This increase may explain the reason why in 1996, for the first time, the number of higher education applicants surpassed the number of places offered by the public and private higher education institutions (Eurydice, 2005).

When it comes to doctoral education, it can be noted that in 2010 Portuguese Universities graduated 1,666 new PhDs, as compared to only 337 in 1990. This shows the increasing capacity of Portuguese Universities in offering PhD programs, but also poses new challenges regarding the need to strengthen their internationalization and the integration with international scientific research networks. The increasing number of PhDs has raised the qualification level of academic staff, which reached 68 percent in 2009 and now they all have a PhD (Heitor & Horta, 2012). In addition, the scientific output of Portuguese research institutions in all scientific fields reached 12,865 internationally refereed scientific publications in 2010, up from 7,407 publications in 2005, and just 4,463 publications in 2000. From another perspective, the number of publications in the Science Citation Index, by total population, reached 832 articles per million people in 2010, up from 483 in 2004. It should also be noted that while people with a PhD are able to be absorbed by the job market, the uptake is mainly by higher education institutions (GPEARI, 2011; GPEARI = Gabinete de Planeamento, Estratégia, Avaliação e Relações Internacionais (Planning, Strategy, Evaluation and International Relations)). However, the number of PhDs in Portugal remains relatively low compared with other European countries and the United States.

Democratization can also be seen as a process. This conceptual perspective can be seen in a positive or optimistic way in that access to higher education is a reality for the Portuguese population, particularly for social groups that previously had little expression in this education system. We note that the concern here has to do with widening access to higher education to previously under-represented groups. It was felt that higher education should be accessible to larger numbers and that it should represent the national diversity. This means that it is important to increase the amount of people that have access to higher education, but more importantly, specific groups that had no chance of access to higher education such

[handwritten margin notes: "Most PhDs work at a higher ed inst"; "Goal is to widen access through democratization"]

as people with disabilities and special needs, women and people from low social class (Pascueiro, 2009). Now they can and this norm was first invoked in respect of the principle of equal access for women. More recently, Mauritti (2003) presented the findings of an investigation, which shows that women represent 58.4 percent of students attending public higher education and 67.2 percent of students in private higher education.

On the other hand, it is possible to have a pessimistic view since the process of democratization is not yet stabilized and continues to reproduce social inequalities. The European data shows that Portugal exhibits one of the highest levels of inequalities in comparison with Spain, the Netherlands, Ireland and Finland, who exhibit far lower levels of inequality (Pascueiro, 2009). For example, in society and in the labor market, all degrees and educational institutions do not have the same symbolic value. A young man or woman, who because of financial constraints attended the course of Psychology at the University of Madeira in Portugal and who belongs to the area of residence, does not have the same symbolic value of a young man or woman from the same area, who took a course of Psychology at the University of Porto or the capital city Lisbon. The second one is most valued by society and by the labor market. Obviously, those are more prestigious than the Universities from the islands, because of their longstanding research tradition and well-recognized faculty teachers. In addition, certain courses like Medicine continue to be frequented mostly by people from the middle and upper classes. Moreover, currently the degree in Medicine has a higher status in society than any other course.

The phenomenon of the democratization of higher education has prompted us to think about the differentiation of Portuguese society which is evident in two distinct poles. Younger populations have a higher level of education, while the adult population, already in the labor market, has low educational qualifications. This generational difference has triggered a problem in terms of the sustainability of the labor market as well as access to equal opportunities. Portuguese society is now discussing the legitimacy of promoting policies of emigration for the younger population, with high education. The education obtained through the public service system was financially supported by the government to young students who couldn't afford it. However, nowadays those students are being asked by the government to leave Portugal because the job market can't absorb them.

Given all levels of education in Portugal, higher education is perhaps the one that, in recent decades, has experienced more changes at structural, institutional, economic, demographic and social levels (Urbano, 2011). Hence it is important to study the higher education system, taking into consideration that there are currently a limited number of studies available in this area. Accordingly, the Board of Rectors of Portuguese Universities has asked the Agency for the Accreditation of Higher Education to conduct a series of studies that will identify the key elements that characterize the higher education system. This will enable them to make informed decisions about the rationalization and consolidation of the network of higher education into the future (Conselho Nacional de Educação (National Council of Education), 2012).

Scientific research has focused mostly on students—analyzing their ingress, success and subsequent access to the labor market. Furthermore, the evaluation systems of higher education and the consequences of policies adopted have also been studied (Urbano, 2011). In this context, it was felt that this chapter may bring something new in relation to the socio-historical analysis of higher education in recent years, in particular with regard to the peripheral regions of Portugal, namely the Autonomous Regions of Madeira and Azores, two of the islands of Portugal.

Special Competitions in the Access to Higher Education

Access to higher education can occur through the general system of public national competition (which includes special quotas, particularly for candidates from the Autonomous Regions of Azores and Madeira) and institutional competition held by private institutions. It is also possible to apply for higher education through special contests directed at athletes, sons and daughters of diplomats, officials of the armed forces and people with physical or sensory disabilities. This means that there are a number of vacancies in access to higher education that are reserved exclusively for candidates from certain groups. If candidates who comply with these conditions are not placed via the dedicated channels, they are included under the general competition.

The special competition was created because not all candidates are truly equal in the access to higher education. The special competition aims to correct imbalances in society through measures that benefit a certain group. In general terms, this form of distribution of candidates allows students with lower grades to enter ahead of others with higher grades. At first this may seem unfair, considering the principle of equality and recognition of merit; however, such perceived discriminations are admissible because they are considered to be positive. Measures of positive affirmation are used in several countries around the world. In Portugal, this positive discrimination covers students who reside in the Autonomous Regions of the Azores and Madeira, are sons of immigrants, provide effective military service or with physical or sensory disabilities.

Higher education institutions have also changed the rules of access of "non-traditional" students. For example, one criteria measure was the change in the regime of access to higher education in special competitions, by lowering the age from 25 to 23 years of age, giving Universities the institutional autonomy in the selection process. Students aged over 23 years old comprised 13 percent of all students enrolled in higher education during the academic year 2008/2009 (Castro, Seixas & Neto, 2010).

The special competitions for candidates with physical or sensory disabilities have been applied since 1986. Focusing the discussion in the Autonomous Region of Madeira, the Regional Decree Law nº 33/2009/M, December 31, established the legal regime of special education. Specialized support to students with special needs occurs in a less restrictive school environment. This support can take place in schools of reference, structured teaching units, units in regular education and special education institutions. For every city, there are still psycho-pedagogical support centers that have technical teams and material resources that facilitate collaboration between schools and families. These centers allow observation, assessment, referral and intervention with children and youth with special needs. These pioneering nationwide support centers lead to an increase in the number of students with disabilities in the higher education system.

The recent expansion of compulsory education and the use of new information and communication technologies seem to have played an important role in increasing the number of students with disabilities in higher education. Universities are challenged to respond effectively to the needs of individual learners, guaranteeing them not only access but also educational success. In recent years, some studies have been conducted in Portugal on the issue of inclusion of students with special needs in higher education (Abreu, 2011; Espadinha, 2010; Faria, 2012; Pires, 2007). The number of students with special needs has nearly tripled in just over a decade, from 244 students identified in the academic year 1994/1995, to 816 in the academic year 2007/2008 (Pires, 2009). However, it is important to mention that some students do not reveal themselves as having special needs to the academic services available to avoid stigmatization. Thus, the number of students with special needs may be much higher.

The inclusion agenda of these students implies the adaptation of contents and pedagogical strategies, the elimination of infrastructural barriers and transformation of the attitudes of University teachers. Some University teachers believe that the inclusion of students with special needs may negatively affect the academic performance of their students, seemingly unaware that research in the area points to the absence of adverse effects (Ferrari & Sekkel, 2007).

Academic success of students with disabilities in higher education correlated, to a degree, with certain institutional conditions such as difficulties in adapting the methodology to learning and teaching strategies, as well as lack of support services and specific regulations. Forms of direct and indirect support for students with special needs have to be revised and could play an important role in improving their academic success in higher education. It could be equally important for institutions to establish a dedicated office to help students with special needs. Furthermore, we believe that there should also be a national policy for students with special needs, which would create a greater standardization of policies.

Another special contest in the access to higher education is for students from Autonomous Regions, like Azores and Madeira islands. The reason for such protection is the insularity of the candidates. At the time when these quotas were created, the conditions of the school education system in the islands were more precarious than in other regions of the mainland and they were, therefore, unable to compete as equals for places in higher education. But it behooves us to assess whether this inequality continues today.

In the 2001 census, levels of education in the Autonomous Region of Madeira were categorized as follows: 17.4 percent without any level of education; 11.2 percent were illiterate; 35.6 percent had the first cycle of basic education (four years of schooling); 13.2 percent had the second cycle of basic education (six years of schooling); 11.6 percent had the third cycle of basic education (nine years of schooling); 14 percent had secondary education and 7.7 percent had higher education. The capital region of Lisbon and Vale Tejo stands out from all other regions with higher levels of education (secondary and higher). In Lisbon, 14 percent of residents had higher education, double the percentage in the Autonomous Region of Madeira. At the other extreme, the Azores islands have 11.9 percent of students in secondary education and 6.7 percent in higher education. Regarding illiterate or no education level, the region of Alentejo (south of Portugal) and Madeira are those with the highest values (Instituto Nacional de Estatística (National Institute of Statistics), 2002). However, this needs to be analyzed against the global panorama. In 2011, 3.5 million Portuguese people had no education or only the first cycle of basic education. Clearly, persistent low levels of even basic education are a serious problem in the country, as well as cultural and economic obstacles.

[margin notes: Not much education on islands; bigger cities = more education]

Furthermore, the actual ratio of students/teachers in the Autonomous Regions and the mainland show no marked difference. The mean of national examination is 10.45 values (ranging from 0–20 in the Portuguese grading system). Madeira presents the average of 9.68 and Azores stands at 9.75. Given this information, we wonder if the inequality between students from the mainland and from the islands exists to an extent that justifies different treatment to applicants from the islands through special competitions. The answer seems to be no. In fact, students from Portalegre and Bragança (cities from the South and North of mainland Portugal) face greater challenges with regard to admission to higher education than students from the islands of the Autonomous Regions of Madeira and Azores. That is because they have lower averages in national examinations.

To use a practical example: in 2011, in the medical course of the University Nova de Lisboa, the lowest ranking student to apply in the general competition had a score of 18.6 (ranging from 0–20 in the Portuguese grading system), the last candidate of Azores had a score of 16.1 and the last candidate of Madeira had a score of 17.2. How does one justify to candidates from Bragança or Portalegre, who even in conditions of poor education, worked and achieved an average of 18.5 that they have not been admitted to the medical course, while a student from Azores with an average of 16.1 has been accepted? These candidates have been discriminated against negatively. This regime allows that, in some situations, students with worse grades have more privileges than the students with better grades (Caldeira, 2012).

However, there are some counter arguments that have been used to justify this special competition, namely that the flights, from the islands to the mainland, are expensive and the students are away from their families when studying. But these arguments are not sufficient enough to justify the quota, because other support, such as scholarships and regional government assistance with travel costs, could be a more appropriate response. It is very important that the region should not become more important than the individual merit of the student.

The report from the General Directorate of Higher Education (DGES) reveals that the special quota for candidates of the Autonomous Regions is the most used. In 2009, 2,076 candidates competed via the competitions of Autonomous Regions. However, it is interesting to note that 50 percent of applicants intended to study in their home region as their first option. This means that only 141 candidates, from all the candidates from Azores and Madeira, wanted to study away from their home region. In terms of the total placed at the University of Madeira, 96 percent were from the same region, while in the University of Azores this number dropped to 78 percent. Therefore, it can be concluded that the candidates from the Autonomous Regions want to study in their home region (Caldeira, 2012).

The creation of the Universities of Madeira and Azores islands was an important step to providing equal opportunities in access to higher education. Thirty years ago, a Portuguese resident in Madeira or Azores was theoretically less likely to obtain a higher education than a fellow resident in the larger cities of Lisbon (the capital of Portugal), Porto or Coimbra.

The geographical question is particularly relevant: there is no strong tradition of Portuguese students' mobility beyond the classical and central teaching units (Lisbon, Porto, Coimbra). Increased local supply of higher education courses in different scientific areas may have resulted in students being able to access higher qualifications closer to home, thus avoiding ongoing travel expenses to the mainland and social isolation from their families and communities. The institutions themselves created attraction criteria, e.g. 50 percent of vacancies in the Universities of Madeira and Azores are reserved for students from the islands (Caldeira, 2012). However, students also have the option of choosing a private institution if they cannot find a place in a public higher institution. In such a case, the student may choose to enroll in a similar course at a local private institution instead of enrolling in a distant public institution. This also means that enrolments in private institutions are almost exclusively local, as students will not be likely to move away from their parents' residence.

It is important to reveal that Portugal has a binary system of higher education that provides both University education and polytechnic education, through the public and private higher education institutions. The two systems of higher education are linked and it is possible to transfer a student from one system to the other (Teixeira, Rosa & Amaral, 2006).

The number of Portuguese students that are studying outside Portugal has consistently increased from 153 in 1987/1988 to 2,825 in 2001/2002. Portuguese

Study abroad begins

students have a stable pattern of preferences with Spain, France, Italy, Germany and the United Kingdom being the major destination countries. This is probably because of linguistic and cultural aspects. Moreover, these countries are closer to Portugal (Rosa, Veiga, & Amaral, 2004).

Although access to higher education does not purportedly include criteria of social distinction (the application's average scores decides the results, and all have equal opportunity of access) this does not reflect the reality. Currently, the Portuguese education system is characterized by a strong social selectivity, visible when comparing the social status of the families of origin of their students in higher education (Eurostudent, 2008).

It is true that the levels of education are different in each region and this has cumulative effects on the opportunities for the younger generations. Although new generations tend to be more qualified than older ones, environments in which educational and cultural resources are scarce may contribute to the maintenance of low levels of education. According to Mauritti (2003), the number of students in higher education from families in which parents have the first cycle of basic education is increasing considerably. About 62 percent of students in higher education are from higher social categories, while 24 percent have origins in lower social classes. In 2001, the probability of a child whose parents were entrepreneurs and leaders being in higher education was eight times higher than a child with laborer parents (Machado et al., 2003). Looking first at fathers and mothers with and without higher education, it was noted that Portugal, Austria, Germany and France exhibit the highest level of inequality in access to higher education (Clancy & Goastellec, 2007). Those who have financial difficulties and social needs, usually the first of the family to get a degree, must strive hard to overcome the quantity and quality of school knowledge acquired by their parents (Sobrinho, 2013).

Like the UK

The levels of educational attainment are not equal across the social classes. Moreover, the criteria of choice of courses and educational institutions are inherited from each social class, which means that the higher education system tends to reproduce the social structure in society (Urbano, 2011).

In evolutionary terms, the elitism of Portuguese Universities has increased. Contrary to what would be expected and desirable, it has been recorded that between 1995 and 2005 there has been a decline in the participation of individuals from lower social classes and an increase in the number of students from middle-class families (Cabrito, 1995; Cerdeira, 2005).

Higher education institutions have created some measures, such as financial support or scholarships, for those students from lower social classes. The funding per student, although relatively low, has increased by over 30 percent in the period 2005–2010. In terms of funding, the social support to students is critical in Portugal, which has a population with a deficit of qualifications and relatively few resources to invest in the education of children (Heitor & Horta, 2012).

In 2007/2008, a new system of students' loans was launched. This system supplemented existing grants, which extended students' options. This solution was designed in a period of severe financial restraints in the public sector, and was based exclusively on public funds.

Financial support for Universities has decreased and it is with concern that we have seen a significant decline in investment in education being translated into a reduction of financial means and human resources. Ensuing financial difficulties have contributed to a decrease in revenues for the functioning of the institutions as well as financial support available for school social action.

With no guarantees of continued funding, the institutions have to compete with each other for students and the fees they pay. Higher education institutions are currently faced with a different reality characterized by increased competition and severe financial constraints. This competition could result in an increasing commercialization of education and knowledge. Education could become a mere commercial product under the laws and regulations of the markets, thus moving away from the concept of higher education as a public asset (Sobrinho, 2013).

There must be greater financial investment in Universities. The consolidation of the education sector requires further investment and collective social responsibility, which includes the education authorities, the different stakeholders and society in general. The actual situation around the economic crisis and rising unemployment is very serious. Therefore, investing in education should be a priority, a way to break the isolation and give more attention to the people and the development and enhancement of their knowledge. Furthermore, it is important to achieve the target suggested by the European Committee: in the coming years, the Portuguese population in the age group between 30 and 34 years must have 40 percent of higher education graduates (Conselho Nacional de Educação (National Council of Education), 2012).

The Implementation of the Bologna Declaration

The Bologna Declaration, made in 1999, represented a major turning point in higher education in Europe. With this statement began the creation of a common space in the European community, which is based on the realization of a system for simple comparability with two cycles of study and with the use of a common system of accreditation. However, there has also been strong disagreement on the duration of two cycles of graduation (from three to six years for the first cycle graduation and one or two years for the second short cycle, equivalent to a master's degree).

The measures were designed to promote mobility between countries, regions, institutions and areas of knowledge. However, this is a challenge for Universities. Considering the open market of the European area, it is important to make curricular revisions that give to Portuguese students the same skills and knowledge as those provided by other European institutions to their students, especially since

Portuguese graduates will compete, within and outside the country, with young people from other countries. We have an obligation to ensure that the competition is based on equality.

Democratization introduces the notion of quality in higher education. Quality generally refers to methods of teaching and learning, administration of courses, competence and formation of teachers and quality of curriculum content. We have become more concerned with the quality than with the quantity, and that more demanding conditions for access to higher education have, again, been introduced, for example in the national examinations at the end of secondary education. It is not enough that education is good and right in terms of bureaucratic, technical and scientific requirements. It is essential that education also contributes to building a better world; a world that is more educated and more evolved culturally and socially.

Institutions need to produce new pedagogical processes that contrast with the traditional pedagogy of higher education. Lectures that were taught to a large number of students are gradually being replaced by practical classes with fewer students. Students and teachers have had to adapt to a new model of teaching–learning. The curricula at the Universities are more open and diversified with the aim of improving the skills and increasing mobility of human resources. However, the resistance of some teachers and staff personnel to this change, and the introduction of new parameters into the teaching profession, has made the process very slow and, sometimes, led to results that may not have reflected the original intention.

Although the Bologna process has the objective of equality between national and European Universities, it is still not a reality. In Portugal, there is a new dependency between Universities, with a small group of Universities that produce knowledge and a vast majority of other Portuguese Universities that consume this knowledge. The unequal distribution of knowledge represents a global imbalance of power, especially regarding scientific and technological advances.

Furthermore, most classes are still taught in the most conservative way, where memorizing contents and reproducing them are the major form of evaluation of students. These need to be upgraded into a new form of teaching new skills to students. Those skills are important to several areas of scientific knowledge, like social sciences, human-computer interaction, biology, etc. University teachers have, with the implementation of the Bologna Process, the opportunity to reflect on their teaching practices, becoming trainers of citizens with knowledge, competencies and ability to manage conflict, solve problems and be creative and innovative (Sousa, 2011).

A New Period of Change

In recent years some new data about students in higher education has been released. Statistics shows that the number of students has declined in Portugal.

One reason is the demographic issue: the birth rates have declined, impacting on the number of children and young people at school age. Other reasons may be linked to the high level of dropout at different stages of education, due to several factors such as unemployment among young graduates and the financial difficulties of their families.

Institutions and systems of higher education are becoming increasingly more complex and diverse. They have been interested in new audiences with benefits for all. With democratization, students gain because they benefit from education in terms of their personal growth and better work opportunities. Society also gains, because more people with higher knowledge and critical reasoning may participate constructively in public spheres of social and political life, increasing community enrollment.

We hope that this chapter constitutes a further contribution to reflection on and implementation of what is meant by democratization in higher education and, ultimately, by a real democratic society.

References

Abreu, S.M. (2011). *Alunos com necessidades especiais: Estudo Exploratório sobre a inclusão no ensino superior.* Unpublished master's thesis, Universidade da Madeira, Funchal.

Cabrito, B. (1995). *Financiamento do Ensino Superior. Condição social e despesas de educação dos estudantes universitários em Portugal.* Lisboa: Educa.

Caldeira, J. (2012). *Do princípio da igualdade nos contingentes especiais de acesso ao ensino superior. O teste da afirmação positiva.* Verbojuridico.

Castro, A., Seixas, A. & Neto, A. (2010). Políticas Educativas em Contextos Globalizados: A expansão do ensino superior em Portugal e no Brasil. *Revista Portuguesa de Pedagogia,* 44(1), 37–61.

Cerdeira, L. (2005). *O financiamento do ensino superior português. A partilha de custos. Dissertação de Doutoramento.* Universidade de Lisboa: Faculdade de Psicologia e de Ciências da Educação.

Clancy, P. & Goastellec, G. (2007). Exploring access and equity in higher education: Policy and performance in a comparative perspective. *Higher Education Quarterly,* 61(2), 136–154.

Conselho Nacional de Educação (National Council of Education) (2012). *Estado da Educação 2012. Autonomia e Descentralização.* Ministério da Educação e Ciência.

Espadinha, A.C. (2010). *Modelo de atendimento às necessidades educativas especiais baseado na tecnologia: Estudo de caso centrado em alunos de baixa visão.* Unpublished master's thesis, Faculdade de Motricidade Humana, Universidade Técnica de Lisboa, Lisboa.

European Commission, Eurydice & Eurostat (2007). *Key data on higher education in Europe – 2007.* Brussels: European Commission.

Eurostudent (2008). *Data reporting module EUROSTUDENT III (2005–2008). National Profiles Portugal.* Hanover.

Eurydice (2005). *Summary sheets on education systems in Europe. Portugal.* Retrieved from http://eng.uvm.dk/Education/~/media/UVM/Filer/English/PDF/081110_summary_sheet_on_danish_education_system.ashx.

Faria, C.P. (2012). *Inclusão de alunos com necessidades educativas especiais no ensino superior: Estudo exploratório sobre as perceções dos docentes.* Unpublished master's thesis, Universidade da Madeira, Funchal.

Ferrari, M. & Sekkel, M. (2007). Educação inclusiva no ensino superior: um novo desafio. *Psicologia: Ciência e Profissão, 27*(4), 636–647.

GPEARI (2011). *Produção científica Portuguesa, 1990–2010: Séries Estatísticas*. Lisboa: GPEARI.

Heitor, M. & Horta, H. (2012). Democratizing higher education and the access to science: The Portuguese reform 2006–2010. *Higher Education Policy*, 1–19. Doi: 10.1057/hep.2013.21.

Instituto Nacional de Estatística (National Institute of Statistics) (2002). *Censos 2001: Resultados Definitivos*. Lisboa.

Machado, F., Costa, A., Mauritti, R., Martins, S., Casanova, J. & Almeida, J. (2003). Classes sociais e estudantes universitários: Origens, oportunidades e orientações. *Revista Crítica de Ciências Sociais, 46*, 45–80.

Mauritti, R. (2003). Caracterização e origens sociais. In J. Ferreira, P. Ávila, J. Casanova, A. Costa, F. Machado, S. Martins e R. Mauritti (Eds), *Diversidade na Universidade. Um inquérito aos estudantes de Licenciatura* (pp. 51–62). Oeiras: Celta Editora.

OECD (2007). *Reviews of national policies of education – Tertiary education in Portugal*. Paris: OECD.

Pascueiro, L. (2009). Breve contextualização ao tema da democratização do acesso ao ensino superior: A presença de novos públicos em contextos universitários. *Educação, sociedade e cultura, 28*, 31–52.

Pires, L.A. (2007). *A caminho de um ensino superior inclusivo? A experiência e perceções dos estudantes com deficiência: Estudo de caso*. Unpublished master's thesis, Faculdade de Motricidade Humana, Lisboa.

Pires, L.A. (2009). *Levantamento nacional dos apoios aos estudantes com deficiência no ensino superior*. Paper presented at the 1st Seminar GTAEDES: Contributions to an inclusive university, Humanities Faculty at University of Lisbon, Lisbon.

Rosa, M., Veiga, A. & Amaral, A. (2004). Portugal. In J. Huisman & M.C. Van der Wende (Eds), *On cooperation and competition: National and European policies for the internationalization of higher education. ACA Papers on International Cooperation in Education* (pp. 139-163). Bonn: Lemmens.

Sobrinho, J. (2013). Educação Superior: Bem-público, equidade e democratização. *Avaliação, 18*(1), 107–126.

Sousa, I. (2011). *Processo de Bolonha e Mudanças na Educação Superior: Um estudo no ensino superior politécnico português. Tese de doutoramento*. Lisboa: Universidade Lusófona de Humanidades e Tecnologias.

Teixeira, P., Rosa, M. & Amaral, A. (2006). The broader church? Expansion, access and cost-sharing in higher education. In P. Texeira, D.B. Johnstone, M.J. Rosa & H. Vossensteyn (Eds), *Cost-sharing and accessibility in higher education: a fairer deal?* (pp. 241–264). Douro Series. Dordrecht, The Netherlands: Springer.

Urbano, C. (2011). A (id)entidade do ensino superior politécnico em Portugal: Da Lei de Bases do Sistema Educativo à Declaração de Bolonha. *Sociologia: Problemas e Práticas, 66*, 95–115.

6

DEMOCRATIZING HIGHER EDUCATION IN THE UNITED KINGDOM

A Case Study

Craig Mahoney and Helena Lim

Introduction: History and Context

The higher education system in the United Kingdom (UK) is complex and diverse with a long and highly regarded history. Higher education courses and qualifications in the UK are offered by a range of institutions, mostly universities and an increasing number of colleges who have been given governmental approval to deliver courses and programmes at higher education level. Providers of tertiary education in the UK are often referred to as 'higher education institutions' (HEIs) and they vary in size, subject focus, research interests, infrastructure, priorities and history. In recent years, the model of funding by which they are supported has begun to diversify extensively across the four nations comprised by the UK.

The Further and Higher Education Act (1992) resulted in university title and status being granted to many institutions previously known as polytechnics. As a collective, these are often referred to as 'new' universities in modern parlance. Universities that predate 1992 are often called 'old', 'traditional' or 'ancient' but are in fact of varying ages. The 'civic' or 'red brick' universities were established in the nineteenth and early twentieth centuries, mainly in larger cities of the UK, whilst some of the colleges from the 'ancient universities', Oxford and Cambridge, date back to the twelfth and thirteenth century respectively, and St Andrews to the fifteenth century. Some were founded in the 1960s following the Robbins Review – a report published in 1963 from the Committee on Higher Education, which called for the expansion of higher education and recommended that university places 'should be available to all who were qualified for them by ability and attainment' (the so-called Robbins principle, Committee on Higher Education, 1963). As a result, higher education across the UK has gone through considerable changes during the last 50 years. There has been a move from an elite basis to a mass system of education.

TABLE 6.1 Student and Staff Numbers Across the UK, 2012/13

2012/13	Students			Staff		
	Undergraduate	Postgraduate	Total	Academic	Non-Academic	Total
England	1499870	445125	1944995	155485	160910	316395
Scotland	162025	52760	214785	17225	22075	39300
Wales	101165	27620	128785	9515	10375	19890
Northern Ireland	40780	10935	51715	3305	3485	6790
UK	1803840	536440	2340280	185,530	196845	382375

Source: www.hesa.ac.uk (HESA, 2014b)

(There were approximately 250,000 students in UK higher education at the time the Robbins report was published compared with today's 2.3 million, see Table 6.1.)

Today in the UK, higher education is sometimes provided by further education colleges that either have their qualifications validated by an HEI or national awarding organisation. Some further education colleges have recently acquired their own awarding powers for Foundation degrees (a two-year non-honours qualification up to level 5 in England or Wales). Others are pursuing full degree awarding powers as part of a relaxation to those who can deliver higher education awards in England, which has also allowed an expansion of private providers. There is now a growing number of private higher education providers (in England) that have been encouraged to deliver higher education, to seek degree awarding powers and pursue university title – the latter having been zealously guarded by UK governments for centuries and only recently has this been relaxed. Today, institutions in England, with more than 1,000 tertiary level students, can apply for university status through a secure process overseen by the Quality Assurance Agency (QAA). Access to public money is still restricted for private providers but this is set to change in the near future.

It has been estimated that the UK's higher education system contributes around £59 billion to the economy and generates some 2.3 per cent of UK GDP (Kelly et al., 2009). Considerable work has established that HEIs contribute significantly to local and regional economies, and according to recent research, international students bring almost £7 billion annually into the UK (UUK, 2013). Alongside the traditional roles of teaching and research, in addition to the valuable contribution to the UK economy as a major export industry, higher education also has a significant impact on social mobility.

UK institutions offer a range of higher-level courses and qualifications. First degree courses, commonly known as Bachelor's degrees, typically take three years to complete when studied full-time in England, Wales and Northern Ireland, or four years when completed in Scotland. Sandwich courses, which include periods of practical work outside the HEI, normally add a further year to the study period. Certain specialist courses and some vocational or professional degrees may take longer, for example, in medicine, dentistry and architecture.

The UK's degree classification system awards students First-class Honours (1st), Second-class Honours, upper division (2:1), Second-class Honours, lower division (2:2), Third class Honours (3rd), an Ordinary-degree (Pass) or a Fail, rather than the Grade Point Average (GPA) often used across north America and many other countries. The UK classification system is broadly based on percentage bands as an aggregate of final year marks, but has recently been labelled as outdated and unfair, favouring older and more established universities and failing to recognise the achievements and additional capabilities of individual students seeking to enter the job market or continue studying. Changes to this long-established system are currently under consideration.

The new Higher Education Achievement Report (HEAR), given to students on graduation, is intended to provide more detailed information about their learner journey and additional personal achievements than the current system, which only records academic outcomes. Based on the European Union Bologna Process, to produce a Diploma Supplement, the HEAR was introduced in 2013, which led to 88,743 HEARs being issued from across 27 HEIs to students with this figure set to increase year-on-year with now over 100 HEIs in the UK participating in the productions of HEARs. The HEAR was developed specifically to provide a more UK centric approach to recording student achievement in addition to the 'academic transcript' and the European Diploma Supplement.

Many UK HEIs offer a range of vocational 'sub-degree' qualifications, such as the Higher National Diploma (HND), the Higher National Certificate (HNC) or the Diploma in Higher Education (Dip HE). These are usually taken over one or two years study. In addition, students in England, Wales and Northern Ireland can now take a two-year foundation degree, which upon successful completion can be 'topped-up' to an honours level Bachelor degree.

Qualifications and Credit Framework

Higher education qualification frameworks provide a useful reference point for awards in the UK and relate to degrees, diplomas, certificates and other academic awards (other than honorary degrees and higher doctorates) granted by HEIs. In England, Northern Ireland and Wales, the levels are contained within the National Qualifications Framework (NQF), superseded by the Qualifications and Credit Framework from September 2008. The Framework was intended to create consistency in how qualifications were recorded and recognised across a scale from entry level to level 8. Higher education qualifications are contained in the Framework for Higher Education Qualifications (FHEQ) and mainly correspond with levels 4 to 8 of the NQF (Table 6.2). Scotland has its own education system and uses a 12-level framework called the Scottish Credit and Qualifications Framework, though there are many similarities between the two Frameworks.

Increasing numbers of students are seeking qualifications beyond their first degree. This often takes the form of a postgraduate course which might be delivered in taught form, conducted through research activity, or a combination of both, with the pattern of study normally part-time or full-time with increasing levels of blended learning in place. Qualifications include research doctorates (PhD), professional doctorates which combine taught study with research activity (e.g. EdD, DBA etc.) or, PhD by publication, where an existing body of research outputs are awarded a PhD, after the candidate provides a coherent summary on how their work has added to the body of knowledge. Taught postgraduate Master's courses typically take one year full-time or two years part-time to complete, and are rigidly based on academic content, not 'time served'. Research programmes, at doctoral level, are typically designed to take three years for full-time students and more than four years for part-time students, but each can vary significantly. Such research programmes will require the student to complete a written thesis and present their research and findings to external scrutiny before the award is granted. Postgraduate courses normally require students to have a degree-level qualification, but the academic level of the course may not always be more advanced than an undergraduate course – for example, a postgraduate law 'conversion

TABLE 6.2 UK Higher Education Qualifications Framework

	Scottish Credit and Qualifications Framework		National Qualifications Framework / Qualifications and Credit Framework	
Scotland	12	Doctoral degree	8	England, Wales, Northern Ireland
	11	Master's degree, Integrated Master's degree, Postgraduate diploma, Postgraduate certificate	7	
	10	Honours degree, Graduate diploma, Graduate certificate	6	
	9	Bachelor's/ordinary degree, Graduate diploma, Graduate certificate	6	
	8	Diploma in Higher Education, HND	5	
	7	Certificate of Higher Education, HNC	4	

course' for non-law graduates is considered equivalent to that of an undergraduate law degree course and similar qualifications in education also exist.

Policy and Funding

Higher education policy is now developed separately in each of the four countries making up the UK, with the Scottish Government, Welsh Assembly and the Northern Ireland Executive each having specific and varying responsibilities for higher education and student policies, whilst the UK government maintains control over the English higher education system.

Each government manages funds to support higher education in each of the four 'home nations' through funding bodies, which provide both financial support and general guidance to institutions. These are the Higher Education Funding Council for England (HEFCE), the Scottish Funding Council (SFC) and the Higher Education Funding Council for Wales (HEFCW). In Northern Ireland, universities receive funding directly from government via the Department for Employment and Learning (DELNI). Funding channelled through the funding bodies typically represents the largest single source of income for most public HEIs, although variations exist between institutions across the sector, in the percentage of their overall funding received from such sources. The UK's public investment in higher education is 0.7 per cent of GDP – well below the Organisation for Economic Co-operation and Development (OECD) and EU averages – and in total the UK spends 1.4 per cent of GDP on higher education, which is only half of the 2.8 per cent spent by the US (OECD, 2013), ranking the UK 11th.

Even though public HEIs receive funding through governmental sources, they are not owned or run by government. They are autonomous and independent legal entities, with governing bodies that have responsibility for determining strategic direction, monitoring financial health and performance and ensuring effective management.

Governmental bodies have no authority, nor any direct responsibility for determining the courses offered by HEIs, or in directing the research undertaken by individual academics. UK HEIs have a zealously guarded reputation for intellectual and academic freedom and their autonomy is considered a key factor in the sector's success in research, scholarship and education.

Student Enrolments

Most students enter higher education at the age of 18 to study a full-time undergraduate degree. Currently, 77 per cent of students are studying for an undergraduate qualification, whilst 23 per cent are pursuing a range of postgraduate awards (HESA, 2014a). Historically, many of these young people attend HEIs located some distance from their family homes, requiring them to become independent and find suitable accommodation on or near the campus, whilst studying. However, in recent years this practice has begun to alter with increasing numbers of UK students studying at HEIs near their home. The UK has just over 2.3 million students with nearly 660,000 part-time students; the majority of these students are over 21 and many are combining study with existing work or other commitments in their local communities. With an increasing focus on flexible learning determined by pace, place and mode of study, it is likely that new models of delivery will feature strongly in the coming years as higher education seeks to offer a relevant, contemporary and cost effective method for students to acquire knowledge and skills, relevant to their transformation objectives.

Student Number Controls

'Student number control' refers to the limit set for each HEI on how many students they can recruit, by funding bodies. HEIs across the UK have traditionally been given a number of places, which they can 'fill' with students registered, to complete a programme of study leading to an accredited award, for example, Bachelor's, Master's or Doctoral degree. These totals have been broadly based on the number of students they have recruited in the past, with adjustments made annually, following negotiations with their relevant funding body. It is normally down to the individual HEIs to determine how these places are distributed across their courses, though courses in education, medicine and some other defined programmes will have numbers controlled on entry. However, a new 'high-grades' policy, introduced in England in 2012, allowed HEIs to recruit as many students with high grades at A-level (grades of AAB or ABB equivalent) as they wish, outside of their student number control. (A-levels are the pre-university entry qualifications studied by most students in England, Wales and Northern Ireland. Students in Scotland study a different pre-university curriculum and complete Scottish Higher awards.)

The cap on student places for all English HEIs will be completely removed from September 2015. This could result in pressure on places and a shift in the demand for higher education across the 'devolved nations'. The perceived prestige of some English institutions has encouraged students from Scotland, Wales and Northern Ireland to seek entry into English HEIs where they can now take uncontrolled numbers of students with the higher pre-university results, thus potentially diminishing demand in the respective home nation.

International Students

The UK remains one of the most popular destinations for students, after the US, and has some of the most 'internationalised' universities to be found in OECD member countries, with international students forming 17 per cent of the student population in the UK. More than 200 countries are represented in this student population with greatest representation from China and India, followed by Nigeria, the US, Malaysia and a number of European Union (EU) countries.

Recent immigration reforms in the UK have been the subject of much international media attention, which emphasised that there are now more stringent regulations associated with studying in the UK. A new visa regime in the UK requires all prospective students to be 'sponsored' by an HEI that has been approved by the UK Border Agency (UKBA) and recognised with highly trusted status (HTS). Student visas are issued through British embassy facilities and are only granted if a prospective student has confirmation of course acceptance from an institution with HTS; shows adequate finances to cover the cost of living and study for their study programme; is adequately qualified to complete the award; and has minimum standards of English language, determined by an approved assessment. Once students arrive in the UK, it is now the responsibility of the HEI to monitor attendance of international students, keep UKBA informed of any changed status for students, arrange for the students' return home, should they fail or when they complete their degree, and take full responsibility for ensuring regulatory requirements for working (not to exceed 20 hours per week during teaching periods) are fully adhered to. These changes have led some countries to perceive the UK as disinterested in supporting the educational aspirations of students from foreign shores; however, the changes have arisen from a rather loose system previously, which failed to adequately track students following arrival into the UK.

Institutions are not restricted on the number of international students they can recruit in the UK. Despite a 7.9 per cent dip in the number of international students enrolled across all HEIs in 2011/12, this is now reversing with acceptances rising by 0.5 per cent and 5.8 per cent in 2012 and 2013 respectively (HESA, 2014a). Recent years have also witnessed an expansion in the number of non-UK students studying for a UK higher education qualification abroad. The Observatory on Borderless Higher Education (2014) recently reported that transnational education (TNE) 'appears to be growing at a rate faster than that of international student mobility', and there are now more international students studying for a UK qualification outside of the UK than in the UK – 503,795 compared to 425,260 respectively (HESA, 2014a).

Quality and Enhancement

As UK HEIs are autonomous institutions, they are each responsible for maintaining the quality and standards of the education they provide – a responsibility that the higher education sector takes very seriously.

A national system based on the principle of peer review ensures that both the quality and standards of awards are broadly comparable (not equal or identical) across the sector. The QAA reviews and reports on how well UK universities and colleges maintain their academic quality and standards. The Higher Education

Academy, an independent organisation, supports change in learning and teaching to improve outcomes for students.

Drivers for Change and Emerging Trends

The UK higher education system is experiencing one of its most turbulent periods for many decades, with change a constant feature arising from the impact of government policy, student choice, economic pressures and funding decisions. Some major drivers for change include funding, fees, globalisation, technology, diversification, access and participation.

Funding

While public funding remains the significant source of funding for UK HEIs, there has been an increasing divergence of national HE funding policies across the devolved governments. Funding for higher education is being channelled away from direct allocation to institutions through core grants with a move towards more indirect allocations via student tuition fee income, though this is mainly true for England rather than Scotland, Wales or Northern Ireland. In the 2011/12 financial year, the HEFCE teaching grant of £4.6 billion accounted for 64 per cent of teaching funding to English HEIs. This is expected to decrease to just over £2 billion (in cash terms) by the financial year 2014/15, accounting for only 25 per cent of teaching funding in that year (UUK, 2013). There is also increasing selectivity and concentration of research funding into a few institutions. In spite of strong assurances from the UK government of its desire to maintain support for what has become the second most prolific research output, behind US academic institutions, pressures on research funding could result in research becoming 'the luxury of the few' (Anyangwe, 2012).

Since 2001, English HEIs have received additional revenue in the form of annual tuition fees, paid by UK students, as a contribution towards the cost of their education. However, various financial support mechanisms, including loans and means-tested maintenance grants, are available to help students pay their fees and meet living expenses while they are studying. In 2010, English universities were given approval to charge fees to a maximum of £9,000 per year from September 2012. This created a hugely variable fees regime across the UK, with different costs for students dependent upon their country of domicile (Table 6.3).

Core grant funding, which constituted 40 per cent of English HEIs' income, fell to 30 per cent in 2011/12, though similar shifts are not so apparent in Welsh, Northern Irish or Scottish HEIs. Given the decrease in core public funding, it is inevitable that HEIs have increasingly sought to diversify their funding. Most UK HEIs also receive additional income from the provision of residence, catering and conference facilities; the delivery of contract research, consultancy and training to businesses; the fees charged to international students; and expansion of the learning

TABLE 6.3 Fee Arrangements Across the UK

Students domiciled in	Students studying in 2012–13 in			
	England	Scotland	Wales	Northern Ireland
England	Variable fee up to £9,000	Variable fee up to £9,000	Variable fee up to £9,000	Variable fee up to £9,000
Scotland	Variable fee up to £9,000	No fees or £1,820 means tested	Variable fee up to £9,000	Variable fee up to £9,000
Wales	Variable fee up to £9,000 (with fees above £3,575 paid by the Welsh Government)	Variable fee up to £9,000 (with fees above £3,575 paid by the Welsh Government)	Variable fee up to £9,000 (with fees above £3,575 paid by the Welsh Government)	Variable fee up to £9,000 (with fees above £3,575 paid by the Welsh Government)
Northern Ireland	Variable fee up to £9,000	Variable fee up to £9,000	Variable fee up to £9,000	Variable fee up to £3,465
EU	Fees as for English student studying in England	Fees as for Scottish student studying in Scotland	Fees as for Welsh student studying in Wales	Fees as for Northern Irish student studying in Northern Ireland

Source: UUK (2013)

year by running summer school and pre-entry programmes to optimise resource utilisation. Some HEIs have also managed to secure significant endowment, sponsorship and match funding. However, with the exception of the Universities of Oxford and Cambridge, and compared to many north American universities, most UK HEIs have so far managed to attract only small endowments (from charitable foundations and business corporations). This will change in the coming years (UUK, 2013):

> At the end of financial year 2006–07, 131 UK institutions reported £513 million in total funds raised from 132,000 donors. Five years later, 152 institutions reported £693 million from more than 204,000 donors. This is equivalent to a 35% increase in funds raised and 54% more donors.
>
> UUK, 2013, p. 58

Globalisation, Marketisation and Competition

Linked to changes in the composition of higher education funding is the increasing commercialisation of the system. Across the UK, a shift to new sources of funding for students and enhanced ability for institutions to attract the 'best' students through the use of the AAB+ (only in England) is creating increased competition. It is worth noting that the cap on student numbers in England will be removed in 2015 and this will signify the biggest step towards marketisation higher education has experienced to date. At that point, English HEIs will be able to expand and contract based on demand for their services, rather than government controls.

Internationally, the globalisation of higher education and the mobility of international student flows will continue to impact on the UK. Demand for higher education, from both 'developed' and emerging economies, continues to grow. Significant investments are being made in higher education in many countries (e.g. China, Malaysia, India) and there is an increase in the number of private 'for' and 'not for' profit providers as they seek to meet this demand. For the UK, there are opportunities for the expansion of its higher education provision abroad; transnational education is a core part of the internationalisation strategies of most UK HEIs. There are also opportunities for the UK to continue supporting the development of mature HE environments outside the UK including India, Nigeria, Vietnam and Cambodia.

Technology

Most institutions in the UK will make use of virtual learning environments as repositories for course outlines, reading lists and study materials. More progressive institutions have used this interactively and enable a blended learning experience comprising classroom contact, tutorial support, peer assisted learning and online support. With the massive and rapidly growing wealth of open educational resources and the explosion in access to 'free' knowledge content, institutions are now able to offer a world learning experience with the best and most creative knowledge being accessed through portals such as 'iTunes U', which are transforming learning into an increasingly social and virtual enterprise. Some investment in the development of the US initiated phenomenon of 'massive open online courses' (MOOCs) is gaining traction in the UK, but it is still in its infancy.

These technological changes open up new learning opportunities, and that means that, potentially, content delivery can be unbundled from tutorial support and assessment, all of which can be provided separately. As content becomes increasingly accessible online, it is no longer monopolised by HEIs and for some this signals a break from the hegemony or 'closed shop' of higher education systems. Open access and 'free' knowledge could be perceived as meeting the social objectives of providing access to education for the disadvantaged or geographically remote countries; but for others, the 'unbundling' of activities are perceived as at once driving and being driven by marketisation and will lead ultimately to the de-professionalisation of learning (Kennie and Price, 2012; Holmwood, 2013). As the internet creates these new forms of knowledge and access to it, the key challenge for HEIs is how to accredit the learning gained online (Anyangwe, 2012).

Institutional Diversification

The prospect of 'unbundling' hints at a higher education system that is becoming increasingly diverse in the UK. Yet, the last decade has seen a reduction of around 10 per cent in the total number of HEIs (Ramsden, 2012). This apparently modest reduction is partly offset by the entrance of several new institutions, mostly from the further education sector, and some private HE providers. Around 50 institutional mergers have taken place in the UK higher education sector in the last two decades, with Wales experiencing the most recent round of rationalisation. There were 15 HEIs in Wales in 1994/95; by the start of 2012/13, this had reduced to eight. However, it does not follow from this that the overall diversity of provision has declined, since the opportunities have, by and large, been carried over into the smaller number of institutions that are now operating. Ramsden (2012) has identified that notions of decreasing diversity in the sector are unfounded and the sector remains highly diverse in many significant respects. For the future, the differentiation of higher education may be brought to bear by new funding regimes and growing market pressures.

Some institutions may be forced to specialise in order to effectively distinguish themselves and compete. The momentum for new institutions and open educational spaces as alternatives to traditional centres of learning may increase (Anyangwe, 2012). Kennie and Price (2012) have argued that mission different-iation will become a key priority.

On the flipside, the legacies of history and tradition may persevere, as the new market forces a fees environment and preserves old hierarchies with a new version of a bi-partite system of a small handful of elite, research-intensive institutions and a larger, less differentiated mass of teaching-intensive HEIs.

Affordability

The UK is a relative newcomer to a marketised higher education system, with much smaller variations in the range of fees charged (up to £9,000). Eligible full-time UK undergraduate students can apply for a tuition fee loan to help them cover the cost of their tuition fees which are only paid back gradually, if and when a graduate begins to earn more than £21,000 a year. After a dip in application rates in 2012, acceptances of UK students to UK institutions hit a record level of 433,612, a 6.7 per cent rise over the previous year. Given that the number of 18-year-olds in the population has fallen, application rates for that age group in the UK are at, or near, the highest levels. In England, 35 per cent of 18-year-olds have applied to start undergraduate courses in September 2014.

Despite gloomy predictions that higher tuition fees introduced in autumn 2012 would put people off applying, figures from the Universities and Colleges Admissions Service (UCAS) demonstrated that numbers applying from the UK are recovering, although not to the levels seen in 2010 or 2011, and those from the most disadvantaged backgrounds are more likely to enter higher education than previously (UCAS, 2014). The longer-term impact of tuition fees remains unknown.

Accessibility and Participation

Linked to the affordability of higher education is also accessibility to it. Widening access to higher education has been a primary aim of government policy in the UK, especially since 1997 when the Labour Government had a target of increasing participation of those aged 18–30 towards 50 per cent by the year 2010. Alongside this policy was a commitment by the Government, announced in its 2003 White Paper (*The Future of Higher Education*), to encourage more people from under-represented groups, particularly lower socio-economic backgrounds, to participate successfully in higher education.

In England, a programme called Aimhigher was set up in 2004 to encourage learners from under-represented groups to participate in higher education – particularly those from non-traditional backgrounds, looked-after children and individuals with learning difficulties and disabilities. Funding for Aimhigher ceased in July 2011. The full responsibility for widening participation outreach is now down to individual HEIs and reported to the Office for Fair Access (OFFA) and HEFCE (Dent et al., 2013).

OFFA was established after the Higher Education Act 2004, which enabled English HEIs to charge variable fees up to £3000 a year, from the 2006/07 academic year, to ensure that '[the] introduction of higher tuition fees in 2007/08 did not deter people from entering higher education for financial reasons [and that] universities and colleges were explicitly committed to increasing participation in higher education among under-represented groups' (OFFA, n.d.).

The funding bodies in Scotland, Wales and Northern Ireland have also provided significant financial support for a range of wider access activities. For instance, Wales established the Reaching Wider initiative in 2002 to break down perceived barriers and widen access to learning. This Wales-wide programme aims to increase higher education participation from groups of people of all ages, which are currently under-represented in higher education.

Higher education participation has expanded dramatically in the last few decades – for instance, in England the participation of young people has increased from just 5 per cent in 1960 to 47 per cent in 2010, bringing it close to the Labour Government's 50 per cent ambition. However, an individual's likelihood to embark on higher education study is partly dependent on their socio-economic background, and research has shown that there are significant differences between different socio-economic groups (Crawford, 2012). Even though participation of young people from the most socially disadvantaged groups has been increasing in recent years, the proportion of young people from the most advantaged groups is still three to four times that of the most disadvantaged group. For instance, while entry rates for English applicants from all backgrounds to higher tariff institutions increased in 2012, the proportion of the English 18-year-old population from the most advantaged backgrounds entering high tariff institutions was 21 per cent compared to 2.6 per cent for those from the most disadvantaged backgrounds. These gaps have remained remarkably consistent over time (Croxford and Raffe, 2011a and 2011b). Likewise, the National Union of Students Scotland statistics, published in *Unlocking Scotland's Potential* (NUSScotland, 2012), reported that just 12.7 per cent of university entrants in 2010/11 came from the most deprived backgrounds, a significantly lower proportion than in England. Some universities had an especially elite intake, with one Scottish institution welcoming just 13 students from the most deprived backgrounds, or just 2.7 per cent of its intake. It would appear that government and institutional commitments to tackle the problem have had little impact on current trends and it will take 40 years for students from poor backgrounds to be fairly represented in Scotland's HEIs.

After taking a dip in recent years, participation rates in higher education rose by 6.6 per cent in the 2013 cycle, with acceptances from UK domiciled applicants rising by 6.7 per cent, reversing the fall in 2012 and resulting in the highest number of acceptances of UK domiciled applicants from any cycle. There was also an increase in applicants (3.6 per cent up to 677,400) and the largest increase in over a decade in the proportion of these applicants accepted – 73.2 per cent acceptance rate in 2013, an increase of 2 percentage points. Over half of these UK domiciled acceptances were from 18-year-old applicants.

This trend appears to be mirrored by 'mature' students. 'Mature' students are defined as those aged 21 and above, and constitute about a quarter of all full-time undergraduate entrants to higher education. Around 12 per cent of all UK domiciled acceptances are from applicants aged 25 or over. Following increases in the 2008 and 2009 cycles, there were consecutive decreases from 2010 to 2012. However, like their younger counterparts, the 2013 cycle saw a 5.8 per cent increase in the number of mature acceptances (UCAS, 2013).

A recent HEFCE report (2013) on the impact of the reforms on widening participation did not identify a clear impact on disadvantaged groups as a result of the changes. The report highlighted the persisting inequalities between them and their more advantaged peers, and also showed significant gaps between particular sub-groups and access to different types of universities, with a considerable drop in acceptances for mature and part-time learners and a continuing gender bias. In spite of early signs of recovery in application rates and sustained demand for higher education, recent figures show that 87,000 more women than men applied for 2014 entry and there are warnings that men are becoming a 'disadvantaged group' in terms of going to university (Times Higher Education, 2014).

In spite of enhanced opportunities for higher education participation, some research points out that there may be reduced equality and that the higher education system may be reproducing and legitimising wider 'social differences' (Shavit et al., 2007; Brennan et al., 2008). While education is the major route to upward social mobility, there has been a change in focus from 'who goes to university?' to 'who goes where?' (Reay et al., 2005). Brown et al. (2004) have identified a 'royal route' (5+ good GCSEs, 2+ A-levels, followed by a full-time degree). Gorard et al. (2006) have identified the polar opposite for those from disadvantaged backgrounds: limited educational chances and achievement; higher prospects of dropping out at all stages; and upon graduation, lower earnings prospects and higher debt. Following the logic of 'effectively maintained inequality' (Lucas, 2001, p. 1642), lower-status students appear to be diverted into lower-status courses and institutions, while high-status students continue to maintain their dominance of high-status institutions. Some researchers have noted the considerable and growing inequalities in UK society, with education being an important agent in the reproduction and legitimisation of these inequalities (Institute of Fiscal Studies, 2008; Toynbee and Walker, 2008; Brennan et al., 2013). This leads us to Watson's question (2006, p. 3): 'Is HE simply a sorting device or does it have transformative possibilities?' and Wolf's (2003, p. 56) damning description of vocational education as being 'a great idea for other people's children'.

Quality

Government policies have sought to encourage HEIs to change by increasing market pressures in the belief that greater competition will put students at the heart of the educational experience, improve teaching, drive down costs and encourage innovations in educational delivery. Even though UK higher education is still far from a fully functioning market, given the lack of price variation, there is growing pressure for better, clearer public information so that prospective students can easily compare *quality* across universities. Green (1994, p. 12) identifies 'quality' as an elusive concept, even though 'we all have an instinctive understanding of what it means, it is difficult to articulate'.

As the UK moves towards a more market-based model in HE, notions of quality in higher education may increasingly be equated to 'value for money', accountability and market position, both nationally and internationally, as HEIs are looking for a competitive edge (Anyangwe, 2012). Additionally, Coiffait (2012, p. 14) identifies the perceived 'risks of private for-profit providers, that free-ride on the wider academic community', as well as identifying an appropriate role for employers. He concludes that 'there are no simple answers, and the sector continues to serve a multitude of masters and purposes', but optimistically, the 'sector will continue to maintain a focus on high quality provision and that will help dictate the pace and degree of change – rather than the reverse'.

A Look to the Future

The UK is faced with uncertainty in a diverging policy environment, in the unprecedented cuts to public funding of higher education, to increased global competition, the rise of new modes of learning and in the increasing marketisation of the system. Against this volatile and fluid economic environment and significant demographic developments, change seems inevitable. The prospects for disruption and reinvention are evident, and out of it there is potential for a new UK higher education ecosystem:

> As lives and society change, so too must the forms of teaching and learning provided by our higher education institutions. Students of the future will choose between universities internationally and demand more flexible forms of learning that enable them to retrain while in work or raising a family. They are also likely to have greater expectations of higher education institutions, given that they are themselves meeting much of the cost of their course. The challenge for our higher education system is to ensure that it is responsive enough to adapt to these more diverse needs and changing expectations.
>
> *IPPR, 2013, p. 13*

As global competition intensifies, public funding diminishes and the concept of a traditional 'university' comes under pressure, various scenarios have been painted (Kennie and Price, 2012; Barber et al., 2013; IPPR, 2013; UUK, 2013). While these are compelling versions of what could happen, it is difficult to predict how these changes will impact on the shape, size and nature of the higher education system. It is also likely that the key transformations will be evolutionary, rather than revolutionary. In the book *The Sun Also Rises* (first published in 1926), Hemingway (2006, p. 141) paints a scenario where one of the key characters is asked, 'How did you go bankrupt?'. His response is 'Gradually and then suddenly.' Change does not happen suddenly; change happens gradually through a series of smaller, incremental changes.

UK higher education now needs to find a path through this continued period of austerity so that it evolves and becomes more self-improving and sustainable. In the days to come, a new 'cast' of characters (e.g. consumers, users, producers, owners) with new roles to play may emerge. The institutional map may become increasingly diverse, fragmented or bi-partite with most, if not all, HEIs seeking and indeed claiming excellence, exceptionalism or distinction. The role of government may also change as public funding decreases and the system moves towards greater self-regulation and marketisation. Some key features of this new landscape may look like those in Figure 6.1.

In spite of the uncertainties in the future, the higher education system has much to be proud of and remains a vital asset to the UK economy and society. Higher education remains a transformative force in society through 'expanding opportunities for our people and supporting a prosperous economy, in which all can share' (IPPR, 2013, p. 10). There remains no doubt that engaging in higher education continues to provide an exceptional opportunity for life-changing

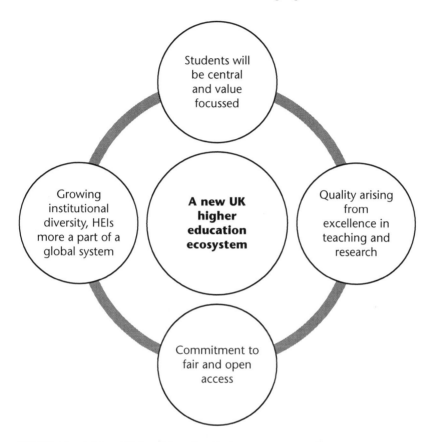

FIGURE 6.1 A New Higher Education Ecosystem

benefits, not only to the participants but also for those with whom participants have to interact in the economy more widely.

UK graduates can expect to earn even more than the government suggests, gaining 157 per cent more (on average) than non-graduates, according to the OECD (2013). Higher education plays a longstanding role in providing 'critical space' within which new and potentially controversial views can be elaborated, of 'taking truth to power', of supporting innovation and change across all sectors of society (Brennan et al., 2008).

References

Anyangwe, E. (2012) *The university of 2020: predicting the future of higher education.* Available at www.theguardian.com/higher-education-network/blog/2012/aug/24/higher-education-in-2020 (accessed on 5 February 2014). .

Barber, M., Donnelly, K. and Rizvi, S. (2013) *An avalanche is coming: higher education and the revolution ahead.* London: IPPR.

Brennan, J., Enders, J., Valimaa, J., Musselin, C. and Teichler, U. (2008) *Higher education looking forward: an agenda for future research.* Strasbourg: European Science Foundation.

Brennan, J., Durazzi, N. and Séné, T. (2013) *Things we know and don't know about the wider benefits of higher education: a review of the recent literature.* BIS Research 133.

Brown, N., Corney, M. and Stanton, G. (2004) *Breaking out of the silos: 14–30 education and skills policy.* London: Nigel Brown Associates.

Coiffait, L. (ed.) (2012) *Blue skies: new thinking about the future of higher education. A collection of short articles by leading commentators,* UK 2012 edition. London: Pearson.

Committee on Higher Education (1963) *Higher education: report of the Committee appointed by the Prime Minister under the Chairmanship of Lord Robbins 1961–63,* Cmnd. 2154. London: HMSO.

Crawford, C. (2012) *Socio-economic gaps in HE participation: how have they changed over time?* London: Institute for Fiscal Studies.

Croxford, L. and Raffe, D. (2011a) *Applicants and entrants through UCAS to the UK's differentiated full-time HE system 1996–2010.* Working Paper 1. Available at www.ces. ed.ac.uk/research/DIFFHE/index.htm (accessed on 5 February 2014).

Croxford, L. and Raffe, D. (2011b) *The social, demographic and educational characteristics of applicants and entrants to full-time HE in the UK 1996–2010.* Working Paper 2. Available at www.ces.ed.ac.uk/research/DIFFHE/index.htm (accessed on 5 February 2014).

Dent, P., Garton, L., Hooley, T., Leonard, C., Marriott, J. and Moore, N. (2013) *Higher education outreach to widen participation: toolkits for practitioners: Overview,* 2nd edition HEFCE: Bristol.

Gorard, S., Smith, E., May, H., Thomas, L., Adnett, N. and Slack, K. (2006) *Review of widening participation research: addressing the barriers to participation in higher education.* Bristol: HEFCE.

Green, D. (ed.) (1994) *What is quality in higher education?* London: SRHE.

HEFCE (2013) *Higher education in England: impact of the 2012 reforms (2013/03).* Bristol: HEFCE. Available at: www.hefce.ac.uk/about/intro/abouthighereducation inengland/impact (accessed on 5 February 2014).

Hemingway, E. (1926/2006) *The sun also rises.* New York: Scribner.

HESA (2014a) *Higher education student enrolments and qualifications obtained at higher education institutions in the United Kingdom for the academic year 2012/13.* Cheltenham: Higher Education Statistics Agency.

HESA (2014b) *Staff at higher education institutions in the United Kingdom 2012/13.* Cheltenham: Higher Education Statistics Agency.

Holmwood, J. (2013) *Unbundling the university.* Available at http://publicuniversity.org. uk/2013/03/14/unbundling-the-university/ (accessed on 5 February 2014).

Institute of Fiscal Studies (2008) *Racing away? Income inequality and the evolution of high incomes,* Briefing Notes 76.

IPPR (2013) *A critical path: securing the future of higher education in England.* London: Institute for Public Policy Research.

Kelly, U., McLellan, D. and McNicoll, I. (2009) *The impact of higher education institutions on the UK economy,* 4th Report. Glasgow: University of Strathclyde.

Kennie, T. and Price, I. (2012) *Disruptive innovation and the higher education ecosystem post-2012.* London: LFHE.

Lucas, S. (2001) Effectively maintained inequality: educational transitions, track mobility and social background effects, *American Journal of Sociology,* 106, pp. 1642–1690.

NUSScotland (2012) *Unlocking Scotland's potential.* Edinburgh: NUSScotland.

The Observatory on Borderless Higher Education (2014) *TNE and the Transnational & Distance Education Barometer.* Available at www.obhe.ac.uk/newsletters/tne_and_the_tne_barometer (accessed on 5 February 2014).

OECD (2013) *Education at a glance 2013: OECD indicators.* OECD Publishing. Available at http://dx.doi.org/10.1787/eag-2013-en.

OFFA (n.d.) History. Office for Fair Access (OFFA). Available at www.offa.org.uk/about/background/ (accessed on 17 November 2014).

Ramsden, B. (2012) *Institutional diversity in UK higher education.* London: HEPI.

Reay, D., David, M.E. and Ball, S. (2005) *Degrees of choice: social class, race and gender in higher education.* Stoke on Trent: Trentham Books.

Shavit, Y., Arum, R. and Gamoran, A. (2007) *Stratification in higher education: a comparative study.* Stanford: Stanford University Press.

Times Higher Education (2014) University applicant numbers hit near-record levels. Available at www.timeshighereducation.co.uk/news/university-applicant-numbers-hit-near-record-levels/2010962.article (accessed on 5 February 2014).

Toynbee, P. and Walker, D. (2008) *Unjust rewards: Exposing greed and inequality in Britain today.* London: Granta Books.

UCAS (2013) *UCAS undergraduate 2013 end of cycle report.* Cheltenham: UCAS. Available at www.ucas.com/sites/default/files/ucas-2013-end-of-cycle-report.pdf (accessed on 5 February 2014).

UCAS (2014) *UK application rates by country, region, sex, age and background (2014 cycle, January deadline).* Cheltenham: UCAS. Available at www.ucas.com/news-events/news/2014/uk-application-rates-country-region-sex-age-and-background-2014-cycle-january (accessed on 5 February 2014).

UUK (Universities UK) (2013) *The funding environment for universities: an assessment.* London: UUK.

Watson, D. (2006) *How to think about widening participation in UK higher education.* Bristol: HEFCE.

Wolf, A. (2003) *Does education matter? Myths about education and economic growth.* London: Penguin.

7

HIGHER EDUCATION IN SCANDINAVIA

A Case Study

Jørgen Lerche Nielsen and Lars Birch Andreasen

Introduction

Higher education systems around the world have been undergoing fundamental changes through the last 50 years, from more narrow self-sustaining universities for the elite into mass universities, where new groups of students have been recruited and the number of students enrolled has increased dramatically. As the general level of education in society is growing, universities are adjusting to the role of being a mass educational institution. Universities have been challenged on how to cope with various external pressures, such as forces of globalization and international markets, increased national and international competition for students and research grants, increased pressure to become more efficient economically and regarding students' length of studies. These various pressures can be seen as expressions of national policy changes from more democratic governance towards new public management principles. In this chapter we will examine how higher education systems in Scandinavia are developing in relation to these challenges. To what extent has the democratic tradition had an impact on the educational systems, and what possible futures can be envisioned?

The area of Scandinavia refers to the three North European countries of Norway, Denmark, and Sweden, which in many ways have a shared history and relatively similar development of welfare societies, where education plays a central role. Another term often used is the Nordic countries, referring in addition to the Scandinavian countries also to Finland and Iceland. In this chapter we will, however, focus on Scandinavia.

Major Trends and Structural Changes in Scandinavia

The oldest universities in Europe were founded in Bologna in 1088 and in Paris in 1208. In Scandinavia, Uppsala University, Sweden, was established in 1477 and the University of Copenhagen, Denmark, was established two years later in 1479. The "modern" university can be traced back to the beginning of the 19th century with the German philosopher, linguist, and educator Wilhelm von Humboldt, who founded Berlin University. The Humboldtian model, which became influential in Scandinavia, underlined the unity between research and teaching, and stressed the process of discovery of knowledge. Thus, lectures, seminars, laboratory courses, and excursions were seen as supporting students' independent pursuit of understanding and knowledge, more than the means of transmitting knowledge (Dysthe and Webler, 2010). Humboldt envisioned university education as a student-centered activity of research: "The university teacher is thus no longer a teacher and the student is no longer a pupil. Instead the student conducts research on his own behalf and the professor supervises his research and supports him in it" (Humboldt, 1809, cited by Clark, 2009, p. 333). Professors and students should together embark on research and thorough investigations, with the purpose of improving society and teaching critical thinking and research.

The underlying value of professional autonomy has been an important feature of the Humboldtian university model. This university organization builds on a collegial perspective stressing consensus, autonomy, and democracy. The faculty has a great deal of academic autonomy as long as it possesses the required competence and qualifications (Fägerlind and Strömqvist, 2004, p. 20).

Until the beginning of the 1970s, university departments were usually organized with few professors carrying out the decisive decisions, but the youth and student revolt in 1968 had a strong impact on the organization of higher education in Scandinavia. In Denmark, the organized student movement succeeded in contributing to major changes regarding content, form, and organization of the universities. As a consequence, the Danish University Act of 1972 introduced election among faculty, students, and administrative staff for participating in the decision-making bodies of the university. Also, heads of departments and study programs, deans, and rectors (university presidents) were elected by the employees and students.

The resulting changes led to a focus on practical and professional application of the content of studies. At some study programs, the organization of teaching and learning processes was no longer directed at individual assignments on fixed questions, but could involve groups of students collaboratively writing projects of up to 100 pages, applying theories and methods from a variety of disciplines to investigate a certain problem. Criticism of the traditional examination and grading system resulted in new ways of assessment and in some places students were examined in groups, where they, on the basis of their written project report, made an oral presentation and the examination was undertaken as an illuminating dialogue.

This development was in a way a combination of interests of various actors. From the students' and reform movement's point of view, the changes led towards more focus on student-led project work, cross-disciplinarity, and improved societal relevance. Parallel with this, the government and ministries had a wish to establish more flexibility and efficiency in the university programs (Christiansen et al., 2013, p. 22), which was also one of the implications of the reform development.

During the 1980s and 1990s, the elected university bodies and the universities as a whole were criticized for being ponderous organizations overloaded with demands from many stakeholders and incapable of responding quickly, efficiently, and flexibly to changing social and industrial demands. New lines of authority were modeled upon those found in corporate structures, mixing traditional academic values with managerial ones (Fägerlind and Strömqvist, 2004, p. 21). In Denmark this led to the University Act of 2003, which abolished the democratic collegiate system and replaced it with professional hired leaders and governing boards with the majority of external representatives from industry, business, and public and private institutions. Another contested change took place in 2006, when the center-right government issued a law that prohibited group exams. Later, in 2012, a new center-left government reversed this law, and it is now up to the educational institutions themselves to decide the form of assessment (Andreasen and Nielsen, 2013, p. 218).

With the University Act of 2003 grew a new kind of institutional autonomy. The state would not govern higher education directly, but rather indirectly through negotiations and through rewarding best practices. Still, centralized decision-making is maintained in many ways, e.g. through performance contracts and control of accreditation of programs, and autonomy is therefore limited (Rasmussen, 2014).

The recent reform agenda for management and financing of higher education institutions is not unique to Scandinavia. Similar patterns seem to appear in many countries worldwide. In Europe, universities have become more autonomous from the state in many ways. At the same time, increasing pressure for social responsibility and accountability has brought about another type of state control. Thus, the decentralization of authority from the central government directly to institutions is seen in combination with more direct links and contracts between the ministries and higher education institutions. New agencies or councils have been created for the purpose of quality control and coordination, and the financing of higher education is changing from basic funding towards performance-based funding.

The Scandinavian welfare model has given high priority to policies regarding health, social welfare, and education; and this has been considered by economists and social scientists to promote economic growth. But a shift in paradigms has taken place with more emphasis on private actors, and it has been stressed by governmentally appointed commissions such as the Danish Productivity Commission (2013) and by OECD (2014) that funds for social welfare and education are not limitless. This is the landscape in which the current developments in higher education shall be seen.

Diversification of Higher Education Institutions

Higher education in Scandinavia has a long history, but from the first establishment of universities until today, institutions of higher education have changed considerably. One period of change took place in the 1960s with a dramatic rise in the number of students applying for university studies and a resulting growth of the existing universities and establishment of new universities. In the political landscape of societal transitions in the 1960s and 1970s, the expansion of higher education institutions served several purposes. In the Scandinavian countries, the locations of new institutions of higher education were often decided partly in order to create regional development and growth.

After a period of regional diversification and growth in the number of higher education institutions in the 1960s and 1970s, the number of educational institutions and programs became more stable. In the beginning of the 2000s, we can notice in the Scandinavian countries a tendency towards merging processes and fusions of institutions into fewer, more centrally governed ones—at times, with local branches.

In Sweden and Norway, as well as in Denmark, a distinction exists between universities and university colleges. In all three countries, universities have the purpose of conducting research and offering long-cycle tertiary education. The term "university college," however, covers different areas in the three countries. In Norway and Sweden, university colleges have a longer history and may not only provide medium-cycle profession-based education, but may partly also cover master's and PhD. Some university colleges in Sweden and Norway are in a transition phase where they expand their research activities and some have become accredited as universities. In Denmark, on the other hand, "university colleges" are relatively new. These were established in 2008 as "professionshøjskoler," merging several local and regional educational institutions, and with the main task of providing medium-cycle higher education at the bachelor level for professions such as teachers, kindergarten/pre-school teachers, nurses, and social workers (called a "professional bachelor"). Therefore, university colleges in the three Scandinavian countries may address different tasks.

Higher Education Institutions in Denmark

In Denmark, the educational system is organized in two parallel strands: an ordinary education system and a parallel system covering adult and continuing education, where the educational levels of the two systems are directly comparable. The ordinary educational system consists of the basic school, youth education, and higher education. Higher education covers three different types of programs: short-cycle programs of one-and-a-half to two-and-a-half years at vocational/business colleges ("erhvervsakademier"), medium-cycle programs of three to four years at university colleges ("professionshøjskoler") leading to a diploma or a professional bachelor degree, and long-cycle programs of five years at universities, usually through a three-year university bachelor followed by a two-year master's degree (*candidatus*) (Schmidt, 2006, p. 522). The various types of education in the ordinary system do not require tuition payment.

A parallel system of lifelong learning makes it possible for people having obtained some years of work experience after having left the mainline education system to re-enter higher education, developing their qualifications further at professional diploma and master levels. The educational offerings of this parallel system are typically financed through a combination of tuition fees from participants and subsidies from the state (Buhl and Andreasen, 2010).

In Denmark, an expansion of the number of educational institutions took place during the 1960s and 1970s, often contributing to the local and regional development. Until the late 1960s, there were only two universities in Denmark—in Copenhagen and in Aarhus—which at that time grew significantly due to the rapidly growing number of students. In order to cope with the continuing rise in student intake, during 1967–75, three new universities were founded—in Odense, Roskilde, and Aalborg. These universities were founded with the intention of not only giving access to education in geographically remote places and supporting regional development, but also with the intention of experimenting pedagogically and modernizing the university traditions (Olesen and Jensen, 1999). Two of the universities—in Roskilde and Aalborg—explicitly favored a project-organized and problem-based learning approach.

All five above-mentioned institutions were established as multi-faculty universities. In the 1990s, a number of single-faculty universities were established, building on already existing institutions of higher education with a specialized focus in technical science, business, pharmaceutics, or education.

Since the millennium, the former multitude of different educational institutions has merged and are now forming fewer, often regionally based, centers, each offering a number of specializations at various locations. Before the millennium, there were 150 different schools, colleges, and seminaries offering short- and medium-cycle programs (Schmidt, 2006, p. 522). In the beginning of the 2000s, 23 "Centers for higher education" were formed, some covering all medium-cycle programs in a definite geographical area, others covering only specific programs. In 2008, these 23 centers were further merged into only seven regionally based "professionshøjskoler"—in English, translated into "university colleges." Parallel with this, the providers of short-cycle programs have merged into nine business colleges, regionally based around the country.

During this time, many universities merged. During 2006–07, 12 universities and nine research institutions merged into eight universities in Denmark. Five of these are multi-faculty universities and three are single-faculty universities covering business, technical science, and information technology. Parallel with this centralization, some of the universities have established branches in various parts of the country.

The rationale behind the fusion of educational institutions has been to create stronger entities, improve quality as well as efficiency and international strength. These processes have also been expressed as a wish to establish better possibilities for cross-disciplinary cooperation, joint teaching activities, and knowledge sharing. Whether the mergers have led to the development in this direction are, however, yet to be seen.

Higher Education Institutions in Sweden

The universities of Sweden were originally founded as places for education of civil servants for the public administration (Nilsson, 2006, p. 46). In Sweden, during the 1960s and through the 1980s, there has also been a regionalization process of the universities. This first happened by locating some of the activities of existing universities in regionally based branches, and later through giving these branches full independence as universities in their own right. The same development towards regional coverage took place regarding medium-cycle programs, as the Swedish university college reform in 1977 ensured that each of the approximately 20 regions of Sweden should have at least one higher education institution (Hedin, 2009, p. 16). In 2013, there were 14 public universities, three independent higher educational institutions, and 20 public university colleges in Sweden (Swedish Higher Education Authority, 2013, p. 16).

Higher Education Institutions in Norway

The first university in Norway was established in Oslo in 1811, while the country was still in union with Denmark. The second university, in Bergen, opened in 1946, just after the Second World War (Nilsson, 2006, pp. 30–31). During the last 50 years, higher education in Norway has developed through three waves of reform. In the 1960s, "the right to nine years of schooling" was decided, and a reform of the high school level was introduced—paving the way for more people entering higher education (Nilsson, 2006, p. 31).

In Norway, as in the other Scandinavian countries, the expansion of educational institutions from 1960 onwards was at the same time a regional development process to develop areas with previously only few educational institutions. In Norway, a new kind of higher education institution—regional specialized public colleges—was established during the 1970s and 1980s (Hedin, 2009, p. 15). In the educational institutional reforms of the 1990s, these almost 100 colleges and other independent higher education institutions were merged into 26 university colleges, each covering a larger regional area. In the late 2000s, a further merging of institutions occurred, which reduced the direct presence of educational institutions in several regions (Hedin, 2009, p. 16). In 2014, there were eight universities, eight specialized institutions at university level, and 19 university colleges in Norway (Government of Norway, 2014).

Across the Scandinavian countries, throughout the 20th century, there has been a diversification and growth in the number of educational institutions at various levels. These were often based regionally and provided a foundation for local and regional development. In the last 20 years, there has been an opposite tendency of centralization through closures and fusion of existing institutions.

Affordability

In the Scandinavian countries, higher education is considered a public good, and it is generally free of charge to enter and participate in a higher education program. With equal rights to education as a central political goal, systems of financial support for students were developed after the Second World War. For example, in Norway in 1948, a State Education Loan Fund was established to give all young people an opportunity for education—irrespective of social background, gender or residence (Nilsson, 2006, p. 31).

In Sweden, higher education has been free of charge for both Swedish students and those from other countries, but since June 2010 citizens of countries outside Europe have to pay an application fee and tuition fees for higher education courses and programs. The higher education institutions are required to charge tuition fees that cover their costs in full for these students (Swedish Higher Education Authority, 2013, p. 20). The same conditions were implemented in Denmark in 2006. Norway is one of the few countries where higher education is free, regardless of citizenship. However, recently the Conservative party, which is now in government, has contested this policy (Grove, 2011).

Beside the free ordinary educational system, as aforementioned, Denmark has a parallel education system with diploma and master's programs directed mainly towards people in jobs. These programs are organized according to the Act on Open Education, and participants pay tuition fees to cover parts of the educational costs.

Financial Support for Students

The Scandinavian countries have systems of financial support for students, which compared to most other countries are at a relatively high level. In Denmark, grants for students are said to be the highest in the world—twice as high as in Norway and three times higher than in Sweden (Danish Productivity Commission, 2013, p. 15). In Sweden, two-thirds of the support is through state-financed loans with low interest and one-third is a grant portion (Swedish Higher Education Authority, 2013, p. 20). Although Scandinavian universities do not charge tuition fees, and even though Scandinavian student welfare is relatively generous, most students need to work to support themselves. They typically leave home when they enter tertiary study and must pay for their own accommodation. In other OECD countries, up to three-quarters of students continue to live with their parents during tertiary studies (Dobson, 2010).

One of the voices in the debate on higher education belongs to OECD. In its regularly published *Economic Country Surveys*, OECD analyzes and recommends on what reforms and political actions are needed. OECD's recommendations for Denmark, published in January 2014, focus on the introduction of tuition fees for higher education, and on reforming the study grant system in favor of programs with higher expected employment rates and in having students complete their education faster (OECD, 2014, pp. 95–96). The Danish Productivity Commission (2013, p. 21) has similar recommendations of introducing "a certain" amount of tuition fee, especially in relation to programs with lower job prospects. These voices are led by an economic rationality that represents a break with the hitherto welfare state-oriented organization of higher education. The current Danish center-left government seems to be open to much of this criticism of the present state of the system of higher education. However, the responsible minister points out that introducing tuition fees is not on the current agenda. A reform of the study grant system seems to be more likely.

Financing Higher Education Institutions

Scandinavian countries have a strong commitment of public resources to higher education. In Denmark, Sweden, and Norway, public resources devoted to higher education represented between 1.6 and 1.8 percent of GDP in 2010, as shown in Figure 7.1. This relatively high level in part reflects traditions of universality and commitment to social welfare in Scandinavia (Hauptman and Kim, 2009, p. 10). As can be seen, private resources to higher education represent a marginal part in Scandinavia, which is in contrast to the USA and South Korea, where private funding is dominant.

The public support for higher education institutions in Denmark takes place partly through relatively fixed yearly allocation of funds for research and for basic administration, while the funds for educational activities are allocated through a performance-based model. This model is called the taximeter principle (Rasmussen, 2014) and depends on the actual number of students that pass exams. A growing part of the research allocations are furthermore directed from basic funding to allocation through performance-based indicators.

In Sweden, after incentive reforms, the direct funding for research and education is based mainly on past allocations, but since 2009, 10 percent of the funding and new resources are allocated on the basis of quality indicators as publications, citations, and research funding from external sources (Swedish Higher Education Authority, 2013, p. 17).

Accessibility

In principle, all citizens in the Scandinavian countries have the opportunity to access higher education, provided that they meet the requirements for admission—which are often defined as having completed high school. In some cases, specific courses or combination of courses are required.

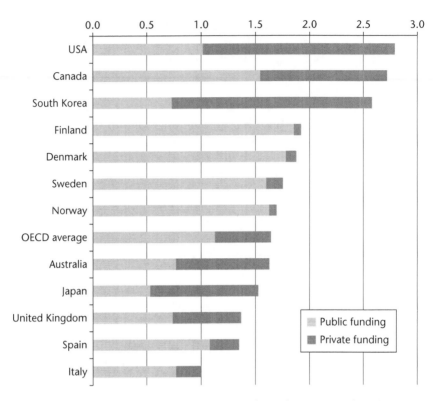

FIGURE 7.1   Public and Private Investment in Higher Education in Selected OECD Countries 2010, in Percentage of GDP

Source: Own adaptation, based on OECD, 2013, p. 193, table B2.3

Even though higher education in the Scandinavian countries was free of tuition fees, after the Second World War only a few fulfilled the requirements for university admission and hence, a small percentage attempted university education. A change to this occurred in Norway not before the late 1950s (Nilsson, 2006, p. 31). Looking at the number of possible applicants for higher education, the same tendency can be seen in Denmark. As shown in Figure 7.2, in 1945 only 5 percent of young people in Denmark completed high school; thus, the numbers of students entering higher education were equally low (Statistical Agency of Denmark, 2014, p. 9). From the end of the Second World War until today, a massive expansion of the number of students has taken place. In 1972, the compulsory schooling in Denmark was expanded from seven to nine years. This led to a major growth in the 1970s and onwards, and the tendency towards the majority obtaining a high school education has continued.

When the influx of students grew significantly after the 1960s, beyond the capacity of the existing as well as the newly established universities, and the public

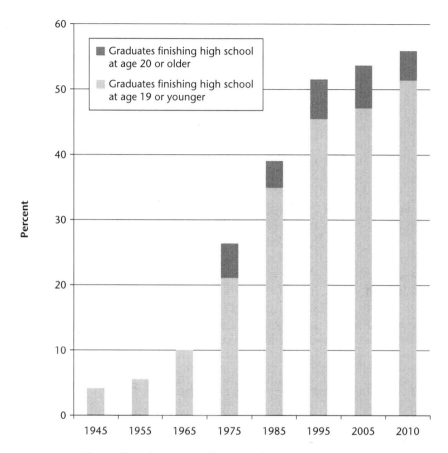

FIGURE 7.2 Share of Population Completing High School Education

Source: Own adaptation, based on Statistical Agency of Denmark, 2014, p. 9

expenses grew correspondingly, the former principle of open access was revised and a system of restriction of access was introduced in order to limit the growing number of students, and to direct the students towards programs that were seen as useful or with better employment expectations. The restricted access was implemented in Denmark by giving a certain maximum of student intake on specific programs.

In Sweden, access is mainly based on school-leaving grades (Swedish Higher Education Authority, 2013, p. 20). In Denmark, access is also mainly based on the applicants' grades from their high school exams (called quota 1). In addition to this, 10–25 percent of the student intake is based on criteria specified by the institutions (called quota 2), which allow for individual assessments with regard to work experience, other education, or study abroad.

The coherence between different areas of the educational system has recently become more open and flexible. It is now possible to get access to some of the master's programs at the universities if you have a professional bachelor's degree from a university college. Earlier, this possibility did not exist, as the medium-cycle programs were not recognized as professional bachelor degrees. Therefore, a student from a medium-cycle program had to start all over again. Additionally, parallel educational opportunities have opened up in the form of diploma and master's programs through Open Education, where people can study part-time while still holding their positions in the private or public sector.

From the perspective of the educational researcher Martin Trow, educational systems can be classified into three ideal types. An educational system can be described as having *elite* access if only a small percentage of the population obtains a higher education. If a share of 15 percent or more completes higher education, the educational system may be described as having *mass* access, meaning that it is generally considered as a straightforward thing to do for a middle-class student to enter higher education. Furthermore, when over 50 percent of a population completes higher education, the educational system may, in the perspective of Trow, be described as having *universal* access, meaning that higher education is considered an even more natural thing to enter for the majority of young people. The implication of this broadening of access is that university education needs to be structured in new ways (Trow, 2010, pp. 94–95).

According to the classification of Martin Trow (2010), the transition of Scandinavian higher education from elite access to mass access occurred in the 1960s, when a great mass of students were seeking further education in connection with the societal development from predominantly agricultural societies to more industrialized societies, with the need of a more skilled workforce. The increase in the number of students was further aggravated by the fact that the baby boomers, the big generation born in the years after the Second World War, had grown up and were able to apply for study. The change from mass access towards universal access to higher education is currently happening in the Scandinavian countries.

Participation

The overall tendency in Scandinavia, as well as worldwide, is that a growing number of people are attending higher education. Additionally, more people are obtaining a higher level of education. This general tendency of an increasing educational level has been particularly prevalent in two periods, the first in the 1960s and 1970s, and the second from 2000 to the present.

Efforts have been made to widen participation in higher education and include groups that traditionally did not participate, e.g. older students, or students from non-academic backgrounds. For the Social Democratic Party, which has been influential in all three Scandinavian countries, the goal of recruiting students from a variety of social, cultural, and educational backgrounds to obtain more educational equity in society has been considered important as a democratic goal. Furthermore, the need for a highly qualified workforce in order to maintain the welfare state has also been considered a crucial factor behind the effort to widen participation. Even though the goal has not been fully achieved, an increasingly diverse group of students from more varied backgrounds than before, and at different life stages, is now found in Scandinavian higher education institutions (Fägerlind and Strömqvist, 2004, p. 245).

The share of the population entering and completing a program in higher education has been growing in all Scandinavian countries, with the actual level of Norway and Sweden a bit higher than Denmark. The level can be measured in many different ways; here, we will mainly refer to data collected by Eurostat—the statistical agency of the European Union—that measures the participation in higher education by analyzing what percentage of people in the age group 30 to 34 years have completed either a short-, medium-, or long-cycle higher education, that is, at least two years of tertiary education (Eurostat, 2014).

Figure 7.3 shows generally a continuous growth in the share of the population achieving higher education, in the Scandinavian countries as well as in the European Union (EU). (The break in the graph of Denmark between 2006 and 2007 may be due to a change in methods of assessment.) The EU has a goal that the share of 30–34-year-olds with a completed higher education should in 2020

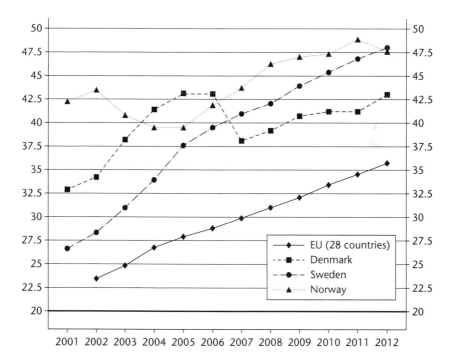

FIGURE 7.3   Share of 30–34-year-olds achieving a higher education, 2001–2012

Source: Own adaptation, based on Eurostat, 2014

be at least 40 percent. Generally this goal is about to be achieved, as in the period from 2002 to 2012 the overall mean for the EU countries has moved from 23.5 percent to 35.7 percent. The Scandinavian countries have already exceeded the EU goal. The Danish government has set different goal in that by 2020, 60 percent of a youth cohort should be able to complete higher education. The difference between the Danish goal of 60 percent and the EU goal of 40 percent is partially due to the difference in the criteria behind measuring the numbers. The EU figures are calculated as the actual share of higher education among 30–34-year-olds. The Danish figures are calculated as the expected future educational level of today's 15-year-olds, based on register data and statistical projections. In Denmark in 2010, 54 percent of the 15-year-olds were expected to complete a higher education. This is an increase from 35 percent from expectations in 1990 (Ministry of Business and Growth, Denmark, 2013, p. 57). Thus, the goal of 60 percent seems to be within reach.

In Figure 7.4, the share of students completing a short-cycle, medium-cycle, and long-cycle higher education is highlighted, showing a considerable growth, especially in relation to long-cycle higher education.

Another relevant aspect regarding participation is the balance between male and female students. Historically, educational systems have been male-dominated, but today there is globally a slight majority of female students. In Denmark in 1945, only 14 percent of the university graduates were female, while in 2012 the

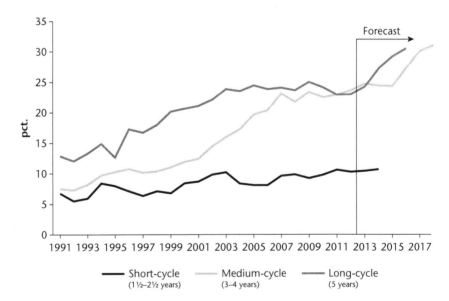

FIGURE 7.4 Share of a Youth Year Group that Completes a Higher Education

Source: Danish Productivity Commission, 2013, fig. 3.4, p. 35

share has grown to 55 percent (Statistical Agency of Denmark, 2014, p. 9). In the Scandinavian countries since 2000, female students' share of the total student population of higher education has been relatively stable. In 2011, the percentage of female students in higher education was 57 percent in Denmark, 59 percent in Sweden, and 60 percent in Norway. In science, mathematics, and computing programs, the share of female students in 2011 was 35 percent in Denmark, 41 percent in Sweden, and 35 percent in Norway (Eurostat, 2014).

Another tendency is that a growing number of students enroll in higher education directly or shortly after completing their qualifying degree. In Scandinavia, students entering higher education have generally been older than students in most other countries, where higher education normally begins early after leaving high school. This difference in age of higher education entrants in various countries reflects social differences and differences in the educational systems. For instance, one factor could be the age at which high school education finishes. In Scandinavia, pupils normally leave high school at the age of 19—which is one of the reasons why higher education entrants are older than in many other countries. Higher education in Scandinavia is also characterized by a major element of lifelong learning (Swedish Higher Education Authority, 2013, p. 8). As shown in Figure 7.5, there is a clear tendency that higher education entrants in Sweden are getting younger.

In Denmark as well, young students are encouraged to enter higher education earlier. Since 2009, students can multiply their average grades from high school by 1.08 if they apply for higher education within two years of finishing high school. Thereby, they will receive an 8 percent increase in their scores. This allows them to more easily enter their program of choice. Danish students are also encouraged to complete their studies faster and a 2013 reform is attempting to increase the study efficiency and cut half a year off the time students take to complete their studies.

Quality

In the wake of the rapid expansion of the numbers of students, quality has become a key general theme for the Ministries of Education in all Scandinavian countries (Andersen and Jacobsen, 2012, p. 24). In Sweden, for instance, the total number of students in 1950–55 was 20,000, while in 1999 the total enrolment was around 300,000. Torsten Husén calls this a process of massification (Husén, 1999, p. 1). How can institutions guarantee quality in this situation? The challenge has been to secure quality while expanding quantity. According to Palle Rasmussen (2014), quality assessment was not an issue in Danish education prior to 1980. All institutions had to adhere to a fairly detailed set of official regulations, and this, in combination with the professional judgment of the teaching staff, was expected to uphold the quality.

Another way of upholding quality in the institutions of higher education happens through the continuous evaluations in the system of examination of

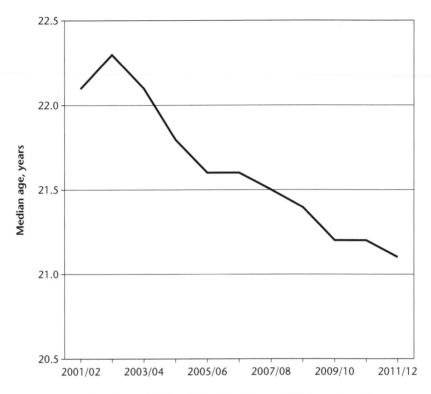

FIGURE 7.5 Median Age of Higher Education Entrants (Without Incoming Students) in Sweden, 2001–2012

Source: Swedish Higher Education Authority, 2013, p. 26

students. In Scandinavia, university exams are generally organized not as questionnaires or multiple-choice-assignments with fixed answers, but through oral and written examinations, where the students are evaluated by two academics, an internal university professor, and an external examiner. Each higher education program is connected to a board of external examiners, with members from other academic institutions as well as relevant businesses and organizations. The members of the boards of external examiners are continually renewed. Through this system of evaluating the students' results, the quality of higher education is continually contested.

In 1992, the Danish Ministry of Education established the Evaluation Center for Higher Education. The goal of the Evaluation Center was to undertake quality assessment of all study programs in higher education; to develop appropriate evaluation methods; to guide institutions in matters of quality development; and to compile national and international experiences on evaluation and quality development in higher education (Rasmussen, 2014). The director of the Evaluation Center has pointed out that Danish higher education institutions did not, until the late 1990s, have a strong tradition for focusing on quality assurance of teaching and learning (Thune, 2001). With the Evaluation Center, all study programs in Danish long-cycle higher education were to be evaluated at regular intervals. However, in 1999 the Evaluation Center was given a broader task comprising the entire educational system, and evaluation of higher education gradually became a minor part of its work (Rasmussen, 2014).

In 2007, a new accreditation institution was founded to strengthen the quality assurance work at the university level in Denmark. New programs have to be approved by the Accreditation Council on behalf of the Ministry before they can be offered to students. The decisions are based on a procedure where universities produce comprehensively documented proposals that are evaluated by expert panels against criteria for coherence, teaching resources, research base, and not least, labor market relevance (Rasmussen, 2014).

The newest development regarding the quality of higher education in Denmark is that a Quality Commission for Higher Education appointed by the government published its first recommendations in the spring of 2014, in continuation of the thoughts and proposals from the above-mentioned Danish Productivity Commission (2013). In November 2014 the Quality Commission published its second report. Focus is on quality, study intensity and relevance in relation to societal needs, job market and how to gear university studies more directly to employment prospects. Within this framing the government has proposed to cut student intake primarily within arts and humanities.

In Norway, a Quality Reform of Higher Education was implemented in 2003. The goal of this reform was to improve the quality of higher education, both at universities and university colleges, and to implement the EU "Bologna model" of 3+2+3 (three years of bachelor, two years of master, and three years of PhD studies) (Dysthe and Webler, 2010, p. 253). Higher education institutions now have their own systems for quality assurance. An independent national body for accreditation and evaluation (Norwegian Agency for Quality Assurance in Education—NOKUT) started operations in 2003 to oversee institutional quality and to accredit institutions and study programs. For institutions that do not follow up on standards, NOKUT can withdraw accreditation (Nyborg, 2007, p. 4).

One of the new initiatives is that students in Norway have to make a kind of agreement with their institutions: they must finish their degrees in a given time, take certain courses, and follow up on the lab classes. The institutions, on the other hand, must provide good and sufficient learning conditions, good lectures, flexible education, supervisors with enough time for supervision, and, in all respects, help the students reach their goals (Rangnes and Haraldsen, 2006).

In Sweden, the higher education institutions are relatively free to decide on their own organization, allocation of resources, and course offerings. The system is based on the principle of management by objectives. The government lays down directives for operations of the higher education institutions in its annual public service agreements. The Swedish Higher Education Authority exercises supervision of the higher education institutions. Through panels of external assessors consisting of subject experts, labor market representatives, and students, the Swedish Higher Education Authority reviews the quality of higher education and the efficient use of resources and public funding at the institutions (Swedish Higher Education Authority, 2013, pp. 17, 34).

Conclusion

In the development of higher education in Scandinavia there are different perspectives on education at play. One perspective sees education as a "public good" that benefits society and therefore should be free and accessible for all students who qualify to be admitted. According to this perspective, one of the main purposes of higher education is to add value to all students, so they can contribute to society. Within the framework of the Scandinavian welfare state, this model has prevailed in the organization of education, health care, and social services.

Another perspective sees education as mainly an "individual investment," and therefore students should pay for attending their education. According to this perspective, one of the main purposes of higher education is instead to select the best among the students, in order to sharpen their market value. The notions of competitiveness and individualism play an important role here. In some of the recent reforms in Scandinavia, as well as in the recommendations of the Danish Productivity Commission (2013), we see this second perspective prevailing.

Even though the current reforms seem to point towards this second perspective and towards principles of new public management, the Scandinavian countries still have educational systems where higher education as a basis is free of tuition fees, students are supported with study grants, and people generally have access to education. The massive diversification of educational institutions during the 20th century, which also provided local access to education, is currently replaced by a process of centralization of higher education and merging of existing institutions. The rate of participation in higher education is, however, still growing—thus supporting the possibility of social mobility, especially when students from families without traditions of education enter the higher education system. In the light of the possible new reforms, it remains to be seen whether this development will continue.

References

Andersen, H. L. & Jacobsen, J. C. (2012). Central concepts in the international educational discourse: a political frame [Centrale begreber i den internationale uddannelsesdiskurs: en politisk rammesætning]. In H. L. Andersen & J. C. Jacobsen (Eds.), *Educational quality in a globalized world – entry of the knowledge economy in higher education [Uddannelseskvalitet i en globaliseret verden – vidensøkonomiens indtog i de videregående uddannelser]* (pp. 17–30). Copenhagen: Samfundslitteratur.

Andreasen, L. B. & Nielsen, J. L. (2013). Dimensions of problem based learning – dialogue and online collaboration in projects. *Journal of Problem Based Learning in Higher Education*, *1*(1), 210–229. Retrieved from: http://ojs.aub.aau.dk/index.php/pbl/article/view/283.

Buhl, M. & Andreasen, L. B. (2010). e-Learning for lifelong learning in Denmark. In B. Kim (Ed.), *e-ASEM White Paper: e-Learning for lifelong learning* (pp. 29–103). Seoul: KNOU Press.

Clark, C. (2009). *Iron kingdom: the rise and downfall of Prussia, 1600–1947*. Cambridge, MA: Harvard University Press.

Christiansen, F. V., Harboe, T., Horst, S., Krogh, L. & Sarauw, L. L. (2013). Development traits in the role of the university [Udviklingstendenser i universitetets rolle]. In L. Rienecker, P. S. Jørgensen, J. Dolin & G. H. Ingerslev (Eds.), *University pedagogy [Universitetspædagogik]* (pp. 17–41). Frederiksberg: Samfundslitteratur.

Danish Productivity Commission [Produktivitetskommissionen] (2013). *Education and innovation [Uddannelse og innovation. Analyserapport 4]*. Copenhagen: Produktivitets kommissionen.

Dobson, I. R. (2010). FINLAND: students: too old and too slow? In *University World News* 25 April 2010, Issue No. 121. Retrieved from: www.universityworldnews.com/article.php?story=20100424175106129.

Dysthe, O. & Webler, W. (2010). Pedagogical issues from Humboldt to Bologna: the case of Norway and Germany. *Higher Education Policy*, *23*(2), 247–270.

Eurostat (2014). *Education and training*. European Commission. Retrieved from: http://epp.eurostat.ec.europa.eu/portal/page/portal/education/data/main_tables.

Fägerlind, I. & Strömqvist, G. (2004) Higher education reform in the global context – what ever happened to the Nordic model? In I. Fägerlind & G. Strömqvist (Eds.). *Reforming higher education in the Nordic countries – studies of change in Denmark, Finland, Iceland, Norway and Sweden*. International Institute for Educational Planning, UNESCO. Retrieved from: http://unesdoc.unesco.org/images/0013/001390/139015e.pdf.

Government of Norway (2014). *Universities and university colleges*. Retrieved from: www.regjeringen.no/en/dep/kd/Selected-topics/higher-education/universities-and-specialised-institution.html?id=491288.

Grove, J. (2011). Last of the free: will Norway's universal no-fee policy endure? In *Times Higher Education*, October 13, 2011. Retrieved from: www.timeshighereducation.co.uk/417752.article.

Hauptman, A. M. & Kim, Y. (2009). *Cost, commitment, and attainment in higher education. An international comparison*. Boston, MA: Jobs for the future. Retrieved from: http://files.eric.ed.gov/fulltext/ED505346.pdf.

Hedin, S. (2009). Overview of Nordic higher education institutions. In *Higher education institutions as drivers of regional development in the Nordic countries.* (Nordregio Working Paper 2009:3). Stockholm: Nordregio.

Husén, T. (1999). The quality dimension of higher education: a Swedish perspective. In I. Fägerlind, I. Holmesland & G. Strömqvist (Eds.) *Higher education at the crossroads. Tradition or transformation?* (pp. 1–13). Stockholm: Stockholm University, Institute of International Education.

Ministry of Business and Growth, Denmark (2013). *Denmark at work. Report on growth and competitiveness 2013 [Danmark i arbejde. Redegørelse om vækst og konkurrenceevne 2013]*. Copenhagen: Erhvervs- og vækstministeriet.

Nilsson, J.-E. (2006). Higher education in the Nordic countries. In *The role of universities in regional innovation systems – a Nordic perspective* (pp. 29–54). Copenhagen: Copenhagen Business School Press.

Nyborg, P. (2007). Higher education in Norway. Fifty years of development. English resumé of: *Universitets- og højskolesamarbeid i en brytningstid: Femti års utvikling*. Oslo: UNIPUB.

OECD (2013). *Education at a glance 2013: OECD Indicators*. Paris: OECD Publishing.

OECD (2014). *OECD economic surveys: Denmark 2013*. Paris: OECD Publishing.

Olesen, H. S. & Jensen, J. H. (Eds.) (1999). *Project studies – a late modern university reform?* Frederiksberg: Roskilde University Press.

Rangnes, K. & Haraldsen, K. B. (2006). Reform of the quality of higher education in Norway – implications for the library teaching. Paper presented at *Creating Knowledge IV. Empowering the student through cross-institutional collaboration*, Copenhagen, August 16–18, 2006. Retrieved from: www.ck-iv.dk/papers/RangnesHaraldsen%20 Reform%20of%20the%20higher%20education%20in.pdf.

Rasmussen, P. (2014). Accreditation and expansion in Danish higher education. *Nordic Studies in Education, 2014*(3), 201–212.

Schmidt, E. K. (2006). Higher education in Scandinavia. In J.J.F. Forest & P.G. Altbach (Eds.), *International handbook of higher education, part two: regions and countries* (pp. 517–537). Dordrecht, Netherlands: Springer.

Statistical Agency of Denmark [Danmarks Statistik] (2014). *65 years in numbers [65 år i tal – Danmark siden 2. verdenskrig]*. Copenhagen: Danmarks Statistik.

Swedish Higher Education Authority [Universitetskanslersämbetet] (2013). *Higher education in Sweden – 2013 status report*. Report no. 2013:3. Stockholm: Universitetskans lersämbetet. Retrieved from: http://english.uk-ambetet.se/download/18.1c251de 913ecebc40e780003403/annual-report-2013-ny.pdf.

Thune, C. (2001). Quality assurance of higher education in Denmark. In D. Dunkerly & W. S. Wong (Eds.), *Global perspectives on quality in higher education* (pp. 70–89). Aldershot: Ashgate Publishers.

Trow, M. (2010). *Twentieth-century higher education. Elite to mass to universal*. Ed. by M. Burrage. Baltimore, MD: Johns Hopkins University Press.

8

HIGHER EDUCATION IN NEW ZEALAND

A Case Study of the Land of the Long White Cloud

Lorraine Stefani

Introduction

New Zealand is a small country located some distance from the economic weight of the world's superpowers of Europe and North America, but closer to the growing economic weight of Asia. As a former British colony, it has inherited British political and legal institutions. The relationship between the indigenous Maori population and the non-Maori European settlers, or *Pakeha*, encapsulated within the Treaty of Waitangi has implications for a number of policy areas including education. However, this relationship is an uneasy one in many different socio-political aspects of life in New Zealand. The historically low educational attainment levels of Maori, and indeed the large population of Pacific Islanders who migrated to New Zealand from the 1950s onwards, create tensions regarding the democratization of higher education. This chapter endeavors to explore the challenges for New Zealand in achieving true democratization of higher education in a complex population and a constrained economic environment.

The Unique History of Aotearoa

New Zealand, also known as Aotearoa, the Land of the Long White Cloud, is a unique country situated in the South Pacific, South East of Australia. Its uniqueness as a country arises from the history of its indigenous population. Polynesian Maori reached New Zealand around AD 800 from a mythical land called Hawaiki (Wilson, 2013). The first European settlers began to arrive from 1642 onward (Wilson, 2013). It is not within the scope of this chapter to give a detailed account of the history of Maori and the European settlers, but this is a topic about which much has been written (e.g. King, 2003) and it has a poignancy regarding the topic of democratization of higher education in New Zealand. In 1840, a year of great significance regarding New Zealand history and culture, Maori chieftains entered into a pact with Britain, known as the Treaty of Waitangi, in which the indigenous Maori population ceded sovereignty to Queen Victoria while retaining territorial rights (Wilson, 2013; New Zealand History, 2014). This Treaty still remains the subject of much ongoing debate, which cannot be comprehensively entered into in this chapter. However, the renowned New Zealand historian, the late Sir Keith Sinclair, writing in 1980 quotes John Eldon Gorst, author of *The Maori King* (Gorst, 1864), giving a glimpse of the consequences for the indigenous peoples of Aotearoa of entering into a pact with Britain:

> The hopes of social advancement which the natives had formed when they first consented to share their country with the stranger, were disappointed. They did not fail to contrast the rapid alienation of their land with the slow improvement of their condition and they feared that at this rate their lands would be gone before they had attained the desired equality with their white neighbors.
>
> *Gorst, 1864*

In his article "New Zealand declared a British Colony" (1980), Sinclair states:

> In every measurable 'social indicator' they (Maori) are worse off, in average income, housing standards, education, even in health, they are not yet equal. There are still not nearly enough Maoris, proportionately, in the universities, teachers' colleges, or in the professions. Undoubtedly some Maoris feel a vain nostalgia for a largely lost Polynesian world, and a deep resentment against what they got in exchange. Many people believe that the greatest threat to New Zealand's stability and progress lies, not in its acute economic problems, but in this crucial weakness in its racial relations.

In the intervening decades since Sinclair's article was published much has been done to redress the balance, particularly in the sphere of education and educational attainment of Maori, but significant inequality of opportunity still exists. It would be a great injustice in a chapter addressing democracy and the democratization of higher education in New Zealand not to present this important background regarding the indigenous population.

Education in New Zealand

The population of Aotearoa is approximately 4.5 million of which some 683,000 are Maori (Statistics New Zealand, 2012). A consideration for the future of democracy in New Zealand is that the Maori population is much younger than the total, which in turn has implications for tertiary and higher education provision and attainment. English is the language spoken by 92 percent of the population. Te Reo Maori, spoken by only 3.9 percent of the population, and New Zealand Sign Language are also official languages of the country (Statistics New Zealand, 2013). With some exceptions, English is the language of instruction throughout the three bands of education, early childhood, schooling and tertiary education (Ministry of Education NZ, 2013). In 1989, the New Zealand government of the day enshrined the single sector approach to post-compulsory education into legislation with the passing of the 1989 Education Act (Education Act 1989). Regarding this significant shift to de-differentiation of the post-compulsory sector, Mahoney (2003, p. 2) stated that "NZ is currently unique in that no other country has clustered its community, vocational and academic education together in quite this way."

Some commentators would suggest that the long-term implications of this move have been an increase in government interference in the direction and goals of tertiary education (Grey and Scott, 2012), while successive governments state their vision of a world-leading education system that equips all New Zealanders with knowledge, skills and values to be successful citizens in the 21st century (e.g. Tertiary Education Strategy 2010–2015).

Tertiary education in New Zealand is delivered by a variety of providers. There are eight universities in New Zealand, all of which feature in the QS World University Rankings top 500, with the largest, the University of Auckland, having a place in the top 100 world universities (QS World University Rankings, 2013/2014). There are 20 Institutes of Technology and Polytechnics (ITPs), 369 Private Training Organizations (PTOs), 451 other funded organizations and three *Wananga* (Profile and Trends, 2012).

The Wananga are seen as critical to Maori educational success and attainment and a brief explanation of this is important to the topic of 'Democratization of Higher Education.'

Maori peoples have traditionally valued knowledge as a means of maintaining their *mana* or status and enhancing their quality of life. The ancient concept of *whare wananga* related to a mental process of learning rather than an institution where learning took place. The classroom was the world in which Maori lived and learning could take place anytime, anyplace—a holistic approach to learning. The Wananga of today are physical learning places with the Mission Statement: "Te Wananga O Aotearoa will provide holistic education opportunities of the highest quality for Maori, peoples of Aotearoa, NZ and the world" (Te Wananga O Aotearoa, n.d.). The importance of the Wananga and their mission to support culturally sensitive learning strategies, which align well with Maori learning orientations, cannot be overstated. There is a significant issue relating to the conflict of pedagogies between the ancient, traditional Maori ways of being and learning and the pedagogies of the dominant culture. Maori students entering into university level education very often have difficulty adjusting to the dominant *Pakeha* pedagogical models and strategies.

The educational attainment levels of Maori have long been a matter of great concern. As stated by Bishop et al. (2009, p. 734): "the social, economic and political disparities within our nation, primarily between the descendants of the European colonizers and the Indigenous Maori peoples continue to be major challenges." The dominant or prevalent educational models and strategies are predicated within a colonial framework. The disparity between these educational models and *matauranga Maori* (Maori ways of knowing) are considered to be at the root of the poor educational attainment levels of Maori peoples. The educational disadvantages historically experienced by Maori at least partially underpin their poor attainment levels (Bishop et al., 2009). This situation naturally impacts on the levels of Maori enrolment into tertiary or higher education (Hood, 2007; Ministry of Education, 2006).

The Complexity of New Zealand Demographics

The other significant population which must be considered with respect to democratization of higher education in New Zealand is the Pacific Island populace, often referred to as Pasifika. Migration to New Zealand by the Pasifika peoples has been ongoing since the 1950s when there was a strong need for migrant labor. The Pasifika population is highly significant because of its youthfulness with 38 percent of this population under the age of 15 and, as of 2012, comprising 6.9 percent of the Aotearoa population. The majority of the Pasifika peoples in New Zealand come from the islands of Samoa, Tonga and the Cook Islands, with others originating from Nuie, Tokelau and Fiji (Statistics New Zealand and Ministry of Pacific Island Affairs, 2010).

Pasifika people in general have much lower incomes than the Pakeha population and this is not unrelated to their educational attainment. As with the Maori population in New Zealand, there have long been concerns over the poor educational attainment of Pasifika people for different cultural reasons. Learning in traditional Pacific Island culture took place everywhere: "at home, during gatherings, in the fields and at sea. Family and community were inextricably interwoven into a coherent 'school' of learning" (Onikama, Hammond and Koki, 1998, p. 1). Once again, the dominant pedagogical frameworks of the colonizing population are at odds with the ways in which the Pasifika peoples learn (Chu, Abella and Paurini, 2013).

The demographic shifts that are predicted to occur over the next decade show that Europeans will increase by 0.4 percent whereas the Maori population will increase by 1.3 percent and the Pasifika population by 2.4 percent (Statistics New Zealand and Ministry of Pacific Island Affairs 2010). It is critical to the future of New Zealand as a modern democracy that we do better for Maori and Pasifika, in social, economic and educational terms. It is however an over-simplification of the concept of democratization of higher education to consider increased numbers of 'minority' population learners entering into higher education as a success. Until we recognize and acknowledge different ways of being and knowing as equally legitimate to the ongoing development of knowledge and blend and shape our pedagogies in a more inclusive manner, it may be said that we are merely paying lip service to the true meaning of democratization.

Education, Enrolments and Economics in New Zealand

Because the universities are part of the tertiary education system in New Zealand, it is difficult to separate out some of the key statistics relating to student numbers and the significant increases in these numbers over the past 10–15 years. In 1991, only 6 percent of New Zealanders aged 15 or over held a bachelor's degree or higher qualification; by 2009 this had increased to 17 percent. In 1994, 139,975 Equivalent Full-Time Students (EFTS) (domestic students) participated in some form of tertiary education, representing a participation rate of 8.8 percent. By 2011, this number of EFTS had increased to 246,482 representing a 10.9 percent participation in tertiary education by domestic students (Ministry of Education, 2010). Approximately 8 percent of tertiary level students in New Zealand are classed as international.

In the New Zealand university system, the eight universities teach approximately 180,000 students (part- and full-time) and employ around 19,500 staff. The University of Auckland is the largest of the New Zealand universities with 32,657 students (EFTS) and approximately 5,000 staff (Full-Time Equivalents, FTE) (Universities New Zealand, 2013). Auckland is the largest city and the Auckland region has the highest population level. Lincoln University, the smallest of the eight universities and originally an agricultural college, has 3,717 EFTS and 618 FTE staff (Statistics New Zealand, 2012).

New Zealand's universities receive approximately 40 percent of their annual income from government grants, with the rest of the funding coming from student fees, research contracts and trading income. The 40 percent in grant income from the New Zealand government or public purse reflects a significant and ongoing downward shift over many years. As commented on recently by the Chief Science Advisor to the Prime Minister: "NZ operates with the lowest expenditure per student of any system in the developed world and this inevitably impacts negatively on New Zealand's efforts to be a significant player in a rapidly changing world" (Universities News, 2013).

Constrained funding for tertiary institutions inevitably pushes more costs on to the learners themselves. Students can access loans and allowances to assist with fees and living costs. Inevitably as the level of government funding for universities decreases, the burden of costs falls on students. Again this seems a contradiction to the idea of democratization of tertiary or higher education. The continuous increase in costs of funding tertiary education is becoming unsustainable, raising an important question over the feasibility of affordable tertiary education opportunities for all who would like to avail themselves of that opportunity.

Students who graduated with a bachelor's level degree and left study in 2010 had an average student debt level of $NZ22,000 (Statistics New Zealand,

2014). Coupled with a shortage of graduate level jobs in New Zealand, the picture is not rosy for our next generation of graduates. This does not sit easily with the claim from the Tertiary Education Commission, NZ in its Statement of Intent (2012) that tertiary education is a major enabler of economic competitiveness in an increasingly knowledge-driven economy.

After the results of the 2013 QS University League Tables showed New Zealand universities to be taking a year on year tumble, the University of Auckland Vice Chancellor stated:

> what we seem to be trying to do in this country is have low student fees, low levels of government investment, low levels of research funding nationally and high numbers of students in universities.
>
> ...We have to decide in this country whether we want cheap universities, or whether we want highly ranked universities. It is very clear – you can't have both.
>
> *Universities News, 2013*

Such prominent figures commenting on government attitudes to university funding give an indication of the mood of the moment. New Zealand is not a wealthy country and it may not have suffered the extreme effects of the Global Economic Crisis that European countries experienced, but nevertheless there are ongoing significant economic impacts. The comments from such leading figures in the higher education sphere regarding the funding challenges are not merely knee jerk reactions to bad news, but rather give a sense of the gap between government rhetoric regarding its goals for education and its willingness to support education institutions in realizing these goals.

On the other hand, there is a quite extraordinary situation in New Zealand. In 2005, the government removed interest from student loans. This was seen at the time as a massive election bribe rather than sound policy making (Meadows, 2013). There is no indication that this policy was drawn up on the basis of a sense of democratizing higher education but it has remained in place and has cost the New Zealand taxpayer up to $NZ3.8 billion in foregone interest. At the same time, student debt is growing at a rate of approximately $NZ1 billion per year. New Zealand economists make comment on the wisdom or otherwise of retaining such a policy, but it is not the kind of information finding its way into scholarly research! Although students must eventually repay the debt, and this is undoubtedly a burden for many graduates, the rate of repayment is inordinately slow (Meadows, 2013).

Higher Education Strategy and Policy Shifts

The two central agencies responsible for policy and funding decisions relating to tertiary education are the Tertiary Education Commission (TEC) and the Ministry of Education. The TEC is the New Zealand government agency responsible for planning, funding and monitoring the government's investment in the national tertiary education and training system. In recent years, as with the situation in many countries particularly since the Global Economic Crisis, the message from the TEC to the sector has more stridently emphasized the economic purpose of tertiary education. A recent Statement of Intent from the TEC (Tertiary Education Commission, 2012, p. 8) leaves no room for doubt that the primary purpose of tertiary education is seen to be to enhance the New Zealand economy:

A world-leading education system is an important first step towards a productive and growing economy that delivers greater prosperity and opportunity for all New Zealanders. The tertiary education sector plays a core role in advancing New Zealand's economic and social development by providing:

- High quality education to prepare and maintain a relevantly skilled, flexible workforce
- High quality research that builds New Zealand's knowledge-base and drives innovation
- International education that contributes to export earnings and strengthens Tertiary Education Organizations

Each point emphasizes the contribution of tertiary education to the economy and the workforce. In the same document, the TEC presents the four key outcomes it is setting out to achieve through its work (Tertiary Education Commission, 2012, p. 2):

- Increasing tertiary education's contribution to economic recovery and growth
- Doing better for Maori and Pasifika
- Enhancing transitions from post-compulsory to tertiary education
- Improving system performance

The emphasis on the contribution of tertiary education, including university level education to the economy, is not unique to New Zealand. New Zealand can simply be seen to be following the trend. As Morley (2012, p. 26) states: ". . . we live in times of policy turbulence and change has been rapid and extreme. Transformation has largely been driven by the perceived needs of the economy rather than by academic imaginaries or social movements." It is something of a mantra that mass higher education leads to higher economic growth, but this depends on the skills produced by an expanding tertiary sector and the utilization or under-utilization of these skills in the jobs available to increasing numbers of graduates (Holmes, 2013).

During the last few years, the TEC has become more strident and blatant about its view of tertiary education as a business to be steered and managed and expected to show tangible return on investment using spurious evaluative measures (Grey and Scott, 2012).

Previous targeted funding from the government prioritized widening participation in tertiary education from all parts of the population, with significant initiatives intended to increase not just the participation but the retention and attainment of Maori and Pasifika learners. However, in recent years the TEC has been placing stronger emphasis on ensuring the quality of educational outcomes, and making demands on the sector to show return on investment made by both funding bodies and learners themselves.

The declarations from the TEC show a familiar mechanistic approach to evaluating the success of tertiary education. While it is clear that there will be demographic shifts in New Zealand and that it is imperative to ensure that previously disadvantaged groups in society achieve positive outcomes, the TEC intends to "hard-wire" (Tertiary Education Commission, 2012, p. 18) performance commitments for Maori and Pasifika achievement outcomes and apply quantitative measures to determining institutional success in improving performance. This performativity agenda tends to use language in a manner that suggests tertiary education institutions are failing in their duty. More worrying is the sense that punitive measures will be imposed on institutions if Maori and/or Pasifika students do not complete their studies or actually fail; the concept of 'failure' being judged by the TEC or the government.

The Quality Agenda—A Democratic or Economic Imperative?

Any government funding higher education institutions is right to have the expectations that these same institutions will produce public value. The New Zealand Academic Audit Unit, now known as the Academic Quality Unit, was set up by the New Zealand Vice Chancellor's Committee in 1993 to provide assurance and quality enhancement services which assist universities in enhancing the learning experience and learning outcomes within research-led academic environments (Kirkwood, 2011). Over this period of time, from 1993 to the present day, there have been shifts in the focus of the quality audits carried out, reflecting changing priorities for the institutions and changes in the government policy framework for tertiary education. The more recent audit cycles have paid increasing attention to the role of governance and management structures and communication, as well as paying attention to learning technologies and learning spaces, and to institution-wide approaches to quality assurance (Kirkwood, 2011). Regarding the auditing of governance and management, this could well be interpreted as increasing levels of interference and steering of the direction of tertiary education, including higher education as suggested by Grey and Scott (2012).

Having robust quality audit and assurance mechanisms is necessary and commendable when public monies are being provided. An interesting question to consider is whether the motives in the present circumstances are necessarily altruistic or whether perhaps institutions now actually have one eye on their own context and one eye on the market, or the education export business. The export education industry is now worth $NZ2.6 billion and is New Zealand's fifth largest export industry according to a report from The Economic Impact of International Education (2012/13). The most significant markets for New Zealand education exports include China, India, Korea and Japan, with other markets such as Saudi Arabia, Malaysia and many European countries growing rapidly.

A government report in 2013 indicated that 18,300 international students were enrolled in New Zealand universities in 2012 (International Student Enrolments in New Zealand, 2013). As reported in *The New Zealand Herald*, the Minister for Tertiary Education suggested that revenue from international students can assist university finances (McCutcheon, 2012)! The education export industry and enticing large numbers of international students into New Zealand may well have its attractions in terms of revenue, but this should perhaps be seen more as the icing on the cake regarding university funding, not an integral aspect. Markets are notoriously fickle and subject to global economic fluctuations.

Interestingly in 2011, the New Zealand government of the day created a Crown Agency, Education New Zealand, to market New Zealand institutions to the international education market. Is this democracy at play or is this the fulfilment of the economic recovery and growth, while at the same time starving the education providers of the necessary funding to fulfil their critical role?

It would be an unusual situation if there were not mechanisms in place to show accountability from any organization still largely dependent on public monies, but despite the extensive efforts being made to assure the quality of tertiary education provision, there are some uncomfortable data to consider regarding student attainment in New Zealand. The numbers of students entering into bachelor degree level study in New Zealand is growing and is considered high relative to other OECD averages. However, the number of students leaving with a tertiary level qualification is low compared with many other countries (Scott and Gini, 2010).

The Student Experience

An interesting question that has a relationship to the democracy or democratiz-ation of higher education relates to the student learning experience. Does the learning experience live up to learner expectations? A survey which takes us closer to understanding the student learning experience is the Australasian Universities Survey on Student Engagement (AUSSE) (Radloff, 2011). This survey is administered by the Australian Council for Educational Research (ACER) in conjunction with participating higher education institutions. It is closely related to surveys run in other countries, particularly the National Survey of Student Engagement in the USA (2014) and the recently established UK

Student Engagement Survey (2014), administered by the Higher Education Academy. These surveys are designed to provide an evidence base for understanding and managing students' engagement in their learning, and insights into how institutions and the programs they provide support and promote engagement. The outcomes of these surveys can play a significant role in enhancing learning processes and outcomes (Radloff, 2011).

By taking part in the AUSSE, New Zealand universities are showing their commitment to enhancing transitions from post-compulsory to tertiary education, particularly university level education, and also to improving system performance. It is well known that the first year of university study poses the highest level of risk for students and the highest levels of attrition.

The outcomes of the AUSSE tell us a great deal about potential or perceived shortcomings of higher education provision in New Zealand, including that New Zealand students are far less engaged in their studies than their counterparts in the USA. Given the very low productivity levels we see in New Zealand, this is a worrying factor which most likely has a negative impact on New Zealand's long-term economic success. New Zealand students also feel lower levels of career readiness than their Australian counterparts. The data from the AUSSE correlates well with the matter of lower numbers of learners graduating with a tertiary education qualification than is the case in other countries (Scott and Gini, 2010).

Of considerable concern is the data revealed through the AUSSE regarding departure intentions. The rates of attrition are of serious concern to universities given the very high costs. From the AUSSE, the New Zealand respondents with departure intentions give reasons which include: convenience or practical (27.2 percent); academic (26.8 percent); to improve career prospects (24.4 percent) and to obtain a better quality education elsewhere (17.2 percent) (Radloff, 2011).

The data obtained via the AUSSE is in essence mission critical to the current and future success of New Zealand's universities. A thorough interrogation of the outcomes and a commitment to developing a culture of engagement within and across our institutions could constitute a major step forward in the democratization of higher education in New Zealand. However, what the universities do with the data and how they address the student voice is variable. The New Zealand Centre for Tertiary Teaching Excellence (Ako Aotearoa, n.d.), set up in 2006 with a mandate to contribute to excellent educational outcomes for learners through a focus on working in partnership with tertiary education organizations to enhance the effectiveness of teaching and learning, has arguably done the most to respond to the AUSSE data. Ako Aotearoa has worked and continues to work with staff from across the higher education sector to address the issues arising from the AUSSE data. Ako Aotearoa, funded through the TEC and in operation since 2007, has committed more than $NZ6 million to support evidence-based, change-focused research that demonstrates positive change for learners. Ako Aotearoa promotes, supports and models best practice in providing authentic, student-centered learning experiences across the entire tertiary education arena.

With both a Maori and a Pasifika caucus, Ako Aotearoa has made outstanding efforts through funded projects, targeted conferences, online resources and professional development events to add value to, and might even be said to be a major democratizing force in tertiary education in New Zealand.

Democratizing Higher Education—The Future?

This chapter has so far focused on issues relating to democratization of higher education via the traditional route for most learners attending a campus university and engaging in degree pathways set out by the institution.

Democratization of higher education may be considered a slightly amorphous phrase under which one can park all kinds of political and economic considerations. One critical dimension of the concept of democratization is that of widening access to studies that lead to useful qualifications, while another is enabling study any time, any place and with any subject combination (Daniel, 2013).

In the New Zealand context, while higher education was formerly largely the province of the elite, there has always been provision for access to a university education for mature students over the age of 21 (Ministry of Education, 2013). For such students, where there is a lack of evidence of academic achievement, a Foundation Program is generally recommended. Until relatively recently, entry to most universities was 'open' in that one only needed to meet the minimum requirements in the school leaving examinations. Today, most courses have selective admissions where candidates have to fulfil additional requirements through their qualifications.

The University of Auckland, the largest higher education institution in New Zealand and the most successful in league table terms, has the highest number of selective entry courses. One might be tempted to conclude that league table success over-rides the democratic imperative of education for all. At the same time, if government policy is steering towards applying punitive measures if student pass rates are not deemed high enough by supposedly arms-length agencies, perhaps it is a wise move to place more emphasis on recruiting students deemed likely to manage the rigors of university level study. However, this may well exclude large numbers and cohorts of students, who, if given the chance of a university level education, might thrive and perform as well as, if not better than, their more privileged peers.

The second element of democratization is to allow people to decide for themselves what, where and when they will study, instead of having higher education institutions select their students according to defined criteria (Daniel, 2013). While the concept of total choice of what, where and when to study would have been inconceivable only a very short time ago, new technologies have opened up new, innovative and creative opportunities for co-creation of new knowledge. Imaginative and creative use of new technologies provides the opportunity for the development of innovative pedagogies that can be tailored and modified for different learning orientations and paradigms.

The most recent addition to our vocabulary and repertoire of teaching and learning is the Massive Open Online Course (MOOC) movement. The MOOC movement started in Canada in 2008 and is now being taken up by many prestigious universities as a marketing tool (Liyanagunawardena, Adams and Williams, 2013). Open to all who can access the technology, MOOCs combine brief talks by world experts with interactive coursework, online assignments, games and quizzes. Learners can access university courses online and enrol for free. They can develop a program of study of their own choice, access lectures and online resources. The downside of the MOOC is the gap between enrolments and completions, and the lack of accreditation or assessment (ibid.).

Not all higher education institutions are necessarily convinced by the MOOC movement but many are interested enough to interrogate the possibilities that it offers. New Zealand universities are no exception. The Vice Chancellor of one of New Zealand's top performing universities, the University of Otago, recently articulated what she considered to be the fundamental problems with MOOCs—that a university education is about much more than knowledge transfer; in a world dependent on science and technology, learners need more, not less, experimental experience in laboratories and field studies; MOOCs are essentially premised on inputs and not outputs. She believes that what New Zealand universities do better than anywhere else in the world "is to put its best, brightest and most productive researchers in all disciplines in front of undergraduate classes" (Hayne, 2013).

Conclusion

While advances in technology may contribute to the democratization of higher education globally, New Zealand will still need to come to terms with the higher level learning needs of its own complex population. It must work towards a better understanding of how to blend pedagogies, taking into consideration the richness that Maori and Pasifika ways of knowing and learning can bring to the dominant colonial approaches to learning and teaching, and full acknowledgment that technology is merely a mediating tool. In combining pedagogy and technology, different ways of knowing and learning must, nevertheless, be accommodated in this new environment.

New Zealand must ask itself serious questions about how it can offer pathways into higher education for its diverse population without crippling graduates with unreasonable debt. As a nation, Aotearoa—the Land of the Long White Cloud—must also grapple with what it really desires for its own population and what its unique attributes might be regarding its provision. Is it committed to higher education on the cheap, or to a fulsome realization of its own rhetoric of a "world-leading education system that equips all New Zealanders with knowledge, skills and values to be successful citizens in the 21st century" (e.g. Tertiary Education Strategy 2010–2015).

References

Ako Aotearoa National Centre for Tertiary Teaching Excellence (n.d.) www.akoaotearoa. ac.nz (accessed 16 April 2014).

Bishop, R., Berryman, M., Cavanagh, T. and Teddy, L. (2009) Addressing educational disparities facing Maori students in New Zealand, *Teaching and Teacher Education* 25 (5), 734–742.

Chu, C., Abella, I.S. and Paurini, S. (2013) *Educational Practices that Benefit Pacific Learners in Tertiary Education: Research Report*, Ako Aotearoa, National Centre for Tertiary Teaching Excellence, Wellington, New Zealand.

Daniel, J. (2013) *MOOCs, Media and the Democratization of Higher Education*, Keynote Presentation, Worldviews Conference Global Trends in Media and Higher Education 2013, Toronto June 19–21.

Education Act 1989 http://legislation.govt.nz/act/public/1989/0080/latest/whole. html#DLM183668 (accessed 10 January 2014).

Gorst, J.E. (1864) *The Maori King* quoted in Sinclair, K. (1980) New Zealand declared a British colony, *History Today* 30 (7), www.historytoday.com/keith-sinclair/new-zealand-declared-british-colony (accessed 10 November 2013).

Grey, S. and Scott, J. (2012) When the Government Steers the Market: Implications for NTEU's Future of Higher Education Conference, 22–23 February 2012, University of Sydney, Australia.

Hayne, H. (2013) Vice-Chancellor's Comment, Otago Magazine, University of Otago, www.otago.ac.nz/otagomagazine/issue35/vc-comment (accessed 5 January 2014).

Holmes, C. (2013) Has the expansion of higher education led to greater economic growth?, *National Institute Economic Review* 224 (1).

Hood, D. (2007) *Retention and Achievement of Maori Students in Secondary Schooling* report to Te Kotahitanga, www.tekotahitanga.tki.org.nz (accessed 10 December 2013).

International Student Enrolments in New Zealand (2013) www.educationcounts.govt.nz (accessed 18 January 2014).

King, M. (2003) *The Penguin History of New Zealand*, Penguin Books, London, UK.

Kirkwood, H. (2011) Quality in common: reflections on findings from NZUAAU Academic Audits 2000–2011. New Zealand Academic Audit Unit, Wellington, New Zealand.

Liyanagunawardena, T.R., Adams, A.A. and Williams, S.A. (2013) MOOCs: a systematic study of the published literature 2008–2012, *The International Review of Research in Open and Distance Learning* 14 (3), www.irrodl.org (accessed 19 January 2014).

McCutcheon, S. (2012) Stuart McCutcheon: International students not answer to uni funding, *The New Zealand Herald*, 30 May.

Mahoney, P. (2003) Tertiary Education Funding – Overview of Recent Reform, Parliament Library.

Meadows, R. (2013) Bitter pill should be swallowed www.stuff.co.nz/business/money/ 8197323/bitter-pill-should-be-swallowed (accessed 4 January 2014).

Ministry of Education (2006) *Nga haeata matauranga: Annual Report on Maori Education*. Ministry of Education, Wellington, New Zealand.

Ministry of Education (2010) Domestic students enrolled by attendance status and selected characteristics, ENR 17. Ministry of Education, Wellington, New Zealand, www.educationcounts.govt.nz/statistics/tertiary_education/participation (accessed 18 January 2014).

Ministry of Education (2013) *The New Zealand Education System: An Overview*. Ministry of Education, Wellington, New Zealand.

Ministry of Education NZ (2013) www.minedu.govt.nz (accessed 20 November 2014).

Morley, L. (2012) Imagining the university of the future, in *The Future University: Ideas and Possibilities* (Ed. Barnett, R.) (pp. 26–35), Routledge, New York and London.

National Survey of Student Engagement (2014) http://nsse.iub.edu/html/about/cfm (accessed 20 November 2014).

New Zealand History (2014) www.nzhistory.net.nz/politics/treaty-of-waitangi (accessed 14 January 2014).

Onikama, D.L., Hammond, O.W. and Koki, S. (1998) *Family Involvement in Education: A Synthesis of Research for Pacific Educators.* Pacific Resources for Education and Learning, US Department of Education, Washington, DC.

Profile and Trends: New Zealand's Tertiary Education Sector (2012) Ministry of Education, Wellington, New Zealand.

QS World University Rankings (2013/2014) www.topuniversities.com/university-rankings (accessed 12 January 2014).

Radloff, A. (Ed.) (2011) Student Engagement in New Zealand's Universities. Australian Council for Educational Research (ACER), Melbourne, Australia.

Scott, D. and Gini, P. (2010) How does New Zealand's education system compare? OECD's Education at a Glance. Ministry of Education, Wellington, New Zealand.

Sinclair, K. (1980) New Zealand declared a British colony, *History Today*, 30 (7), www.historytoday.com/keith-sinclair/new-zealand-declared-british-colony (accessed 10 November 2013).

Statistics New Zealand (2012) www.stats.govt.nz (accessed 12 December 2013).

Statistics New Zealand (2013) www.stats.govt.nz (accessed 14 January 2014).

Statistics New Zealand (2014) www.stats.govt.nz (accessed 27 March 2014).

Statistics New Zealand and Ministry of Pacific Island Affairs (2010) *Demographics of New Zealand's Pacific Population.* Wellington, New Zealand.

Tertiary Education Commission: Statement of Intent (2012/13–2014/15) www.tec.govt.nz/Documents/Publications/Statement-of-Intent-2012.pdf (accessed 10 January 2014).

Tertiary Education Strategy (2010–2015) www.minedu.govt.nz/NZEducationPolicies/TertiaryEducationStrategy (accessed 25 January 2014).

Te Wananga O Aotearoa (n.d.) www.two.ac.nz/Te-Whare.aspx (accessed 3 November 2013).

The Economic Impact of International Education (2012/13) www.newzealandgovt.nz (accessed 14 April 2014).

UK Student Engagement Survey (2014) www.heacademy.ac.uk/resources/detail/engagement_survey/pilot_call_2014 (accessed 18 January 2014).

Universities News (2013) University of Auckland rankings fall a big worry: VC, www.universitiesnews.com/2012/05/01/new-zealand-university-rankings-fall-a-big-worry/ (accessed 12 January 2014).

Universities New Zealand: Te Pokai Tara (2013) www.universitiesnz.ac.nz/nz-university-system (accessed 13 January 2014).

Wilson, J. (2013) 'History – Maori arrival and settlement', *Te Ara – The Encyclopaedia of New Zealand,* www.TeAra.govt.nz.en/history/page1 (accessed 14 January 2014).

9

HIGHER EDUCATION IN SOUTH AFRICA

A Case Study

Mandla S. Makhanya and Jeanette C. Botha

Abstract

The study has made use of qualitative historical research methodology, which is defined as the systematic and objective location, evaluation and synthesis of evidence in order to establish facts and draw conclusions about past events (Borg 1963; Cohen, Manion and Morrison 2002:159). Primary data resources, for example, legislation and policy documents, charters, archives, records, files, letters, official publications, newspapers, magazines, films, research reports, written and oral testimony, witnesses or the actual participants in an event; and secondary resources, such as textbooks, quoted material and other reproductions of material of information have been used in charting the transformation, development and progress of South African higher education since the advent of democracy in 1994.

Introduction

This study traces the trajectory of higher education development in South Africa, from a highly fragmented, exclusionary and inequitable higher education model and practice that mirrored the undemocratic Apartheid regime pre-1994, to a radically engineered, inclusive and democratic model that is still engaged in redress, reform and transformation 20 years after South Africa's first democratic elections in 1994. The narrative provides clear evidence of a society that continues to grapple with its legacy of gross socio-economic and political inequality as it forges ahead with the transformation of higher education in a very challenging national and global environment. The research demonstrates very clearly that there is no "silver bullet" solution to transformation on this scale and that the democratization process is likely to be iterative for some decades to come, in line with national socio-economic and political transformation.

South African Higher Education on the Cusp of Transition

Education in South Africa has undergone a radical transformation since the ideologically based Apartheid (racial segregation) system of governance was abolished and the first democratically elected government assumed power in 1994. Prior to 1994, under the Afrikaner Nationalist Government and in terms of the Bantu Education Act, 1953 (later renamed the Black Education Act, 1953) (South Africa (Union) 1953), South African education was structured along racial and language lines with deliberately engineered, unequal and inferior standards of education (so-called "Bantu Education"[1]) for all so-called "non-white"[2] South Africans. This inequitable status did not only pertain to the quality of education and the allocation of educational resources, but also to the number and caliber of educators: a legacy that endures to the present (DoE 2006:6–9). While enfranchised white South Africans enjoyed largely free first world standards of education and educational facilities, the vast majority of disenfranchised "black" South Africans did not. Essentially, while education prior to 1994 purported to reflect and serve the cultural and linguistic diversity of South Africa, there were legislated divisions and distinctions aimed primarily at ensuring the survival of Apartheid ideology *Bantu Education* (Mnguni 1999:150; Barnes, Baijnath, Sattar 2010).

The global opposition to Apartheid and the imposition of sanctions and boycotts against the South African government across a range of social, economic and political domains took a toll on South African higher education institutions, which became increasingly isolated and insular. The political "struggle" reached a tipping point in 1976, sparking the historic "Soweto Uprising"[3] and culminating in the transfer of power to an entirely new government and political regime in 1994. For the first time all South Africans were able to vote freely and without fear, thus heralding the first truly South African Government and State.

Education emerged from almost two decades of active struggle with a spectrum of deficits that continue to impact on the sector today. Over and above the dynamic socio-political environment, the historical systemic and structural levels of fragmentation and inequality contributed to a serious lack of coherence and dialogue amongst higher education institutions in South Africa and further afield and inevitably led to stagnation and a lack of currency, especially with regard to such vital areas as research and global higher education trends.

The first democratically elected government that assumed office in 1994 inherited a country that was deeply divided and fragmented, isolated and, to some extent, alienated from prevailing higher educational trends. These challenges had to be addressed within a framework of similar disarray and redress needs, nation-wide (Botha 2011:9).

South African Higher Education: 1994–2014

South African higher education has been completely restructured since 1994. To date the restructuring has comprised two "phases". The first phase comprised a complete overhaul of higher education policy and legislation in the period immediately following the assumption of power by the new government, to enable the vision of a single national coordinated higher education system. Crucial considerations such as equity and redress, democratization, quality, development, academic freedom, public accountability and efficiency and effectiveness were embedded as foundational concepts in all of the legislation, policy and regulations. This phase commenced shortly before 1994 and continued until 2009, which marked the separation of the Department of Education (DoE) into two entities: the Department of Basic Education, and the Department of Higher Education and Training and the incumbency of a new Minister in that portfolio.

The second phase is marked by a shift in focus, in 2009, from university education as the key pillar of higher education, to a focus on post-school education and training, with a clear strategic positioning of vocational and skills development as the national higher education strategic priority. This culminated in the release of a new White Paper for Post-School Education and Training: *Building an Expanded, Effective and Integrated Post-School System* (Republic of South Africa (RSA) 2014) on 15 January 2014, which was conceptualized within the context of South Africa's national development strategy as set out in seminal national policy documents (mentioned in Phase 2 below). This phase reflects higher education's response to the changing realities and dynamics of South Africa's socio-economic and political journey of transformation.

Phase 1: 1994–2009: Reconfiguring the Landscape

Under the Nationalist Apartheid Government, the number of higher education institutions designated for whites far exceeded those designated for blacks despite an inverse population ratio. All higher education institutions were further split along demographic, language and cultural lines. Barnes, Baijnath and Sattar (2010:1) explain:

> English-speaking whites had the universities of Cape Town, Natal, Rhodes, and the Witwatersrand. The University of South Africa operated through the medium of distance education. Afrikaans-speaking whites had the universities of Stellenbosch, Pretoria, Rand Afrikaans, Orange Free State and Potchefstroom. The University of Port Elizabeth was officially bilingual in English and Afrikaans. African students were accommodated at the universities of Fort Hare, Bophuthatswana, the North, Venda, Zululand, the Medical University of South Africa (Medunsa), the Transkei and Vista University. Indian students were served by the University of Durban-Westville and coloured students by the University of the Western Cape.

One of the key priorities of the new government was to completely restructure the higher education landscape through a new raft of higher education policy and legislation. Key amongst these was a document entitled *A Framework of Transformation* (NCHE 1996), which set out the prevailing status of South African higher education and made comprehensive proposals on a new higher education dispensation. These proposals informed the subsequent Green Paper of 1996 (DoE 1996) and culminated in the *Education White Paper 3. A Programme for the Transformation of Higher Education* (DoE 1997). The *White Paper 3* outlined the framework for change from a multi-systemic, disparate agglomeration, into a single national coordinated system. The *White Paper 3* was concretized in the *Higher Education Act, 1997* (Act no. 101 of 1997) (RSA 1997), which wrote into law the establishment of a single national higher education system and repealed in their entirety the former higher education acts that undergirded the previous higher education model in South Africa.

Also of significant policy import, the Council on Higher Education (CHE) was established in terms of the *Higher Education Act, 1997* (Act no. 101 of 1997) as a key higher education policy advisory and monitoring body, also responsible for quality assurance in South Africa (RSA 1997). The CHE has been responsible for the re-engineering of South Africa's higher education quality regime in line with the transformation of the higher education sector. A key national quality assurance body, namely, the Higher Education Qualifications Committee (HEQC) was formally established in May 2001, to this end. All South Africa tertiary qualifications are quality assured in line with internationally benchmarked norms and standards, thus ensuring a level of education commensurate with the best in the world.

A raft of additional discussion documents, policies and legislation was introduced from 1997, the more seminal of these being the National Students Financial Aid Scheme (NSFAS), a national bursary scheme for financially disadvantaged but academically deserving students; the incorporation of colleges of education into universities and technikons; a revised higher education funding formula (which is currently undergoing yet another iteration) and a new language policy (Botha 2011:109).

The actual physical restructuring of the higher education landscape commenced with the so-called *Size and Shape* exercise, "an overarching exercise designed to put strategies into place to ensure that our higher education system is indeed on the road to the 21st century" (CHE 2000:4), and culminated with the National Plan for Higher Education (NPHE) (MoE 2001), which was grounded in the provisions of the Higher Education Act (1997) and which mapped out the aims and objectives, as well as the implementation, of the new structure. The NPHE announced, amongst others, the intention to reduce the number of public higher education institutions from 36 to 23 by means of a series of mergers and incorporations. Included in this number were six new *comprehensive* institutions, a new institutional type created through the mergers of universities and technikons.[4] The Programme and

Qualifications Mix (PQM) of *comprehensive* universities reflected their academic and vocational heritages. (It should be noted that most of the previously "white" or historically advantaged research-intensive universities were not merged, providing some level of stability and continuity in their operations and outputs.) A complex and difficult merging process followed for most higher education institutions, changing irrevocably their leadership, structures, cultures, traditions, visions, systems and processes, and their staff and student profiles, adding accretive levels of destabilization and complexity to an already fragile system, and impacting negatively on sustainable, effective and efficient higher education delivery in South Africa.

It is evident that the closing of many colleges of education, and the incorporation of the remaining few into universities, has had serious ramifications for South African higher education 20 years on. There has been a decline in the number of teachers that the country produces, and in quality teacher education, at a time of very significant growth in student enrollments at both the basic and post-school levels in the country. This has given rise to the need for more, well-qualified, experienced teachers. Furthermore this lack has impacted on the caliber and preparedness of the students entering higher education, placing a sometimes intolerable burden on universities in terms of bridging courses, for example, to ensure students' readiness to embark on a university curriculum. In retrospect, it is generally agreed that the so-called "Asmal"[5] model for a single national coordinated system that essentially spelt out the demise of teacher training colleges, may have been too radical and possibly shortsighted, especially given that the new White Paper (2014) has re-introduced a college system. However, it must simultaneously be acknowledged that the underlying driver of equity and redress remains a constant in South African higher education.

The NPHE (MoE 2001) expressed the intention to achieve transformation through *institutional steering* (using planning, funding and quality) and specific legislation (new legislation, as well as amendments to existing legislation) (MoE 2001:3). From 2003, the Ministry of Education (MoE) directly linked the funding of higher education institutions to the approval of institutional three-year "rolling" operational plans (ibid.:15).

The Ministry also implemented a system of various earmarked funds to realize particular policy objectives. However, the effective use of funding as a steering mechanism necessitated the development of a new funding formula based on the funding principles and framework outlined in the White Paper (ibid.:16). This initial funding framework has seen subsequent iterations, aligned to emerging socio-economic/education needs and priorities. Additionally, and more recently, in terms of new (draft) reporting regulations, higher education institutions are more stringently monitored, evaluated, audited and held accountable for responsible, transparent and effective governance in line with the King III Report, as well as ethical financial management and stewardship over their grants, funds and allocations. Compliance, particularly regulatory reporting compliance, is now an audited operational requirement.

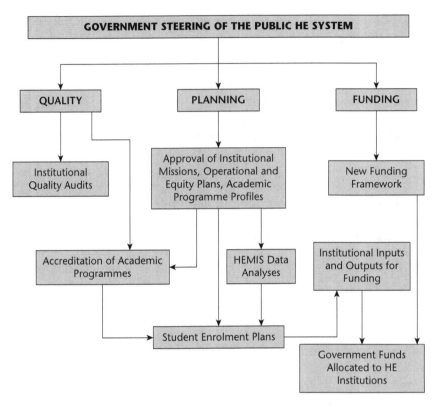

FIGURE 9.1   The System of Government Steering of the Public Higher
Education System

Source: DoE 2004

Phase 2: 2009–2014

On 10 May 2009, the DoE was split into two departments, each with its own
Minister. The responsibility for South African education would be shared by two
ministries. The Department of Basic Education would deal with all schools from
Grade R to Grade 12, and adult literacy programs, while the Department of
Higher Education and Training would deal with universities and other post-
school education and training, while also coordinating the Human Resource
Development Strategy for South Africa.

It should also be noted that Minister B. E. "Blade" Nzimande is simultaneously
the Minister of Higher Education and Training and the General Secretary of the
South African Communist Party (since 1998), one of the three alliance partners
comprising the African National Congress (ANC), which is the ruling party in
South Africa. It could be argued that the ideological leanings of the new Minister
have, to some degree, also shaped the higher education trajectory in South Africa
since his assumption of office.

Whereas the NPHE (MoE 2001) conceptualized a university sector with distinct responsibilities and accountabilities, the new White Paper (2014), discussed below, introduces a reconfigured, differentiated post-school education and training sector, in which universities are part of the post-school sector. Instead, there is a concerted focus on the FET sector, which is reconfigured and renamed the Technical and Vocational Education and Training (TVET) sector, and the introduction of so-called community colleges.

South African Higher Education into the 21st Century

This section outlines the current status of higher education and the challenges faced by universities in South Africa today, as they re-organize and re-prioritize around global pressures and trends and changing national needs. What is evident is that in South Africa, higher education is becoming increasingly regulated (as mentioned above), and that higher education institutions now need to have built-in agility that allows for the seamless accommodation of changing demands and emerging trends, as well as far greater levels of cooperation with a variety of higher education stakeholders, towards the optimal leveraging of existing infrastructure, resources and capacity, and a more inclusive and integrated model of higher education delivery.

South Africa's socio-economic status has worsened incrementally (in line with global dynamics such as the 2008 global recession) and this has impacted on South African education. Nationally, higher education is regarded as a key pillar of socio-economic development for the country, placing significant pressure on higher education institutions to lend the necessary impetus to national development through well-qualified, well-equipped and capacitated graduates who are able to merge seamlessly into the workplace.

However, this expectation is not being matched by increased funding. To the contrary, higher education institutions, and universities in particular, are expected to do more with less, to raise additional funds through third-stream income[6] and to leverage additional income, resources and capacities through partnerships, collaborations and multi-stakeholder engagement.

Furthermore, South Africa has to deal with the critical issue of the so-called NEETs (Not in Employment, Education or Training). NEETS comprise almost 4 million unemployed youth between the ages of 16 and 24, and it is widely acknowledged that left unaddressed, they pose a serious threat to social stability and national development. Equally important, South Africa is engaged in massive infrastructural development projects, which require artisan skills that are in critically short supply in the country. The move to rebuild and expand the TVET sector has to a very significant extent been prompted by these two concerns.

In a seminal Budget Speech on 30 June 2009, the newly appointed Minister of Higher Education and Training, Minister B. E. Nzimande (2009), alluded to a

number of initiatives that signaled this changing policy direction. Amongst others
he spoke of a concerted drive to increase enrolments in FET colleges:

> I also intend to establish a coherent college sector which includes the
> 50 Further Education Training (FET) colleges and other career specific
> colleges such as agricultural colleges the latter being crucial for rural skills
> development.... It is still our intention to increase the student enrolment at
> FET colleges to at least 1 million by 2015. I also intend improving student
> articulation between the college and university sectors. To this end, my
> department will be finalising a national policy outlining the minimum entry
> requirements to university study requiring the national vocational certificate
> offered at colleges.
>
> *Nzimande 2009*

Confirmation of this direction came in the form of the 2012 legislation
reverting functions of the FET colleges to the Department of Higher Education
and Training. In 2012/13, R1, 24 billion was allocated to the FET colleges' bursary
scheme and 122,911 students were being supported by bursaries and loans. The
establishment of the Department of Higher Education and Training (DHET) in
2009 also necessitated the development of a new Education White Paper to
facilitate this policy direction, and on 15 January 2014 the New White Paper for
Post-School Education and Training, *Building an Expanded, Effective and Integrated
Post-school System* (RSA 2014), was released, setting out a distinct strategic shift
towards a focus on vocational education and training.

The New White Paper:

> focussed its attention on the vision ... for an integrated system of post-
> school education and training, with all institutions playing their role as parts
> of a coherent but differentiated whole.... These institutions include the
> colleges and universities whose main purpose is the direct provision of
> education and training and, in the case of universities, the conduct of
> research. They also include institutions that support the education and
> training process such as the Sector Education and Training Authorities
> (SETAs), the National Skills Fund and the advisory, regulatory and quality
> assurance bodies such as the South African Qualifications Authority (SAQA)
> and the Quality Councils.
>
> *RSA 2014:vii*

This new landscape provides explicit acknowledgement of the apparent blunder
that was made in subsuming the colleges into the university sector as per the NPHE
(MoE 2001), as well as a clear ideological shift towards vocational and skills training,
evidenced in the repositioning and renaming of the higher education sector as the
Post-Secondary Education and Training Sector. Nevertheless, the (new) White Paper is

envisaged to be a vehicle that will "drive and deepen the transformation of the entire post-schooling sector [and] provide a framework to build on the achievements of our democratic government since 1994" (RSA 2014:viii).

The executive summary in the White Paper[7] contextualizes and provides a comprehensive exposition of the new policy direction and structure of South African higher education, and has been drawn on extensively in this section of the narrative. As mentioned above, the White Paper forms a key policy pillar of South Africa's national development strategy, and ranks alongside other seminal policy documents, which include:

- the New Growth Path: Framework (RSA 2010);
- the National Development Plan: vision for 2030 (RSA 2011);
- the Human Resource Development Strategy for South Africa (HRD-SA) 2010–2030 (RSA 2009);
- the Industrial Policy Action Plan: Economic Sectors and Employment Cluster (IPAP 2013/14–2015/16 (RSA 2013)).

As of 2014, South Africa's post-school system comprises all education and training provision for those who have completed, not completed or never attended school. The following institutions fall under the purview of the DHET:

- 25 public universities;
- 50 public TVET colleges;
- public adult learning centers, which will be absorbed into the new community colleges;
- registered private post-school institutions, both higher education institutions and TVET colleges;
- the SETAs[8] and the National Skills Fund (NSF);
- regulatory bodies responsible for qualifications and quality assurance in the post-school system (SAQA and the Quality Councils).

RSA 2014:4

A number of state-owned post-school institutions exist under the authority of several other national government departments, mainly (but not exclusively) training public service workers, and some institutions are operated by provincial governments and municipalities to train their own personnel, and the DHET is also responsible for assuring the quality of provision and the registration of the qualifications on offer in these colleges.

The White Paper articulates a strategy for a PSET (Post-School Education and Training) system to meet the country's needs, outlining policy directions to guide the DHET and pertinent institutions towards the attainment of a developmental state characterized by a vibrant democracy and a flourishing economy. Its main policy objectives are:

- a post-school system that can assist in building a fair, equitable, non-racial, non-sexist and democratic South Africa;
- a single, coordinated post-school education and training system;
- expanded access, improved quality and increased diversity of provision;
- a stronger and more cooperative relationship between education and training institutions and the workplace;
- a post-school education and training system that is responsive to the needs of individual citizens, employers in both public and private sectors, as well as broader societal and developmental objectives.

RSA 2014:4

The DHET's key PSET strategy is the expansion of the TVET sector and their establishment as institutions of choice for school leavers. Total head-count enrolments in this sector have increased from just over 345,000 in 2010 to an estimated 650,000 in 2013; they will increase to 1 million by 2015 and 2.5 million by 2030 (RSA 2014:xii). However, the TVET system is currently fragmented and in disarray, and for this lofty aspiration to be realized, there will have to be a very significant improvement in their management and governance, infrastructural development and management, quality of teaching and learning, student support, and their responsiveness to, and relevance for, local labor markets.

The new White Paper also announced the introduction of community colleges, mainly for youth and adults who do not qualify to study at TVET colleges and universities, as well as the establishment of the South African Institute for Vocational and Continuing Education and Training (SAIVCET) to provide curricular, technical and pedagogical support and capacity development, as well as to facilitate dialogue and articulation, and monitoring and evaluation in the sector.

The White Paper further asserts that South Africa needs a university sector which is purposefully differentiated to increase the diversity of the system, and it sets out principles to guide the ongoing differentiation of the university sector and the formulation of institutional missions, identities, variety in program offerings and increasing articulation in and between the universities and the rest of the system.

Participation rates in universities are expected to increase from the current 17.3 percent to 25 percent—that is, from just over 937,000 students in 2011 to about 1.6 million enrolments in 2030 (RSA 2014:xiv). As participation increases, universities are simultaneously tasked to focus their attention on improving student performance. Improving student access, success and throughput rates is a very serious challenge for the university sector and is a priority focus for all institutions, particularly in regard to improving access and success for those groups whose race, gender or disability status had previously disadvantaged them. Of particular importance in this regard is the development of the scarce and critical skills needed for South Africa's economic development.

The DHET asserts that it remains committed to progressively introducing free education for the poor in South African universities as resources become available, although the likelihood of this seems to be quite remote given the lack of, and reduced, funding. Thus, despite ongoing student demands and protests in support of free education, nothing has been forthcoming from government over and above the increased funding of the National Student Financial Aid Scheme for students from disadvantaged backgrounds. This has resulted in severe pressure on the scheme and concomitant pressure on higher education institutions that are obliged to deal with students' frustrations and anger at what they perceive to be unfilled promises.

Other issues which are identified in the White Paper for attention are: increased research and innovation; improving the quality of research; building on areas of strength identified as important for national development; university staffing; and the study and development of the African languages in universities.

An attempt will also be made to coordinate, centralize and extend data collection on private providers to contextualize, understand and regulate this sector more fully, especially in terms of quality assurance.

While recognizing and appreciating the role of private institutions, the DHET believes that the public sector is the core of the education and training system and that government's main thrust, therefore, should be to direct public resources primarily to meeting national priorities and to provide for the masses of young people and adult learners through public institutions.

The DHET also intends to develop a strategic policy framework to guide the improvement of access to, and success in, post-school education and training for people with disabilities, to facilitate awareness creation, capacity building and improved access to all levels of post-school institutions.

Importantly, especially in terms of the monopoly of South Africa's hitherto sole, dedicated comprehensive distance education institution, the University of South Africa, the White Paper also sets out the intention to create a post-school distance education landscape based on open learning principles. This landscape will complement the traditional campus-based provision, and will consist of a network of education providers supported by learning support centers and/or connectivity for students. Such a network aims to make available a wide range of learning opportunities to potential students irrespective of their locations and appropriate to their contexts. Other advantages will include the development and availability of well-researched, high-quality national learning resources (made available as open education resources [OER]), collaborative development of learning resources, more efficient use of existing infrastructure and an increasing emphasis on independent study as preparation for subsequent lifelong learning (RSA 2014:xv).[9]

Universities, especially comprehensive universities and universities of technology, will be encouraged to expand distance higher education for vocationally oriented diploma programs. Presently, this area is less developed than distance education for the purely academic programs. The DHET will also encourage all universities to expand online and blended learning as a way to offer niche programs (RSA 2014:xvi).

The White Paper asserts that the DHET will seriously investigate the possibility of providing distance education programs at the TVET and community college level, including dedicated staff and equipment. This includes the theoretical component of apprenticeships.

Continuing professional development for full-time staff in the post-school sector, and increasing staff numbers in line with growth in distance education enrolments, will receive concerted attention, as will the expansion of equitable access to ICT resources. This point is of crucial importance to the successful conduct of Open, Distance and eLearning (ODeL) in South Africa, as current constraints and challenges around access to the internet and appropriate ICTs pose a serious barrier to successful ODeL delivery. Globally, quality assurance is similarly a key concern in regard to ODeL, more so in the light of its potential expansion in South Africa, and this will be given specific attention by the DHET and the Quality Councils.

The design of training systems, including curricula, requires close cooperation between education and training providers and employers, especially in those programs providing vocational training. The period just prior to and post 1994 (mid-to-late 1980s) saw a steady deterioration in the apprenticeship system in South Africa, which resulted in a shortage of skills that is quite critical in some areas, such as, for example, the engineering and construction fields. Re-establishing a good artisan training system is therefore an urgent priority, and the current target is for the country to produce 30,000 artisans a year by 2030. Other forms of on-the-job training, including learnerships and internships in non-artisan fields, will also be expanded. The SETAs have a crucial role to play in facilitating such workplace learning partnerships between employers and educational institutions (RSA 2014:xvi–xvii).

The existing structures and remits of the Quality Councils will remain largely unchanged, but individual Councils will have greater flexibility to quality assure qualifications on NQF levels from which they were previously restricted (RSA 2014:xvii).

South African Higher Education: Facing the Future

South African higher education remains in a state of flux, impacted by global forces and dynamics that include a deleterious recession, the potential and pitfalls of rampant technology (which purports to offer feasible solutions to virtually every higher education challenge), and the growing phenomenon of internationalization. Nationally and in line with global trends, ongoing demands for access have placed an onerous burden on higher education institutions as they struggle to cope with masses of students vying for a limited number of places. In South Africa, this has resulted in a veritable explosion in enrolments in Open and

Distance Learning (ODL) to the extent that ODL students comprise more than one-third of all university students in South Africa. This has prompted ODL providers, more particularly the University of South Africa (UNISA), which enrolls more than one-third of all South African higher education students, to investigate moving more concertedly into online teaching and administration as a means of coping with masses of students (in excess of 400,000) and the concomitant administrative burden that they bring with them.

Given the current higher education environment, higher education providers will need to ensure that their institutions have built-in agility (in their strategies and operations) which allows them to move and adapt in good time to changing dynamics, so as to best accommodate emerging challenges and best utilize nascent opportunities.

However, in the case of South Africa, this is easier said than done, because such agility presumes institutional stability, continuity and a very sound foundation. Unfortunately for most South African higher education institutions, especially the historically disadvantaged institutions, the Apartheid legacy, the years of the *struggle* and the subsequent restructuring of the higher education landscape have had a dire impact on the entire education sector. Basic education at both primary and high school levels is struggling to overcome inherited legacies, and there has been a serious decline in both the quality of education and the caliber of students who eventually find their way into South African universities. This is particularly noticeable when it comes to ODL students who often come from more underprivileged backgrounds than those students who meet admission criteria for contact institutions.

As is the case with many emerging nations, South Africa is also facing serious socio-economic challenges. South Africa has the highest Gini-co-efficient in the world: a socio-economic pattern that is echoed in the profile of students enrolled at its institutions of higher learning. South Africa also has serious deficits in its provision of internet access to the population, which poses complex challenges when it comes to education in our 21st-century digitized environment. While there is virtually blanket mobile phone access (3-G) in the country, access to the internet is well below 30 percent and provided mainly in the wealthier provinces and municipalities. Of this percentage, the bulk of access is by business and the more affluent members of society. There are critical shortfalls of internet access in the rural areas of South Africa, which poses many complex challenges for institutions such as UNISA whose mode of delivery is vested in technology and whose student profile reflects the harsh disparities that are to be found in South African society.

It is, however, positive to note the relative speed at which the State is tackling this challenge, especially since South Africa now lags behind a number of its African counterparts in internet provision and cost. It is envisaged that the provision of internet to the broader population will have a significant impact on education access and delivery.

South Africa is faced with significant education challenges that are being addressed systematically and in line with national development needs. However, it would be equally true to assert that globally, most higher education practitioners face their own contextualized challenges as they too re-adjust to a world that is undergoing a fundamental reorientation and whose higher education future is opaque to say the least.

Notes

1 The Minister of Native Affairs at the time, Hendrik Verwoerd, stated that:

> There is no room for him (the Bantu) in the European community above the level of certain forms of labour … for that reason it is of no avail for him to receive a training which has as its aim absorption in the European community, where he cannot be absorbed. Until now he has been subjected to a school system which drew him away from his own community and misled him by showing him the green pastures of European society in which he was not allowed to graze.
>
> *Bloch, 2009: 44–45*

2 "Non-white" was the official term for all South Africans who did not belong to the white race, and included Black South Africans, South Africans of Indian descent (this group included a variety of sub-categories) and so-called "Coloureds" who are South Africans of Malay origin. The term is now considered to be derogatory and in this study is used solely in reference to and within the context of the Apartheid system.

3 The Soweto Uprising was a mass uprising led by school children, against the use of Afrikaans (the language of the Nationalist Government and the then *lingua franca*) as the medium of instruction in schools. The uprising generated an unstoppable momentum that culminated in nearly two decades of violent and vociferous struggle, the eventual demise of the Apartheid government and the ascendancy of the ANC-led government under the Presidency of Nelson Mandela.

4 "Technikon" is the South African nomenclature for a technical college that offers mainly vocationally oriented courses and training. Further Education and Training (FET) colleges offer apprenticeships in trade related vocations. Colleges of Education were dedicated to the training of teachers.

5 Minister Kadar Asmal was the Minister of Education from 1999–2004, and is largely credited with crafting and driving the NPHE (MoE 2001) plan to its complete implementation. Minister Naledi Pandor succeeded Minister Asmal and remained in office until 2009, when Minister Nzimande, the current Minister of Higher Education and Training, was appointed.

6 Third-stream income is income derived from sources other than state funding and student fee income, and includes income from, for example, research, entrepreneurial or commercialization activities, fund-raising initiatives and investments.

7 Given the very recent launch of the White Paper for Post-School Education and Training: *Building an Expanded and Integrated Post-School System* at the University of South Africa on 15 January 2014, and the seminal importance of the White Paper in the new higher education trajectory in South Africa, the Executive Summary is referred to extensively for a more informed understanding.

8 SETAs are Sector Education and Training Authorities. There are 21 SETAs, each of which is responsible for managing and creating learnerships, internships, unit-based skills programs and apprenticeships within its specific jurisdiction. Every industry and occupation in South Africa is covered by one of the 21 SETAs.

9 A useful definition of open education resources is provided by the United Nations Educational, Scientific and Cultural Organisation (UNESCO), which states that they are "educational resources that are openly available for use by educators and students, without an accompanying need to pay royalties or licence fees" (Butcher 2011:5).

References

Barnes, T., Baijnath, N. and Sattar, K. (Eds.) (2010). *The Restructuring of South African Higher Education: Rocky roads from policy formulation to institutional mergers, 2001–2005*. Pretoria: Unisa Press.

Bloch, G. (2009). *The Toxic Mix: What's wrong with South Africa's schools and how to fix it*. Cape Town: Tafelberg. Available at: www.sahistory.org.za/sites/default/files/Graeme_Bloch_paper.pdf.

Borg, W.R. (1963). *Educational Research: An introduction*. London: Longman.

Botha, J.C. (2011). *The Role of Higher Education Policy in Distance Education Provision in South Africa*. Unpublished doctoral thesis: University of South Africa.

Butcher, N. (2011). *A Basic Guide to Open Educational Resources (OER)*. Eds. Kanwar, A. and Uvalić-Trumbić, S., Commonwealth of Learning, Vancouver, British Columbia and UNESCO: Section for Higher Education, Paris, France.

CHE (Council on Higher Education) (2000). CHE. 2000 Shape and Size of Higher Education Task Team. *Towards a New Higher Education Landscape: Meeting the Equity, Quality and Social Development Imperatives of South Africa in the 21st Century*. Pg. 4. Pretoria: Compress.

Cohen, L., Manion, L. and Morrison, K. (2002). *Research Methods in Education*. 5th edition. London and New York: Routledge/Falmer.

DHET (Department of Higher Education and Training) (2011). *Statistics on Post-School Education and Training in South Africa: 2011*. Republic of South Africa: Department of Higher Education and Training.

DoE (Department of Education) (1996). *Green Paper on Higher Education Transformation*. Pretoria, South Africa: Department of Education.

DoE (Department of Education) (1997). *Education White Paper 3. A Programme for the Transformation of Higher Education*. 24 July 1997. Notice 1196 of 1997. Pretoria, South Africa: Department of Education.

DoE (Department of Education) (2004). Presentation to the Portfolio Committee on Education. 24 August 2004. In *Council on Higher Education. Review of Higher Education in South Africa. Selected Themes*. August 2007. Pretoria, South Africa.

DoE (Department of Education) (2006). *The National Policy Framework For Teacher Education and Development in South Africa. More Teachers; Better Teachers*. Pretoria, South Africa, pp. 6–9. Available at: www.info.gov.za/view/DownloadFileAction?id=70084.

Mnguni, M.H. (1999). Education as a social institution and ideological process: from the négritude education in Senegal to Bantu education in South Africa. In *European Studies in Education*, Vol. 9. Germany: Waxmann.

MoE (Ministry of Education) (2001). *National Plan for Higher Education*. Gazetted 9 March 2001. Government Gazette. Vol. 4. No 22138, Notice No. 230. Pretoria, South Africa.

NCHE (National Council on Higher Education) (1996). *Discussion Document: A Framework for Transformation*. NCHE. National Education Policy Initiative. Pretoria. Available at: www.che.ac.za/documents/d000066/HEandSocialTransformationReport_25Feb2004.pdf.

Nzimande, B.E. (2009). *Budget Speech of the Honourable Minister of Higher Education and Training Dr B. E. Nzimande MP, June 30, 2009.* Available at: www.polity.org.za/. . ./ sa-nzimande-budget-speech-by-the-minister-of-higher-education-and-training-parlia ment-30062009-2009-06-30.

RSA (Republic of South Africa) (1997). *Higher Education Act, 1997* (Act No.101 of 1997). Government Gazette No.1655. Volume 390. No. 18515. Pretoria, South Africa.

RSA (Republic of South Africa) (2002). *Transformation and Restructuring: A New Institutional Landscape for Higher Education.* 21 June 2002. Government Gazette no 23549. Notice No. 855. Pg. 4.

RSA (Republic of South Africa) (2009). *The Human Resource Department Strategy for South Africa* (HRD-SA) 2010–2030. Available at: www.gov.za/documents/download/ php?f=117580.

RSA (Republic of South Africa) (2010). *The New Growth Path: Framework.* Republic of South Africa: Economic Development Department.

RSA (Republic of South Africa) (2011). *The National Development Plan: Vision for 2030.* National Planning Commission. 11 November 2011. The Presidency.

RSA (Republic of South Africa) (2013). *The Industrial Policy Action Plan: Economic sectors and employment cluster* (IPAP 2013/14–2015/16). Republic of South Africa: Department of Trade and Industry.

RSA (Republic of South Africa) (2014). *White Paper for Post-School Education and Training: Building an Expanded, Effective and Integrated Post-School System.* Pretoria, South Africa: Department of Higher Education and Training.

South Africa (Union) (1953). *Bantu Education Act, 1953,* Act No. 47 of 1953. Pretoria, South Africa: Government Printer.

10

MODERNIZATION OF RUSSIAN HIGHER EDUCATION

Progress and Opportunities

Natalia Moscvina and Olga Kovbasyuk

Introduction

Traditionally, the main functions of higher education in Russia aimed to address three areas: cultural (in-depth development of an individual and culture communication), economical (professional education, which preconditions the priority of the connection between the educational services market and the labor market), and social (higher education as a major means of vertical mobility and means of "smoothing" social inequality).

In recent years, education, in general, and higher education, in particular, have undergone and continue to undergo considerable transformation in Russia. This is due to changes occurring in the world as well as the internal transition from the post-Soviet (1990s) to modern (2000s) era (Stepanischev, 2002).

New trends and functions of higher education are becoming more and more significant in the 21st century. Among them are democratizing and entrepreneurial orientations, increasing mobility, and strengthening the innovative and research functions of higher education institutions. All of these issues are widely discussed in Russia today. Radical contradictions in existing views on education confirm that the situation in this sphere is controversial and cannot be evaluated from one single perspective. These contradictions also reveal that different political or ideological parties advocate different perspectives on education (Porus, 2009).

In this chapter, we endeavor to analyze the current transformations in higher education in Russia in light of its modernization. According to initiatives (for Education 2020), adopted by the Russian government, modernization of Russian education is to aim for democratization. Some authors call such a declaration "democartic rhetoric" (Panfilova, 2012). We will provide the empirical documentation along with the authors' own expertise in the subject to present the diverse perspectives on whether higher education in Russia is progressing toward democratization or whether this is still a pathway.

We will start with brief historical information on the state of higher education in the Russian Empire of the 18th century to the beginning of the 20th century, when the first universities were founded, and thereafter, move to the Soviet era (1917–1985) when education primarily served the centralized national economy. The focus will be on the current changes in higher education with its adaptation to the Bologna process.

Historic Overview

Higher education in Russia is relatively young. The first higher education institution in Moscow was called Slavic Greek-Latin Academy and opened its doors in 1685. By the beginning of the First World War (1914) there were four first-class imperial universities. All of these universities were founded by the state and inside the state, as governmental agencies. This is the major difference of Russian universities from Cambridge and Oxford in the UK, and many old universities in Italy or France, which did not grow from inside the state and thus remained more independent while becoming integrated into the state system later.

First, "private universities" in Russia were founded at the beginning of the 20th century, although one cannot say these universities were entirely independent. State control over the spheres of public life has always been very strong. In reference to higher education, state control has been extremely strong throughout, with little, if any, changes until today.

At the turn of the 20th century, higher education in Russia began developing rather intensely. For example, within the two decades before the First World War, the number of university students doubled (Druzhilov, 2012). Historical development of education after the 1917 revolution (often called October Revolution) turned extremely complicated. After this tragic event, university faculty became a victim of the "red terror" and Bolsheviks ensured the liquidation of the intelligentsia in order to achieve the goals they had set up for the Bolshevik party (Volkov, 2009).

By the end of 1919, when the majority of university faculty had either died of hunger or left the country, the Soviet government introduced food allowances for professors and their families to not let them die out completely (Druzhilov, 2012, p. 242). Although the Soviets did not intend to destroy all universities, they succeeded in eliminating them in order to re-orient the values espoused by the university in relation to society in general. The Soviets started enforcing new proletarian values and tasks. According to these new policies, workers and peasants received preferences when accessing higher education; a new professorship was "baked" to implement the new desired tasks. Only a small part of the former professoriate, loyal to the new power, was allowed to continue teaching. Consequently, the quality of higher education dramatically decreased during this period of Soviet history.

Only by mid-20th century did the situation in the country begin to stabilize. The major reasons for this were the processes of industrialization and collectivization, initiated by the Communist Party (Stepanischev, 2002). These processes demanded educated professional labor to develop industry and agriculture. Thus, the government became more attentive to higher education and this resulted in the improvement of the quality of education. This resulted in educational advances in literacy, engineering, technical, health, and economic sciences.

However, focusing primarily on the needs of the national economy has considerably narrowed the scope of sciences and research at the universities. In accordance with the needs of the centralized economy, the Soviet Union policy controlled the number of students in higher education institutions. Hence, enrollment in universities was restricted to certain planned numbers.

Since then, in modern Russia, multiple transformations have been taking place in order to keep up with the quality and the aim toward democratization. We will view the most important of such transformations in the next sections before we offer analyses of the current changes and trends.

Higher Education in Modern Russia

The Russian Federation Constitution (Art.43), adopted in 1993, confers the rights to free higher education, based on a competitive basis, to all Russian citizens who receive this educational opportunity for the first time. The new Law on Education, which came into effect in 2013, empowers state government Federal Educational Institutions to ensure state guarantees on enforcement of this right (Art.6, p.1.2.). The Law refers to higher education as the domain of professional education, which includes both secondary level professional and higher professional education. The latter includes baccalaureate, specialist programs, and master's courses (Art.10.). In accordance with the former Law on Education, postgraduate and doctorate programs remain as post-university education.

In the context of social justice and democracy, equal access to education illustrates one of the priorities of educational policy in Russia. In order to put this policy into force, the government took the following actions: non-governmental institutions of higher education and secondary level education were opened; state universities were granted the right to enroll a number of students on a fee paid basis; the network of university affiliations was extended in many regions of the country; and the Unified State Exam (USE) was introduced and became the unified criteria to enroll students into universities. However, despite these developments there is a substantial gap between what has been declared and the reality of existing tendencies in education. For example, the equal access of students to universities remains a challenging issue due to the existing social inequality in Russia and the increasing gap between the rich and the poor. Under such conditions, many legal state initiatives aimed at democratizing the education system are doomed to failure (Larionova and Meshkova, 2007).

One of the possible interpretations of this existing controversy of perspectives on the equality of access to education in Russia is given by Porus who states that:

> The opponents of the existing education system from the "left" parties indicate the obvious reasons of the current crisis, such as extremely small budgets directed towards education and science, the speedy commercialization of educational institutions, and the transformation of education as a means of further stratification of society. They are correct because a country that does not invest much and does not prioritize the development of education and science is doomed to underachieve in its development. However, the opponents on the political "right" are also correct in saying that quality higher education must be an investment for the future, and consequently, it should be costly. One cannot have illusions that all the people can have equal access to costly services, although higher education should not be transformed into the privilege of the elite.
>
> *Porus, 2009, p. 19*

The existing system of higher education in Russia is the result of its lengthy extensive development. Education was funded from the state budget until the beginning of the 1990s. It was free for the population of the country until that time. The Law on Education of 1992 sanctioned non-governmental institutions to provide fee-based education, along with granting the state institutions the right to attract additional funds, including tuition fees. It all happened when the state significantly decreased funding for education in general. Researchers hold that the extensive period in higher education development started in 1995 and finished in 2005. This very decade is characterized by a high demand for higher education in Russia. As a consequence, a great number of private educational institutions were founded, which resulted in a great number of university graduates. In Moscow, for example, 42 percent of the population held university diplomas at this time. Universities could open new departments and introduce new forms of education. One such initiative was distance education. For example, almost half of the existing institutions (around 500 out of 1,100) opened distance education departments, and modified their curricula to meet the public demand.

In such a way, education became diverse regarding the academic content and forms of its realization in schools; it also became more flexible regarding developing academic standards to improve accessibility to higher education institutions (Artamonova, 2013). In fact, it was during this period that a significant shift to democratization of higher education in Russia was made.

However, the major limitation of this whole process within the decade of 1995–2005 was the inability of schools to ensure a sufficiently high quality of education, due to the fact that qualified faculty did not staff the growing number of educational institutions. Besides, there occurred a lack of balance between the educational preferences of schools and the quality of professional education, which led to dramatic consequences. To clarify, despite lack of qualified faculty, universities reacted to the needs of the market by extending the number of students enrolled in economic and law departments. Hence, the quality of professional education suffered and graduates could hardly find jobs in the years to follow.

The situation for higher education began improving around 2006, even as the microeconomic situation in the country was improving at that time and thus, the state funding of higher education was also gradually growing. By 2008, positive transformation in the education system became evident. Schools were able to develop innovative programs and purchase new equipment; faculty was motivated to work and self-develop. However, the global financial crises influenced the situation for the worse in regard to the income and psychological wellbeing of people. The demographic decline in the country made it even worse. Both negative factors gradually resulted in the collapse of the education market in Russia (Abankina et al., 2012).

The higher education sector in Russia currently continues to shrink; therefore, it is hard to give the exact number of existing universities at the moment. The latest numbers were given at the 2012 round table discussion held at the editorial office of the journal *Higher Education in Russia*. According to that data, there were 1,100 higher education institutions in Russia. These included 600 state institutions and 400 non-governmental ones (Idea of the University, 2012). There were around 2,000 affiliations, in addition to existing institutions, although the numbers seem to differ across different publications (Kovalev, 2012; Bodrov, 2012). The numbers look impressive if we compare them with the number of higher education institutions in operation during the Soviet era. Before the 1990s there were only 300 higher education schools (Kovalev, 2012); according to other publications there were up to 514, but still there were at least half of those that provided higher education. All the schools were state-owned institutions (ibid.) and thus were under state control, which secured standard quality education on the competitive basis. This argument became the most important one for the Ministry of Education to justify its decision to decrease the number of higher education institutions in the country. Additionally, the number of university students has been decreasing for the last three to four years due to the demographic decline in the country, which started around 1991. Today, most university students (62 percent) pay tuition fees, indicating an increase in accessibility for the wealthy and 50 percent of students study via correspondence—which does not guarantee quality education.

Current Transformations in Higher Education: Views and Perspectives

The Russian system of education has been reformed intensely during the post-Soviet period. However, the evaluations of these reforms remain very controversial:

from moderate to radical ones. The statement "Fundamental Russian education has been destroyed" can represent the latter perspective and prevails in modern society (Alpatova, 2012).

Around the world, the current crisis in education can be primarily attributed to the changing role it plays in society.

> It was only in the last century that it was recognized as a social, rather than personal, concern, as something that brings critical benefits for the whole of society and humanity at large, above and beyond individuals. Now education is one of the main domains of public policy.
>
> *Leontiev, 2013, p. 24*

Some researchers in Russia consider that this current lasting crisis in Russian education has been underway since the end of the 1940s. This allows them to assume that the current state of education is not the transitional one any longer, since transitional states do not tend to last that long. According to Karmanova, Russian education has turned into a new model (Karmanova, 2013), which relates to the current public policy and is being interpreted in Russia from different perspectives.

Although almost all Russians agree that education in Russia is undergoing crises, people often express contradictory ways of how to cope with these crises. One of the ways being suggested is to transform the Russian education system to align with global shifts. The alternative view held by other parts of the population is to return to the "best Soviet education" as the only possible way forward. We consider there is merit to each of these perspectives. We also believe that those in charge of reforms should seek a balance between the two. The first perspective is based on the understanding that education is a bridge connecting Russia with the world, which sounds very reasonable. The second view suggests that education is an inseparable part of the national culture, and that culture is the basis for self-identification of the people, which does have its meaning too. In summary, both perspectives need to be taken into consideration when creating a strategy to cope with the crises.

The strategic decisions ultimately taken could be more relevant to the existing situation, if all the factors of the crises are considered. Karmanova believes that the educational crises in Russia could be attributed to the following two external factors: (a) discrepancy between the content and quality of professional education in schools and the local and world market demand, and (b) the inability of Russian graduates to become engaged in the global processes due to the fact that most Russian diplomas are not recognized abroad. She holds that the critical internal factor of the crises is the discrepancy between the traditional education system, which aims at knowledge transfer, and the new education system in demand, which aims at developing skills and competences for the young people to succeed in the new global society (Karmanova, 2013).

In the next few paragraphs, we will view the two major strategies the Russian government has been undertaking to eliminate the crisis factors and to modernize the education system. These include joining the Bologna process and raising the prestige of Russian higher education internally and in the global arena. Both strategies overlap regarding the targets to progress in the quality of education and to become a part of the Common European Education Space. In the next sections of the chapter, we will describe the positive outcomes and the pitfalls in relation to the enactment of these strategies in Russian education. Based on recent publications, we will attempt to analyze the advantages and limitations of the actions taken to implement the new polices.

In 2003, Russia joined the Bologna process, which sounded very promising in terms of bridging the gap between the education systems and progressing in the quality of education. Initially, like many European countries that have been gradually adapting their national education systems to reflect the common European system, the Russian government intended to combine the best of national and European educational practices. As Baidenko, one of the Russian researchers of the Bologna process, stated: "The Bologna process aimed at triggering further transformations, which would enable universities to advance the national higher education systems to a new level along with the revival of genuine academic values"(Baidenko, 2010, p. 352). One of such genuine academic values used to be the fundamental character of Russian education, which meant the significance of the profound theory in the academic curricula. However, in time, it became evident that it would be difficult to restore this element, as theory had to be combined with the multifaceted nature of European education, as required by the Bologna process.

Major attractive ideas of the Bologna declaration for Russia were that the two levels of higher education would meet the demands of the market regarding employees' competences, competence-building approach, self-directed learning, and academic mobility. In the next few paragraphs, we will comment on how each of these ideas has been implemented in Russia. Just to mention that, along with the progressive ideas, the Bologna system does have some limitations, which have been recognized almost in every participating country within the process of its realization (Baidenko, 2010). As aforementioned, the Bologna system could not be prototyped but had to be adapted to each of the national systems, with regard to its specific nature. Otherwise, as happened in Russia, the process could have led to diverse distortions in the national education.

Let us start with *the idea of the two levels in higher education* (baccalaureate and graduate level), which is novel to Russia—although fundamentally reasonable for introduction, in light of creating the unified education space in Europe. However, the specific elements of the former system could remain in operation, such as the five-year education program in Russia. It appears more rational to keep the five-year education program for such specializations as medicine, engineering, and math, for example. As experts view it (Vinokurov, 2012), these specialties require a lengthy educational cycle with practical internship in comparison with humanities and/or social sciences, where the baccalaureate can be more reasonably justified and easier to introduce into professional education. Some experts consider that in order to maintain the unified terminology, there should be an option to maintain five-year programs in the baccalaureate and call them higher baccalaureate (ibid.).

The government should have been more accurate when introducing graduate schools in Russia (ibid.). As demonstrated in many European countries, upon graduating from colleges, young people are admitted to graduate school after they gain practical experience working for at least two years in a company. Moreover, it is desired that the practical work of graduate school applicants should relate to their area of expertise. These requirements regrettably did not become a prerequisite for graduate students in Russia, which made the whole process of transferring for the students from the baccalaureate to graduate studies difficult. In fact, 90 percent of graduates from the baccalaureate continue their education in the graduate schools right after they graduate from colleges. According to the survey, they study in the graduate schools in order to receive a formal diploma, which "better corresponds to higher education" than a bachelor degree. Having said that, the two level higher education has been gradually introduced in Russia for the last 15 years, although only 10 percent of the existing educational institutions fully function on the Bologna scheme.

The next attractive character of the Bologna process is the *competency-building approach to education*. It is extremely timely in Russia, as well as globally, as it implies experiential education viewed both as a philosophy and methodology in which educators purposely engage with learners in direct experience and focused reflection in order to develop skills and competencies. These experiences directly engage students in ways that enable them to experience and co-construct new knowledge, which is meaningful to them, thus motivating them for further self-development (Kovbasyuk and Blessinger, 2013). This approach, if appropriately realized in education, could be highly productive for society and the economy. What is meant by appropriateness here is that the market, education, and the state should join their efforts to work out the competencies required for the economic and social development of the country. In Russia, regrettably, employers are rarely included in this process of decision-making regarding education strategies. Hence, academicians often define the market competencies within the academic environment. The consequences of such a policy leads to a more distant relationship between the two. Thus, the traditional skills and knowledge remain the basis for the "newly" defined competencies. In reality, all of the current documents, representing "new education standards" do not represent the real market requirements (Suhomlin, 2013).

Independent work or self-directed learning of students in higher education institutions is another attribute of the Bologna process. Self-directed learning can be viewed as a key attribute of the meaning-making process, which in turn can be initiated by experiential learning. Formally, supporting development of independent students' work has become a priority in higher education in Russia. According to the new curricula, the independent students' workload has been considerably increased. Regrettably, this is also a more formal innovation than the real case. The issue here is that the traditional education system in Russia was and still remains, to a greater extent, teacher-centered and based on teacher supervision of all the students' activities conducted in and outside class. As a result, students stay passive and considerably lack motivation to study independently. They are more interested in getting the formal document (diploma), rather than self-development. It takes time to change the mindset of both students and faculty.

Other reasons why this self-directed learning often does not work for Russian students and faculty may be due to the following: some students have to earn their living when studying, so they do not have enough time to cover the material assigned for self-studies; faculty is often overloaded (a professor's teaching load is 700–750 hours a year including class hours, research, and methodology), so they often control the independent students' work formally rather than profoundly; faculty is also overloaded with abundant paperwork, so they often cannot do research and produce publications in order to meet the standard state requirements for university professorship (Schelkunov, 2013).

Under the Bologna process, *academic mobility* is entirely recognized as a very attractive idea by the state and the public. However, it created challenges for the Russian education system to correspond to the European education system in regard to the credit transfer and curricular requirements. The systems differ in what to teach and how to estimate progress along with the workload for both students and faculty. In addition, academic studies in Europe are not affordable for many Russian families. Fluency in English is another challenge for a substantial number of Russian students. All these factors make it difficult to fully implement the mobility attribute in Russia. Instead, one could think of the internal mobility of students within the vast territory of Russia. This could have definitely enriched students' social and academic experience. However, the difficulty here is the relationship with the system of state funding. As each state university's funding is based on the number of students enrolled, this indicates that if students move from one university to another one, the former university would experience the financial deficit. The fund transfer between the schools appeared to be an obstacle to student mobility within the country.

To sum up, there are quite a few major Bologna process ideas, such as a two level professional education, competence-building approach, self-directed learning, and mobility, which have gradually been adjusted to the Russian system of education for the last 15 years. However, the process remains highly challenging and full of certain limitations.

The strategy outside the Bologna process, which the Russian government undertook to modernize higher education in the country, is connected with raising the prestige of Russian education internally and on the global arena. According to the Presidential Law on the state policy toward education and science (adopted on May 7, 2012), not fewer than five leading Russian universities would be ranked among the 100 world-leading universities by 2020. The Russian government has recognized that in order to achieve this task and to develop sustainable innovative universities, this would need the modernization of the entire higher education system. Among other tasks, the modernization of higher education is aimed at renewing the research infrastructure and investing funds in its development. In order to achieve these tasks, the Russian government undertook a number of measures to create supportive conditions toward research-based innovative entrepreneurial activities in institutions of higher education. One of the most effective strategies was the institutionalization of the categories of the National Research Universities and Federal State Universities.

The Presidential Law sanctioned the formation of National Research Universities on May 7, 2008 (http://elementy.ru/Library9/niu.htm). Since then, this status can be granted to Russian universities that provide effective undergraduate and graduate professional education that conduct fundamental research within a wide spectrum of sciences. In terms of the concept of creating a network of National Research Universities, as published on the Ministry of Education website, a National Research University can be defined as an institution that integrates education and research activities. It is characterized by the following distinctive attributes: capacity to generate knowledge and effectively transfer it to the economy; a wide spectrum of fundamental and applied research; preparation of highly qualified specialists up to and including master's level; and graduate and retraining programs.

The Federal Universities were formed to optimize regional higher education systems and to strengthen the links between universities and the economies of the federal regions. The concept of the Federal Universities involves a number of key strategic issues. A Federal University is defined as an autonomous institution that provides education, research, and innovation activity in a wide spectrum of directions, and seeks to provide integrated professional training of the personnel to be employed in highly scaled federal and regional projects. The priority for such a university is training and retraining of professionals, and conducting research to foster the innovation development of the region and the country.

We believe that the aims that the government set for the Federal Universities could have been set for all the universities in the country. The fact that they set it only for the Federal Universities proves that the government considers it impossible for all the universities to reach such goals. As a result, the number of higher education institutions in Russia has been decreasing since 2008. The latest trend in this direction is merging a few universities into one, which leads to public protests because the criteria of selecting schools to merge with each other look vague and disputable. The Ministry of Education applied these disputable criteria in 2012 to announce 136 "ineffective" universities and 450 affiliations (out of 502 existing universities and 930 affiliations). The criteria they applied were the following: square meters per student; number of international students enrolled in a school; "pass" grade of the Uniform State Exam; funds earned by a school; and rate of employment of graduates. Many experts consider that not one single factor from the above-mentioned criteria may testify to the efficiency of the university and call these criteria absurd (Klyachko, 2013, Malier-Matiyazova, 2013). To further prove the irrelevancy of certain criteria, we provide a few illustrations regarding each of them.

The Uniform State Exam pass grade is an index of high school rather than higher the efficiency of the educational institution. Moreover, the grade point average (GPA) is often connected with the prestige of the university profile (agriculture or law), rather than representing the efficiency of the school. In addition, the GPA is much higher in Moscow than in other regions, since one of the major roles of the Uniform State Exam was to attract talented students to Moscow. Higher GPA, in this case, is "the fee" students "pay" to study in a school, located in the capital of the country, rather than the index of efficiency of the university.

The next criterion they applied to distinguish between effective and ineffective schools is the funds schools earned or attracted. This criterion is especially disputable if applied to research in humanities. Some kind of fundamental research can be conducted without huge finances, whereas lots of funds can be wasted on non-significant research. There have been many recent publications on how education and research interrelate in academia, but this should not imply one could evaluate the efficiency of education by what funds have been attracted to do research.

The number of international students is another criterion under discussion. This number can hardly add to the efficiency of a university, in public opinion (Nekludov, 2012). According to Nekludov, the major task of higher education in the country is to provide high-quality national education to advance the economic and social development of Russia (ibid.). We concur with a different opinion, as presented by Panfilova (2012), that the influx of international students and researchers can be very enriching to both sides and bring inspiration through dialogue. We also believe that this type of international mobility is an important factor to take into consideration when estimating the effectiveness of higher institutions.

The criterion of square meters per student may sound ambiguous. On the one hand it does indicate certain things in the quality of institutions. On the other, the square meters can hardly add to the quality of teaching and learning. Employment of university graduates as a criterion to estimate the effectiveness of an institution can also be questioned regarding its relevance in the given context, as employment in general depends on a number of economic and individual factors, which may, or may not, be relevant to the efficiency of the school.

What causes additional criticism of the applied criteria and rating of universities is the unified approach to all of the existing types of universities. Humanities and pedagogical universities (liberal arts) appeared especially vulnerable under the circumstances, which can present a real danger to the intellectual and moral status of society. If this policy continues, the country will lack teachers in the very near future. The prestige of the teaching qualification in the country remains low, and in comparison to other fields the teachers' working conditions (huge teaching load and low wages) are miserable. Besides, teachers have to work under rigid administrative systems; they have to do more paperwork than working one-on-one with students, which again does not contribute to improving the quality of education.

In essence, the merging of schools often happens mechanically, without taking into account the consequences of that process for faculty and students. What often happens is that big schools swallow ineffective small schools and continue to operate under the former teaching/learning schemes. The number of students and faculty in each of the newly reconstructed schools is considerably decreased to save the funds, which leads to faculty unemployment and students' drifting along the life streams. It becomes evident that this seemingly easy way of solving the complicated problem is full of limitations, one of which is the so-called "social vault." Auzan describes this phenomenon:

> Our school prepares good people, although they are not well educated at times. However, our resource-based economy does not require either good or well-educated people. Where do the young people go after graduating from school? Army is not the best option for most of them. The so-called 'ineffective' universities educate specialists, who are not in demand by economy. However, these young specialists who are often graduates of ineffective schools, constitute the Russian middle class, which is vastly different from the middle class in the West. It is a cultural and social phenomenon, a very important 'product' of the mass higher education in Russia, which is characterized by certain value and behavioral patterns. If the country does not need them any longer, where do they go now?
>
> *Auzan, 2013, p. 271*

The term "ineffective" universities is no longer applied in such contexts by the Ministry.

Conclusion

It is important to analyze the tendences in the development of higher education in Russia within a historical context because, starting from the first universities which were founded by the state in the 18th century to serve its own interests, the state has always controlled education in the country. Political and economic transformations in Russia have been directly affecting education in terms of the curriculum, admission, and funding (Panfilova, 2012). During some brief periods of Russian history, education became more independent from the state (for example, after perestroika in 1985 to the 1990s), while to date, the predominant attitude from the state toward education has remained authoritarian and with little to no change.

Modern higher education in Russia is in crisis. The factors of the current crisis are various. Some of them are lengthy and connected to the internal transition from the post-Soviet model of the Russian state. Others are conditioned by the global economic crises. The third group of factors are due to the demographic decline in the country.

In an effort to modernize and democratize higher education, the Russian government plays its stake on including Russian education within the European education space via the Bologna process. The process reveals lots of limitations and distortions when managed formally and without taking into account public opinion. In an effort to raise the prestige of Russian education, the Russian government introduced the rating system for universities. The government provides financial support to the leading schools, which are getting bigger as a result of merging with the so-called "inefficient" schools. The process raises public concern regarding the consequences of this policy. A step toward democratization could be a public expertise on the activities of the effective and ineffective schools. The results of such an expertise could serve as the basis for the accreditation of schools.

The current transformations in Russian higher education, called modernization, are being introduced by the government consistently and often in spite of public opinion and against the interests of the the subjects of these changes. The lack of reflection from the state and from the public on how the transformation process goes often causes distortions, which decrease the efficiency of the undertaken measures.

In general, the modernization of higher education in Russia is being conducted under the strengthening role of the state, which has resulted in decreasing independence of schools and bureaucratic pressure on faculty. Thus, the effectiveness of schools and faculty is formally evaluated, and yet, we can hardly apply any criteria to estimate the progress of modernization.

References

Abankina, I., Abankina, T., Filatova, L. and Nikolaeva, E. (2012). Trends in social demand for higher education in modern Russia. *Education Issues*. 3:88–112.

Alpatova, E.S. (2012). Modern higher education in Russia and abroad: problems and challenges of the time. Modern Science: problems of theory and practice. *Annual Review in Economics and Law*. 5:2–24.

Artamonova, M. (2013). Education: publications of 2011–2012. *Education Issues*. 2:68–70.

Auzan, A. (2013). The university's mission: view of an economist. *Education Issues*. 3:266–277.

Baidenko, V. (2010). *Major trends in higher education: global and Bologna measures*. Moscow: Research Center Publishing. 352–353.

Bodrov, E. (2012). *The crisis in education. Searching for a new paradigm of education at the turn of the 20th–21st centuries*. The Moscow Humanitarian University. www.mosgu.ru/nauchnaya/publications/2009/professor.ru/ accessed 02.10.2012.

Druzhilov, S. (2012). The tragedy of the national higher educational system during the post-revolutionary chaos. *Education Issues*. 3:241–257.

Idea of the University: challenges of the modern era: round table (2012). *Journal of Higher Education in Russia*. 7:35–63.

Karmanova, D. (2013). Crisis of Russian higher education: aspects of the problem. *Journal of Social and Humanities Research "Labyrinth"*. http://journal-labirint.com.

Klyachko, T. (2013). Education in Russia: key challenges and possible solutions. Moscow: Publishing House "Business". 48–50.

Kovalev G.P. (2012). Myths and reality of higher education in Russia. http://kprf42.ru/ accessed 07.07.2013.

Kovbasyuk, O. and Blessinger, P. (Eds.) (2013). *Meaning-centered education: international perspectives and explorations in higher education.* New York: Routledge.

Larionova, M. and Meshkova. T. (Eds.) (2007). *Analytical report on higher education in the Russian Federation.* Moscow: Publishing House HSE.

Leontiev, D. (2013). Emerging contexts and meanings in human education. In Kovbasyuk, O. and Blessinger, P. (Eds.) *Meaning-centered education: international perspectives and explorations in higher education.* New York: Routledge. 24–25.

Maler-Matyazova, E. (2013). *The reform victims.* http://polit.ru/article/2013/10/01/rsuh/ accessed 11.12.2013.

Ministry of Education of the Russian Federation (n.d.). http://minobrnauki.rf/.

Nekludov, S. (2012). *Guillotine as an effective remedy for migraine.* http://polit.ru/ article/2012/11/27/edu/ accessed 12.10.2012.

Panfilova, T. (2012). *Reformation of higher education in Russia: democratization or bureaucratization.* http://netreforme.org/news/t-v-panfilova-reformirovanie-vyisshego/.

Porus, V. (2009). Higher education for the 21st. century. *Alma Mater* 2:17–22.

Shchelkunov, M. (2013). *Bologna process in Russia – "shooting down" the fundamental Russian education?* http://info.tatcenter.ru/article/26328/.

Stepanishchev, T. (2002). *History of Russia.* Moscow: Nauka.

Suhomlin, V. (2013). *Innovations in Russia defeated education.* http://netreforme.org accessed 01.03.2013.

Vinokurov, M. (2012). Higher education and science in Russia: problems and prospects. *Arguments of the week.* 21:313.

Volkov, S. (2009). *Red Terror witnessed.* Moscow: Iris Press. 34–56.

11

DEMOCRATIZING HIGHER EDUCATION IN CHINA'S HONG KONG

Between Rhetoric and Reality

Hei-hang Hayes Tang

Introduction

Pierre Bourdieu (1984) once maintained that: "in a period of 'diploma inflation', the disparity between aspirations that the educational system produces and the opportunities it really offers is a structural reality which affects all the members of a school generation" (p.143). Development and reforms of Hong Kong higher education in recent decades, with a particular purpose of "democratizing" the access to it, expound quite well the "structural reality" faced by the local school generation situating in this China's special administrative region.[1] This chapter chronicles with critical assessment the massification pathway of Hong Kong higher education since the British colonial era. Undertaking two waves toward massification, Hong Kong has liberated the access to post-secondary education from 30 percent of the school generation at the turn of the twenty-first century to nearly 70 percent in the 2010s (University Grants Committee, 2010). However, close and critical examination into the reality encountered by the students and graduates of different tiers of the higher education sector may uncover that elitism is still prevalent in this Chinese city— which in the meantime faces structural impediments to political democratization (for example Vogel, 2011, p.508). This chapter suggests that without effectual policy responses addressing the "structural reality," the extent to which the recent education reforms have been democratizing its higher education sector is highly speculative, if not definitely determined as a democratic rhetoric.

Supply of Elite Higher Education amid Socioeconomic Development (1912–1983)

Higher education was never central to the economy and citizens' everyday life in colonial Hong Kong. Considered neither as a citizen right nor a commodity, higher education was offered to elite students in Hong Kong and beyond. The growth of higher education—out of an elitist conviction—was limited through control by the Hong Kong colonial government; therefore, many aspiring Hong Kong students without exceptional intellectual caliber needed to look for higher education overseas. All the while, the University of Hong Kong stood as the one and only university in the colony for more than half a century, since its official opening in 1912. Over the decades, in the early twentieth century, the university functioned as an elite training ground for the colonial bureaucracy and professionals, in particular medical and engineering professions.

While economic development in post-World War II Hong Kong brought along prosperity and peace, the provision of higher education by the colonial government also saw some adaptations to the changing society. Not unlike other post-war societies, Hong Kong's developmental state advanced with birth booms, emerging in the 1940s through the 1960s. The mounting population of local schoolchildren gave rise to an unprecedented demand for school teachers. In response, the government set up three teacher training colleges during the period of 1941–1960 to answer the demand for local school teachers.

The provision of higher education in the early period of post-war Hong Kong can also be observed through the establishments of some small liberal arts colleges. After the establishment of Baptist College in 1956 as the first liberal arts college, the other two liberal arts colleges—Lingnan College (which is associated with an American Christian background as Baptist College) and Shue Yan College (a privately run four-year college)—were founded in 1967 and 1971, respectively. Meanwhile, the second university, named the Chinese University of Hong Kong, was instituted in 1963. It was a realization of the Hong Kong government's 1959 plan for a new university, essentially an institutional merger plan of the three liberal arts colleges: Chung Chi College, New Asia College and United College. With a bilingual language policy and a four-year undergraduate curriculum, the Chinese University of Hong Kong is characterized by its emphasis on the Chinese tradition of higher learning and the Oxbridge tradition of college education. The two universities were publicly funded under the auspices of a buffer organization, namely, the University Grants Committee (UGC), which was established in 1965 following the principles and practices of the British UGC (University Grants Committee, 2007; Tang, 2014).

Technical training and education, on the other hand, is another dimension of higher education provisions in post-war Hong Kong, in particular during the rapid industrialization since the 1970s. Hong Kong Polytechnic, founded in 1972, assumed the role of technical education provision at the tertiary level. The City Polytechnic of Hong Kong joined the ranks of technical education in 1984 as the second polytechnic in the territory. Apart from the more sizable polytechnic institutes, four small technical institutes were separately set up through the decade of the 1970s. That said, the degree-granting power was limited to the two universities—and the access to higher education was merely available to an insignificant number of young citizens. Democratic access to higher education had not been an item in the policy agenda of the colonial Hong Kong government. Directions of the Hong Kong higher education policy—which was embedded in the colonial governance at large—were reconsidered by the government when the political future of Hong Kong was negotiated, and perceived problematically by the citizens in the mid-1980s.

Decolonization and the First Wave Toward Higher Education Massification (1984–1997)

The year 1984 is the watershed of Hong Kong political reality that affected the higher education development thereafter. The 1984 Sino-British Joint Declaration affirmed the political future of Hong Kong that the Chinese government would resume its sovereignty over Hong Kong in 1997. Family migrations to other Anglo-Saxon democratic countries are among the responses in dealing with the Hongkongers' anxiety about their uncertain future. Children of the immigrant family would also adjust their study plan to overseas higher education. The Hong Kong government, as a result, initiated a number of decolonization measures with a view to raising citizens' confidence about the Hong Kong future. New higher education policies played an indispensable part in the decolonization project as such. The first wave toward higher education massification began to take shape with an ambitious plan for founding the third university in the colony.

Two years after the declaration, Governor Sir Edward Youde marshaled the plan for establishing a new and innovative university in 1986. The idea of instituting the third Hong Kong university was conceived with the vision to set the Hong Kong knowledge-based economy in motion through nurturing innovative leaders and entrepreneurs, be they scientists, engineers or global business managers. It was then named the Hong Kong University of Science and Technology. In conjunction with the establishment of a new degree-granting institution, the government furthered its decolonization agenda to gradually liberate the access to university education.

Moving toward higher education massification, Hong Kong was astounded by the Tiananmen student democratic movement, which broke out unexpectedly on June 4, 1989 in China's Beijing. The Chinese turmoil heightened the worries about Hong Kong's political future and it induced a large-scale emigration from the colonial city. Within the single year of 1989, a total of more than 65,000 people, mostly from managerial and professional sectors, lost faith in the future security of Hong Kong and moved their families to Canada, Australia, the United States and some other places with a higher guarantee of stability. The situation demanded an instant response from the colonial government—for the sake of social stability and government legitimacy. In November 1989, Governor David Wilson proclaimed in the Policy Address that university places would be increased about 50 percent from 10,500 to 15,000 by 1994–1995, implying that

18 percent of the relevant 17- to 20-year-old age group be admitted to a higher education institution in the territory (University Grants Committee, 1996). Massification of higher education was considered a solution of the colonial government to the perceived crisis of people's confidence and government's credibility (Morris, McClelland and Yeung, 1994, p.138).

In the face of the 1989 public sector reform wherein many government departments underwent various processes of downsizing, the higher education sector, however, experienced a remarkable expansion in the 1990s. In 1990 the government approved the increase of degree-course places by Baptist College, City Polytechnic of Hong Kong, Hong Kong Polytechnic and the two universities (Chinese University of Hong Kong and University of Hong Kong). One year later, the Hong Kong University of Science and Technology was commenced (as the third university) within a mere five years' time since it was planned, due to the tremendous support by the government. In 1992 the Hong Kong Academy of Performing Arts was approved to offer degree courses, whereas shortly afterwards the five teacher training schools were combined to form the Hong Kong Institute of Education in 1994 and the two polytechnics were re-titled as universities in 1995. In 1997, the year when it returned to mainland China, Hong Kong also saw the retitling of the Open Institute of Hong Kong to the Open University of Hong Kong, while maintaining its self-financing operation mode. Currently there are eight institutions[2] operated under the funding of the UGC and they are considered the conventional higher learning institutions by the Hong Kong general public.

As chronicled above, the sociopolitical history shaped the making of Hong Kong higher education policies, which transformed the elitist higher education system toward a relatively massified one. Amid the massive expansion of opportunities for undergraduate education, accountability for education outcomes and maintenance of academic quality became public concerns. The local community, to which the publicly funded institutions are accountable, raised questions regarding efficiency, cost-effectiveness and economy of service (Postiglione and Mak, 1997). After the very wave toward massification in the 1990s, challenges were ahead for consolidating higher education and managing citizens' expectations for it in a post-colonial circumstance.

The Second Wave of Higher Education Massification in Post-colonial Hong Kong (1997–2010s)

In the very year that Hong Kong's sovereignty was returned to mainland China in 1997, the Asian region was confronted by an endemic financial crisis. In response to the financial crisis, Mr. Tung Chee Hwa, the first Chief Executive of the newly established Hong Kong Special Administrative Region (HKSAR), announced in his 1997 Policy Address that the higher education sector called for comprehensive consolidation, right after a decade's time of rapid expansion. To that end, the government implemented the Education Reform in 2000, carrying the financial implication that an initial funding cut of 4 percent would be enforced on the higher education sector. Conducive to the second wave of higher education massification, a new agenda that pertains to a higher target of massification was devised by the Chief Executive: 60 percent of secondary school graduates can pursue tertiary education by 2010 (HKSAR Government, 2000). But the expansion should only be materialized by private initiatives. The American system of associate degree programmes was then introduced and has become part of the Hong Kong higher education structure. An array of different institutions were encouraged by the government to join forces to supply higher education for the second wave of massification, comprising the UGC-funded universities, post-secondary colleges, the Open University and continuing education providers (Education Commission, 2000).

More significantly, "community colleges" (as a type of post-secondary college) were established by the department for continuing and professional education of the UGC-funded universities, sometimes in collaboration with and sponsorship by local charitable organizations. Among the pioneers, we find the University of Hong Kong and the Hong Kong Baptist University, which launched associate degree programs in the Fall semester of 2000. The higher diploma programs of City University of Hong Kong were also converted into associate degree programs at the same time. Thereafter, the supply of the self-financed "sub-degrees" (associate degrees, higher diplomas, etc.) underwent a tremendous growth from 2,468 places in the 2000/2001 school year to 29,608 places in the 2009/2010 school year (Figure 11.1). As shown in Figure 11.1, we can see that the provision of self-financed sub-degrees has made a significant contribution to the second wave of higher education massification in post-colonial Hong Kong. With reference to the University Grants Committee (2010), the overall supply of higher education has increased from around 30 percent of the corresponding age group in 2000/2001 to nearly 70 percent in 2007/2008 (p.153), showing that the result of the expansion was even higher than what the government aimed at. The statistical figures, as reported in government documents, appear to demonstrate that the reform is deemed to be a great success, regardless of the economic downturn caused by the Asian financial crisis in the period.

At the outset, a key purpose of the Education Reform in 2000 is to develop a "diversified, multi-channel, multi-layer higher education system" (The Federation for Continuing Education in Tertiary Institutions, 2001, p.1). According to the HKSAR Education Bureau, post-secondary education shall "ensure that no qualified students are denied access to higher and post-secondary education due to a lack of financial means" (Education Bureau, n.d. a). The policy rhetoric is in reality materialized by offering students various types of study loans, comprising means-tested grants, low-interest loans and non-means-tested loans bearing a higher interest rate. By the same token, the new secondary school curriculum and Hong Kong Diploma of Secondary Education (HKDSE) were implemented in

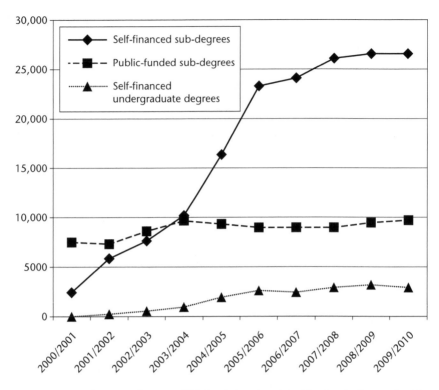

FIGURE 11.1   The Second Wave of Higher Education Massification in Post-colonial Hong Kong

2009, claiming to reform the secondary education of Hong Kong in the hope of providing multiple pathways that lead to various manifestations of "success" (Education Bureau, n.d. b).

Has Hong Kong higher education been massified? Martin Trow (2006) defines "elite higher education" and "massive higher education" numerically and theoretically (pp.243–244). In an elite higher education, the number of students involved in the system is not more than 15 percent of the overall population in the schoolchildren age group, and such education is to prepare the students for the "elite roles" by shaping their mind and character, whereas in a mass higher education, 16–50 percent of the corresponding age group are given access to higher education, with the purpose of preparing the younger generation "for a broader range of technical and economic elite roles" by skills transmission (ibid., p.243). According to Trow's definition, this article argues that Hong Kong higher education is therefore considered, literally, a massive higher education.

In reality, the local society generally perceives its higher education sector in the current form as a two-tier system (for example Kember, 2010, p.172), in which the government/UGC-funded programs are recognized more favorably as the "orthodox" ones making the first tier[3]; whereas all the sub-degree programs operated on a self-financed model (be they emerging, consolidating or fading out according to the market situations) constitute the second tier. Chan and Ng (2008, p.491) suggest that the government has not fully left the development of the second-tier non-elite higher education to the private market, but adopts a "public-private mix mode," in which the government provides financial assistance to the institutions which run the programs. In the school year 2009/2010, the number of self-financed programs have taken up more than half (55 percent) of the overall supply of post-secondary education (University Grants Committee, 2010, p.157), echoing the government's intention to leave the sector of second-tier higher education to take shape in response to the market forces (Chan and Ng, 2008; Kember, 2010).

Nonetheless, the local society perceives that sub-degrees should be regarded as a stepping-stone to (the "proper" study pathway in) the first tier of higher education section (Wong, 2011, p.11) rather than the "destination" of education (Kember, 2010, p.175). This predominant societal perception, reinforced by the vibrant local mass media and social media, poses a challenge to the democratizing project of Hong Kong higher education initiated at the turn of the new century. In practical terms, local employers are quite uncertain about the vocation-preparedness of some sub-degree graduates (for instance, whether they should be better accepted as generalists or skillful practitioners) and their competitive advantages compared with secondary school graduates (Kember, 2010, pp.173–174; Wong, 2011, p.8). In light of reflecting the issues and debates which frustrate the democratizing plans through the new tier of Hong Kong higher education, the following discussions are surrounded by some aspects of the subject: (1) positioning, identity and perceptions among the stakeholders; (2) strategic orientation of the curriculum; and (3) the market-driven developmental mode of operation.

Positioning, Identity and Perceptions among the Stakeholders

The introduction of sub-degree programs, in particular programs matriculating toward an associate degree, into the Hong Kong higher education system in the 2000s was a new—and bold—initiative (Postiglione, 2009). In form, colleges which offer the Hong Kong associate degrees bear a resemblance to the once popular American community colleges. But in substance, the market-driven mode of operation of the Hong Kong associate degrees differentiate themselves from the American counterparts, which are largely government funded, offering democratic access to higher learning for citizens from all walks of life by inexpensive programs. With flexible study modes, the American programs can cater for the different personal interests and learning needs of the citizens at different levels (Cohen and Brawer, 2003). But the purpose of the Hong Kong associate degrees is mainly to provide the specific group of high school graduates some alternative study opportunities if they fail to obtain access to the conventional under-graduate programs provided by the government-funded institutions. Positioning, identity and perceptions of the Hong Kong sub-degrees among the various stakeholders become important issues in the Hong Kong society.

Upon the launch of the associate degree system in Hong Kong, the Education Bureau commissioned the Federation for Continuing Education in Tertiary Institutions to research the position of the "Associate Degree" (AD) in the Hong Kong education system. In the 2001 publication *The Associate Degree in Hong Kong*, the consultancy study reported that there was no common descriptor of an AD internationally nor nationally whereas the consistence of AD and higher diploma or diploma programs were unusual in most of the other education systems. The report advised that the meaning of AD should be allowed to evolve liberally in response to the changing circumstances (The Federation for Continuing Education in Tertiary Institutions, 2001, p.4). Exemplifying an interim evaluation of the Hong Kong associate degree system, another consultative process by the UGC (2010) assessed that the associate degree, as a privately provided sub-degree education in the system, "has neither established a clear identity in the public mind nor much legitimacy as a stand-alone attainment" (p.40). The fact that it bears a questionable identity and ambiguous recognition by the society at large can be associated with its enormous degree of expansion—essentially in response to market forces. On the whole, the extent to which the democratization project for Hong Kong higher education is successful depends on the level of acceptance by the different stakeholders toward this new "tier" of education.

Within the milieu of a Confucian culture, which places an exceptionally high value on intellectual achievement,[4] Hong Kong students and parents embody an educational desire (Kipnis, 2011) seeking a more advanced academic credential. Most of the eligible secondary school graduates in Hong Kong are keen on entering the first-tier government/UGC-funded undergraduate programs. But for a significant percentage of the eligible graduates who failed in the university admission, they are quite likely to proceed to the sub-degree programs primarily looking for a second chance. Yet, places available for articulating to a second-year government/UGC-funded baccalaureate program are insignificant (for example, there were only 210 vacancies opened in 2004 (Postiglione, 2009)). In spite of the plan that the government has pledged to increase the respective places to 4,000 in the academic year 2014/2015, the majority of the sub-degree graduates are still unable to articulate toward first-tier undergraduate programs which are favorably sought driven by a shared "educational desire." It becomes an issue if there is a significant proportion of students with decent intellectual competence who are denied access to higher education solely due to the insufficient quotas offered by the government. They have limited options but to pursue a further study through the pathway of self-financed "top-up degree" (usually operated in collaboration with overseas universities). Interestingly though, Postiglione (2005) notes that universities in the United States are more willing than the local universities in Hong Kong to admit the graduates of associate degrees from Hong Kong (p.12).

Apart from the questionable identity among students and parents concerning this new tier of sub-degree studies, local employers are also uncertain about the competitive edges those graduates possess if they choose to terminate their study at, for example, associate degree level. Kember (2010) argues that most of the associate degree programs tend to be general-knowledge-oriented—with no practical usage to enhance students' immediate competitiveness in the labor market. Employing the paradigm associated with the notions of cost-effectiveness and competitiveness (which is not uncommon in many societal and media discourses in Hong Kong), the Hong Kong general public consider that the value of an associate degree has no important difference from that of a secondary school education. The situation leads to voices querying the cost-effectiveness of spending an extra two years acquiring a sub-degree. It is argued that the main problem of the current associate degree program is the misalignment between the curriculum design (as a liberal arts education nurturing generalists) with the vocational expectation by Hong Kong employers (for instance, Kember, 2010, p.176, who cited the refusal case of accrediting a nursing associate degree program). The ethos of the Hong Kong economy and society—which is with some levels of pragmatism and also elitism embedded—would take the policy makers to reconsider the strategic orientation of the sub-degrees' curriculum so as to align the expectations among the different stakeholders, and to address the cultural and structural realities given rise by credential inflation.

Strategic Orientation of the Curriculum

Elitism in Hong Kong higher education is manifest in an oddly low percentage of young citizens who are admitted to local university for a "full" under-graduate degree. The situation is unusual, in particular when the Hong Kong figures are contrasted with those of the other national cases globally. Notwith-standing the enormous expansion of the second tier of Hong Kong higher education provision, the admission rates to the Hong Kong universities by either secondary school graduates or sub-degree students are still below 20 percent, which is about a quarter of the percentages regionally and internationally (see Table 11.1). Given this circumstance, institutional leaders should strategically re-orient the sub-degree curricula, instead of one-sidedly following market demand, which is driven by the educational desire for a higher and more prestigious academic credential.

Apart from justifying the inclusion of general education in most of the asso-ciate degree curricula, academics in charge of the curriculum design can fine-tune the curricula with realistic consideration. In particular, the curricula can enhance students' communication skills, problem-solving competency, creativity and entrepreneurial mindset, which can be relevantly and readily transferred to

TABLE 11.1 Higher Education Enrollment Rates, 2013

Country/Higher Education System	Enrollment Rate
Australia	96
China	27
Germany	62
Hong Kong	18(60)
Japan	61
Korea	98
Singapore	27*
United Kingdom	62
United States	94

Source: The World Bank (2014)
*2012 data from the Singapore Government (2012)

workplace and personal careers; whereas the curricula can equip the students with common knowledge in career planning and "career literacy." While workplace-university/education misalignment has been criticized for deteriorating the unemployment rates of university graduates globally, if institutional administrators and academic leaders can address the timely issues in this respect, they can position this tier of higher education in an advantageous and competitive status. Such a strategy can sharpen the identity and enhance the positive perceptions about this aspect of Hong Kong higher education among different stakeholders.

The Market-Driven Developmental Mode of Operation

The consultative study report released by the UGC (2010) succinctly reveals that "the expansion over a period of time has also resulted in a fragmented and complex post-secondary education system with a degree of incoherence and duplication" (p.1) and "the quality of some private provision appears sub-optimal" (p.37). As aforementioned, the supply of the second-tier programs has actually grown over ten times in the past decade. The growth rate was even higher under the double cohort in 2012, when the last batch of the Hong Kong Advanced Level Examination (HKALE) candidates entered the tertiary education field together with the first batch of Hong Kong Diploma of Secondary Education (HKDSE) candidates, resulting in doubled demand for the higher education seats, be they in the first or second tiers. Over-heated competitions were observed in the years 2012 and 2013 with a tremendous number of new self-financed undergraduate degree programs opening and some brand-new institutions being established tentatively. Most of those programs charge costly tuition fees, which are about double those of the government-funded programs. The trend would possibly bring about the third wave of Hong Kong higher education massification, as well as a new phase of "diploma inflation." The UGC (2014) recognizes this new sector as the "local self-financing degree sector" and allocates several competitive research funding schemes for institutions in this sector.[5] Due to the diploma inflation, many sub-degree programs faced difficulties in enrolling adequate numbers of students as planned for the academic year 2014/2015. There are also signs that the market has reached a saturation point (Zhao, 2014a; 2014b). Worse still, population trajectory informs higher education managers of the weak market situation due to excepted lowering birth rates in the upcoming cohort over the next decade or so. The market-driven developmental mode of operation in this aspect of Hong Kong higher education will create tensions among the self-financing institutions and harms the ethos of the Hong Kong academic profession.

Conclusions: Some Policy Recommendations for a Democratic Future of Hong Kong Higher Education

This chapter has chronicled the development and reforms of Hong Kong higher education in recent decades, with a special reference to the two waves toward massification of higher education, which attempted to democratize access to it. Nonetheless, results of critical examination into the reality encountered by the students and graduates of different tiers of the higher education sector uncover that elitism is still prevalent.

Education is not a commodity. The value, meaning and long-term significance of an academic program cannot be solely determined by market forces, namely the supply–demand situation. To explain the incoherence and duplication of functions in the increasingly fragmented and complex Hong Kong post-secondary education system, marketization should be counted as one of the causes. Laissez-faire economic policies once enabled Hong Kong to become an "economic miracle," but laissez-faire education policies would not make education more effective and meaningful. Unlike companies, higher learning institutions should be best preserved as an intellectual community with history, heritage and legacy shared by and inherited through generations of students and alumni. As the Hong Kong higher education sector has already developed with a public–private mix mode, the government should show commitments in monitoring the market and sustaining the operation of some well-performing institutions. Government grants can be offered on a competitive basis for quality teaching, academic research and long-term institutional planning, in light of narrowing the gap between the conditions in the first and second tiers of Hong Kong higher education.

In the 2014 Policy Address, the Chief Executive of Hong Kong Special Administrative Region, Mr. C.Y. Leung, proposed a progressive increase of intake of senior-year undergraduate places in government-funded institutions by a total of 1,000 places from the academic year 2015/2016 (HKSAR Government, 2014). Out of the basis of merits, 5,000 sub-degree graduates will be able to articulate to subsidized degree programs each year by the 2018/2019 academic year. The government will also consider subsidizing up to 1,000 students per cohort to pursue self-financing undergraduate programs in selected disciplines. To tighten the alignment between higher education and the workplace, the government will seek to foster vocational education with employment support, particularly through the Vocational Training Council's apprenticeship training program. The Vocational Training Council will be allocated recurrent funding to provide industrial attachment opportunities for sub-degree students.

To further materialize the democratizing projects in Hong Kong higher education, this chapter, based on the above-mentioned data and discussions, suggests the following recommendations for the corresponding stakeholders to consider: (1) The government should put greater investment in higher education. It should liberate access to university education by providing sufficient funding for UGC to open more year-one and senior year articulation places into year two of undergraduate programs. It should also offer funding support for some well-performing self-financed institutions to narrow the gap between the conditions in the first and second tiers of Hong Kong higher education. (2) The higher education institutional leaders should reassess the strategic orientation of their curricula, in particular, acknowledging the diverse purposes and positioning of different tiers of Hong Kong higher education. (3) The government can encourage some non-profit making, well-established and globally connected sponsoring bodies into the higher education sector, for instance, the Jesuit Society. Since some of them aim to address the global poverty problem through education (for example, by providing scholarship support for students in need), fewer young citizens will be denied access to higher education due to financial constraints. (4) The government can seek understanding and gain the trust of Hong Kong society in acknowledging the diverse and democratizing pathways of higher education (for example, through public relation projects).

To recapitulate, the democratic conception of education gives individuals the habits of mind that secure social changes and bestow on citizens the freedom from the subordination of the individual to the institution (Dewey, 1916). As for the case of Hong Kong, without effectual policy responses addressing the "structural reality" faced by the majority of young citizens who fail to gain access to the government-funded (meanwhile top tier of) higher education, the extent to which the recent education reforms in Hong Kong have been democratizing the higher education sector is highly speculative, if not definitely determined as a democratic rhetoric.

Acknowledgments

The author gratefully acknowledges the support of the HKU SPACE Research Grant (Research Project No.: RG899900000053) by the School of Professional and Continuing Education, University of Hong Kong. The chapter also benefits from the research assistance of Mr. Angus Man-hei Chan. All mistakes remain the sole responsibility of the author.

Notes

1 Hong Kong was governed as a British colony during the years 1841–1941 and 1945–1997. The sovereignty of Hong Kong was resumed to the People's Republic of China on July 1, 1997, and Hong Kong has become one of its "special administrative regions." In the colonial circumstances, the Hong Kong education sector was developed closely mirroring the British colonial model, which is significantly different from the other education systems in Greater China (namely mainland China, Taiwan, Macao). For variations in Greater China's higher education systems, see Tang (2014).

2 The eight UGC-funded institutions are: Chinese University of Hong Kong, City University of Hong Kong, Hong Kong Baptist University, Hong Kong Institute of Education, Hong Kong Polytechnic University, Hong Kong University of Science and Technology, Lingnan University, and University of Hong Kong.

3 Kember (2010) unequivocally regards the UGC-funded programs as the "elite" education, "providing undergraduate education for top performing secondary school students" (p.171).

4 In this regard, the status of "university" is an essential concern (which may not always be the case in other cultures which accommodate some very prestigious higher education institutions bearing the name "institute," "school" or "college"). Among the recent cases, Hong Kong Shue Yan University acquired the university title in 2006, whereas the applications for "status upgrade"/renaming by Hong Kong Institute of Education (HKIEd) and the Chu Hai College are yet to be approved, despite previous attempts.

5 Institutions in this new Hong Kong local self-financing degree sector include: Caritas Institute of Higher Education, Centennial College, Chu Hai College of Higher Education, Hang Seng Management College, Hong Kong Shue Yan University, The Open University of Hong Kong and Tung Wah College.

References

Bourdieu, P. (1984). *Distinction: a social critique of the judgment of taste*. (R. Nice Trans.). Cambridge, MA: Harvard University Press.

Chan, D. and Ng, P.T. (2008). Similar agendas, diverse strategies: The quest for a regional hub of higher education in Hong Kong and Singapore. *Higher Education Policy* 21, 487–503.

Cohen, A.M. and Brawer, F.B. (2003). *The American community college*, 4th Edition. San Francisco, CA: Jossey-Bass.

Dewey, J. (1916). *Democracy and education: An introduction to the philosophy of education*. New York: Macmillan Co.

Education Bureau (n.d. a). *Post-secondary education*. Retrieved March 1, 2014, from www.edb.gov.hk/en/about-edb/policy/postsecondary/index.html.

Education Bureau (n.d. b). *Multiple pathways for senior secondary graduates*. Retrieved March 1, 2014, from http://334.edb.hkedcity.net/EN/multiplepathway.php.

Education Commission (2000). *Review of the education system: Reform proposals*. Hong Kong Special Administrative Region: Education Commission.

HKSAR Government (2000). Tertiary education – diversity and flexibility. *The Policy Address 2000*. Retrieved March 1, 2014, from www.policyaddress.gov.hk/pa00/p66e.htm.

HKSAR Government (2014). *The Policy Address 2014*. Retrieved June 1, 2014, from www.policyaddress.gov.hk/2014/eng/.

Kember, D. (2010). Opening up the road to nowhere: Problems with the path to mass higher education in Hong Kong. *Higher Education* 59(2), 167–179.

Kipnis, A.B. (2011). *Governing educational desire: Culture, politics, and schooling in China.* Chicago, IL: University of Chicago Press.

Morris, P., McClelland, J.A.G. and Yeung, M. (1994). Higher education in Hong Kong: the context of and rationale for rapid expansion. *Higher Education* 27(2), 125–140.

Postiglione, G.A. (2005). China's global bridging: The transformation of university mobility between Hong Kong and the United States. *Journal of Studies in International Education* 9(1), 5–25.

Postiglione, G.A. (2009). Community colleges in China's two systems. In R.L. Raby and E.J. Valeau (Eds.). *Community college models* (pp.157–171). Dordrecht, The Netherlands: Springer.

Postiglione, G. A. and Mak, G. C. (Eds.). (1997). *Asian higher education: An international handbook and reference guide.* Westport: Greenwood Publishing Group.

Tang, H.H.H. (2014). Academic capitalism in greater China: Theme and variations. In B. Cantwell and I. Kauppinen (Eds.). *Academic capitalism in the age of globalization* (pp. 208–227). Baltimore, MD: The Johns Hopkins University Press.

The Federation for Continuing Education in Tertiary Institutions (2001). *The associate degree in Hong Kong: Final report of a consultancy study commissioned by the Education and Manpower Bureau and undertaken by the Federation for Continuing Education in Tertiary Institutions.* Hong Kong: Federation for Continuing Education in Tertiary Institutions.

The World Bank (2014). School enrollment, tertiary (% gross). Retrieved from http://data. worldbank.org/indicator/SE.TER.ENRR/countries?order=wbapi_data_value_2012+ wbapi_data_value&sort=desc.

Trow, M. (2006). Reflections on the transition from elite to mass to universal access: Forms and phases of higher education in modern societies since WWII. *International Handbook of Higher Education* (pp.243–280). Dordrecht, The Netherlands: Springer.

University Grants Committee (1996). *Higher education in Hong Kong.* Hong Kong: University Grants Committee.

University Grants Committee (2007, April 3). *University Grants Committee: Brief History.* Retrieved from www.ugc.edu.hk/eng/ugc/about/overview/history.htm.

University Grants Committee (2010, December 1). *Aspirations for the higher education system in Hong Kong – Report of the University Grants Committee.* Retrieved from www.ugc.edu. hk/eng/ugc/publication/report/her2010/her2010.htm.

University Grants Committee (2014, August 29). *Competitive research funding for the local self-financing degree sector.* Retrieved from http://ugc.edu.hk/eng/rgc/sf/sf.htm.

Vogel, E.F. (2011). *Deng Xiaoping and the transformation of China.* Cambridge, MA: Harvard University Press.

Wong, Y.L. (2011). Community college students in Hong Kong: Class differences in various states of cultural capital and their conversion. *Journal of Literature, Culture and Literacy Translation* 2, 1–12.

Zhao, S. (2014a, April 3). Colleges struggling to fill self-financed courses. *South China Morning Post*, CITY3. Hong Kong.

Zhao, S. (2014b, April 4). 300 places, 19 filled . . . but don't judge sub-degrees. *South China Morning Post*, CITY3. Hong Kong.

12

DEMOCRATIZATION OF HIGHER EDUCATION IN INDIA

A Case Study

Arputharaj Devaraj

Preamble

The fundamentals of Higher Education (HE) in India are deeply rooted in India's antiquity, continuity and sanctity. These three strands of Indian HE are intertwined in India's geography, history and politics.

Geographically, India is a continent; historically, it is a sub-continent; and, politically, it is a nation.[1] India never kept its doors closed to any concept, ism, theory or ideology. It never barred the entry of a culture with an iron curtain as seen in Russia, or with a great wall as that of China. Precisely speaking, India never remained in splendid isolation. The very fact of India being a refuge to many ideologies, cultures and religions is reflected in its traditional, ancient higher education.

The sanctity of education could be deciphered from the ancient Sanskrit dictum, '*Matha, pitha, guru, devo*', still lingering in the mouth of every educated Indian. The Sanskrit saying grades the obeisance: mother, above her father, above him teacher, and above all, God. The place of *guru* (teacher) was so divine that he was placed next to God.

A retrospective glance at the history of Indian HE brings to focus: (i) the high standards of the ancient wisdom; (ii) the spread of the fame of Indian HE through the well-known residential universities like Nalanda and Vikramshila (in Bihar), Taxila (now in Pakistan), Kanchi (in Tamilnadu) and Vallabhi (in Gujarat) attracting scholars from abroad; and (iii) the amazingly dizzy numbers that now get enrolled in HE and the earnest attempts at democratizing it.

This chapter takes a synoptic look at:

(i) the history of the Indian HE in three segments (Pre-historic, Middle and Modern Periods);

(ii) the evolution and growth of HE;

(iii) the process of democratization: (a) in the expansion and widening of the reach of HE to every section/stratum of Indian society through the budgetary allocation of government funds ensured by the five-year plans; (b) starting from the firm grip of the government and growing more liberally in private hands; (c) bringing an autonomous administrative and academic set-up in the HE institutions; and (d) making the stakeholders of HE realize their roles;

(iv) the multi-layered evolutionary process of democratization in HE;

(v) the rise of autonomous institutions as an ultimate product of this democratization;

(vi) the formulaic concept of autonomy; and finally,

(vii) the challenges in the process of democratization.

History

The history of Indian HE starts from the Pre-historic times and runs perennially with ups and downs, necessarily accommodating the impact created by frequent invasions. The unusual aspects of its chequered history attract our attention. Education in ancient times was with a particular class, viz., *pundit*, supported by the royalty. Over the millennia, especially during the repeated foreign aggressions and subsequent subjugation, education became one of the State subjects, getting heavily influenced, skewed and biased.

Pre-historic Era

During the Pre-historic times, *guru-kula* (teacher-centred learning) was the learning paradigm. *Sishya* (student) went in search of *guru* (teacher). *Guru* resided at his own place, having a *patasala* (school) nearby where he initiated his disciples in holistic learning which included spiritual science, arts, applied arts, humanities, languages, literature, maths, astronomy, strategic, defence and diplomatic studies, and martial arts. Students, in turn, did all the manual work for the guru, besides paying something in gratitude, in cash or in-kind. *Guru-kula* system was absolute, autocratic and unequivocally controlled by the whims and fancies of the *guru*. There was no institution to benchmark the quality of the knowledge dissemination. The internal communication was mostly top-down and the student implicitly carried out the teacher's instruction.

Middle Period

From the sixth century BC till the twelfth century AD, there were leading universities in India, with scholars from Greece, Persia, Afghanistan, China, Nepal, Bhutan, Burma, Thailand, Mongolia, Cambodia and Sri Lanka. Scholars from abroad enjoyed a residential learning. The visitors from China, including Fahian and Hiuen-Tseng, have left long notes on the fame of these universities. A pleasant stay, definitely set syllabus, designed curriculum and calculated hours of teaching attracted talents from abroad. The education in these monasteries was more centralized and standardized.

From the twelfth to eighteenth centuries, the culture and education of India were in a flux. The *patasalas*, which taught Sanskrit, were to be closed for want of royal support, and with the support of Muslim rulers who promoted the teaching of Arabic, Persian and Urdu, the *madrasas* (Islamic schools or colleges) came into existence. At the time of the Muslim invasion and advent of Islam, Sanskrit and Hindi were replaced with Persian and Urdu. Persian became the language of the legal courts and Urdu, the royal courts. In both the *patasalas* and *madrasas*, rote learning was the learning paradigm.

In the south, thanks to Chera, Chola and Pandiya kings, the ancient Tamil remained intact as a language of higher learning, besides Sanskrit, which was learnt out of interest, especially by the Brahmin pundits. The history of a very high standard of higher education has been available in classical Tamil language right from Pre-historic times. The First, Middle and Last Tamil *Sangams* (*Sangam* is a Tamil term for 'association' or 'union'), lasting until the eighth century AD, groomed and nurtured all the possible disciplines in classical Tamil language. It is interesting to note that of all the five classical languages in which the classical learning was available, Tamil is the only surviving classical language to date, and most of its ancient knowledge, recorded in palm-leaves, was either lost because of the colonizer having smuggled it back to the colonizer's country or due to lack of preservation. Still, the treasure trove of this ancient wisdom is preserved in the archives in Chennai, Tanjore and Madurai – cities in the State of Tamilnadu.

Modern Times

It is again a rare coincidence that the very first English-medium schools were set up in Tamilnadu. 'The earliest efforts to introduce any form of education beyond the indigenous had emanated from the missionaries. Schwartz's schools in Tanjore, Ramnad and Shivaganga in the 1770s and 1780s were among the first to teach English to Indian children' (Raza, 1991). In 1830, under British colonial rule, the British Parliament allotted Rs.1 lakh (0.1 million) for HE in India. W. W. Hunter argued for 'Oriental Education' in an oriental language. Sanskrit was already fast receding from usage in the classrooms. Hindi was spoken only in the north. Tamil was spoken only in the south. Hence Hunter's argument went into oblivion without any taker. Lord Babington Macaulay put forward his famous 'Filtration Theory' and the need for creating a Comprador Class by introducing an education in English. Raja Ram Mohan Roy, the Bengali intellectuals and Lord Bentinck stood by it. Edmund Gosse deplored the big loss of the intellectual development that had happened over the years in the vernacular mode of learning, by abruptly introducing English.

The modern Indian HE in English came to stay during the nineteenth century. The old, glorious, holistic ancient knowledge of India was replaced with English-centric fragmented specializations in every field. Though there were several colleges existing in India enjoying full-fledged autonomy, the first university in India was started in Calcutta in 1857, followed by the setting up of the universities in Bombay and Madras. When India won its freedom in 1947 and became a Republic in 1951, there were only 25 universities and 700 colleges with student enrolment of 0.1 million (Agarwal, 2009).

This Anglo-centric education had a tremendous impact. Even the most illiterate Indian started using nearly 1,600 words in English. No other Indian language had this currency. The impact of HE in English could be seen in Indian culture too. This cultural invasion is tremendous: (i) dining table, table manners, bakery in day-to-day life; (ii) bun, bread, butter, jam, cake and pastry for breakfast; (iii) eating a quick lunch with fork and spoon; (iv) European dress; (v) games like cricket and cards; (vi) the use of guitar, violin, mandolin, saxophone and the like in Indian music; (vii) the parliamentary and legislature systems in national and state politics; (viii) the legal system; (ix) the Brahmo Samaj infusing the ten Commandments into the basic tenets of Hinduism and creating a Protestant Hinduism, which is still avidly followed in the West Indies; (x) every third word in any television soap opera in English; and above all, (xi) a definite university pattern, are but a few examples.

Post-independence

Free India needed a liberated and democratized HE. The Government of India instituted a Commission on Education, headed by Dr S. Radhakrishnan in 1948.

University Education Commission, 1948, outlined these points: (i) the importance of general education right from school to college; (ii) the role of universities as centres of research and advancement of knowledge; (iii) the need for sustaining and increasing the funding for research; (iv) the necessity of research facilities and better salaries for university teachers; (v) university education to be brought under the concurrent list; (vi) the Government at the Centre to be responsible in funding the infrastructure in the universities; (vii) outlining the standards of efficient administration of universities; (viii) focus on a smooth relationship between universities and R&D Institutes of national importance; (ix) the establishment of the University Grants Commission; and (x) the government colleges evolving into constituent bodies of the universities, to be ultimately made into stand-alone institutions or unitary universities (Ministry of Education, 1948).

Four years later, the Government of India constituted a *Commission for Secondary Education*. Having Arcot Lakshmanaswamy Mudaliar as its chief, the Commission sketched the contour of the Indian Higher Education, by suggesting the 10+2+3 paradigm (Naik and Nurulla, 1974).

Creation of the University Grants Commission (UGC)

In order to create and maintain high standards in HE, by an Act of Parliament in 1953, a non-statutory body was first carved out to initiate the process of setting up the UGC. In 1956, under the chairmanship of C. D. Deshmukh, the UGC came into existence as a statutory organ of the Central Government, for the promotion and coordination of university education and for the determination and maintenance of standards of teaching, examination and research in universities (The UGC Act, 1956). As a statutory university education wing of the centre, the UGC distributes the funds it receives from the centre to the universities and colleges. Thanks to the UGC, the scientific, technological and application-oriented research has grown several fold. Besides the UGC, a host of post-secondary-education-oriented, nodal, controlling and funding bodies came into existence, to speed up the democratization of Indian HE: (1) HRD Ministry, (2) National Council of Educational Research and Training, (3) National Staff College for Educational Planning and Administration, (4) All India Council for Technical Education (AICTE) and (5) Central Advisory Board of Education. Of all these, the UGC tops the list in helping the Government of India in the reallocation of funds. Nevertheless, there is a general accusation from some quarters that the UGC has been giving preferential treatment to the central universities in providing funds (Azad, 1975).

Sixth Education Commission

Commissioned in 1964, the *Sixth Education Commission*, under the chairmanship of Kothari, interacted with 9,000 personalities of social, academic and economic standing, and established the link between education and job-placement. It reiterated the 1952 recommendations by the Lakshmanaswamy Commission. This precisely paved the tarmac for a speedy take-off for Indian HE into the realms of democratization. It is from the submission of its report in 1966 that university education in India began embracing autonomy, the actual process of democratization – in terms of generous intake of students, appointment of more teaching faculty, departmental promotions, finalizing the courses and syllabi, teaching methods and addressing problems related to research. Concurrently, there was a focus on autonomy of the university departments as well as of the colleges. It was this Commission that took into cognizance the stakeholders of higher education – viz., the government, the UGC, universities, colleges, teaching faculty and students.

National Education Policy, 1968

Accepting the Kothari Commission recommendations, which reiterated Lakshmanaswamy's 10+2+3 paradigm, the Government of India spelt out its National Educational Policy in 1968. This was followed by a series of special committees, which took closer looks at the Indian HE institutions.

With the creation of the Planning Commission etching the sketches for five-year plans, the way for the evolution, growth and the democratization process of HE in India was paved. The *I Five-Year Plan* (1951–56) laid emphasis on the importance of investing in human resources. The Plan deplored the sorry state of affairs at the universities where power and position coincided with a professor's capability in garnering votes in academic elections, and not showing his strength in the teaching-learning process (Reddy, 1997). The I Five-Year Plan witnessed 0.72 million students studying in 32 universities and their affiliated colleges. The *II Five-Year Plan* (1956–61) apportioned a low amount, Rs. 5.7 million (95,000 USD) for education. The number of universities grew to 46. The real democratization step that touched the borders of rural India was in the Human Resource Development (HRD) ministry's move in creating ten rural deemed universities during this period. The *III Five-Year Plan* (1961–66) witnessed the democratization in HE by way of giving scope for planning more relaxed evening colleges, correspondence and continuing education, to spread HE. The *IV Five-Year Plan* (1969–74) consolidated the gains of the third five-year plan in accelerating the democratization process: more number of faculty, better equipped libraries, improved facilities and equipment for laboratories. The *V Five-Year Plan* (1974–79) continued the good work of strengthening, augmenting and consolidating the infrastructure and the facilities of the postgraduate courses, research, evening college courses, correspondence and part-time courses. The number of universities went up to 112, with 4,558 Arts & Science Colleges having 4.65 million student enrolments. Central instrumentation centres, pooled-in computer facilities and advanced centres of study and research came into vogue. Faculty Development Programmes, Orientation Courses and Summer Training Camps were introduced.

Only in 1975 did education come under the concurrent list. This enactment gave the centre an edge over the states in shaping a National Educational Curriculum. By this time the Teachers Union also grew into an influencing factor, claiming a better salary. To create a strong, transparent and democratic India, people were to be educated and enlightened en masse. This brought in the Rural Functional Literacy Programme, National Non-Formal Education and Adult Education Programme. State Resource Centres were established to train adult education teachers, trainers and resource persons. This accelerated the speedy democratization of HE in India.

Bringing education into the central budget made several progressive steps possible: (i) it aimed at bringing in uniformity in education spreading across nearly two dozen states and seven union territories across India; (ii) it enabled improved salary structure and service conditions for HE teachers; (iii) it regulated university admissions; (iv) it vocationalized Higher Secondary Education; and (v) it brought in a regulated and uniform examination system. This elicited more funds from the centre to be spent on universities and colleges across the states in India (Reddy, 1997).

In 1978, India introduced autonomy to colleges. Until this time, the affiliated colleges were sheepishly beating the drums according to the rhythms of the syllabus designs and dictates of the affiliating universities. A few colleges which were performing very well at the national level – including St. Stephen's and Sri Ram in Delhi, St Xavier's in Bombay and Calcutta, and Loyola in Madras – were granted autonomy with a contingent grant. They started designing their own curricula, syllabi and courses. They constituted their board of studies (BoS), academic council, and conducted the tests and examinations by themselves. The *VI Five-Year Plan* (1980–85) took a critical view of the non-performing institutions of HE. Tertiary level institutions were equipped with community service centres and student extension services. Though there was a critical and often cynical review of Indian education as a surrogate of English education, there was still no doubt the standard of intellectual work was growing in India. During this period, many self-supporting HE institutions started providing technical and professional education for a higher cost.

National Education Policy (NEP), 1986

When the UGC was established in 1956, there were hardly 35 universities. Thirty years later, a number of agencies were controlling Indian HE in 164 universities: AICTE in technical education, Indian Council of Agricultural Research for agricultural science, Indian Medical Council for medical education, Indian Bar Council for legal studies, and Indian Council of Architects for the professional education of architecture (Swamy, 2003). In order to create an umbrella organization coordinating all these fields, the Government of India announced the National Education Policy (NEP), preparing the country for the next millennium. It expected at least one Open University in each state of India. Of the 25 states at that time in India, only six states came forward to establish such universities (Dahiya, 1996). The major thrust areas of the NEP include: (i) autonomous colleges, (ii) redesigning courses, (iii) State Councils of HE, (iv) Accreditation and Assessment Councils, (v) National Eligibility Tests for College & University Teachers and (vi) Orientation and Refresher Courses for HE Teachers.

The *VII Five-Year Plan* (1985–90) made the autonomous colleges and the performing universities set a benchmark in HE. It also cast a concerned look at the most backward section of society. Special UGC grants were awarded to colleges and universities in running remedial programmes for the weaker sections of the student community. Indira Gandhi National Open University (IGNOU) was established to offer courses in HE in an open learning concept. It also trained professionals in producing learning materials for countrywide consumption.

Liberalization, Privatization and Globalization

The Indian Parliament Act on Liberalisation, Privatisation and Globalisation (LPG) in June 1991 opened the floodgates of Foreign Direct Investment (FDI) in every possible sector. This took the democratization concept to zooming heights by helping the HE institutions to garner funds from abroad from the non-resident Indians (NRIs) seeking 'payment seats'. It also made it easy for Indian students seeking admission to educational institutions abroad. LPG enhanced the quality-consciousness of an average Indian, seeking quality education from reputed and well-established institutions of HE. It is interesting to note here that India started its post-independence journey as a 'mixed economy', leaning on socialism. Even the Preamble to the Indian Constitution describes India as a 'Sovereign, Socialistic, Secular, Democratic Republic'. Surprisingly enough, within four decades after it became a republic, India opted for privatization – a definite step towards capitalism. This showed that rather than sticking to precepts, India wanted tangible results.

The *VIII Five-Year Plan* (1992–97) allocated 8 per cent of its spending to HE (Reddy, 1995). There was 125 per cent tax exemption given to industries and corporatations for helping science and technology innovations in the HE institutions. The National Assessment and Accreditation Council (NAAC) was established in July 1994 in order to assess, accredit and rank the colleges. The challenges thrown up by globalization and their impact on local culture could be seen in terms of a new demand and supply in the sphere of HE in India and a greater sophistication among the students and scholars, eliciting a better and qualitative delivery of knowledge from the institutions of HE. The common Indian dictum of 'cheap and best' got replaced with a new dictum, 'quality with a cost'.

The process of democratization got a quantum push during the *IX Five-Year Plan* (1997–2002) through (i) government grants, (ii) public sector funding (from banks and research institutions), (iii) private sector funds (tuition fees, etc.) and (iv) endowment funding. Above all, HE came to be seen as a matter of consumption. This shook the centrality of the conservative authority of the HE provider. The consumer paid for the expensive education and thus became one of the stakeholders of HE. The consumer also began to question the ways and means of delivery of HE. By this time, 12,000 colleges accommodated 8 million students.

During the *X Five-Year Plan* (2002–07) the number of universities went up to 399 and the number of affiliated colleges to 18,064. Rs. 96 billion [1.6 billion USD] was allocated to HE during the Tenth Plan. In spite of enormous funding for the aided HE institutions, the number of students who got enrolled in the self-financed institutions and self-supporting courses grew at an alarming rate. These private, self-supporting HE institutions do not get financial support from the UGC. They have to self-generate funds. Most of these HE institutions started collecting an exorbitant capitation fee, besides a regular tuition fee. In spite of this, a good number of students getting enrolled in these institutions signalled the growth of the middle-class and its affordability. Also, a good number of students started moving out of India in search of HE institutions abroad.

National Knowledge Commission (NKC)

The National Knowledge Commission (NKC), which came into being in the first decade of the new millennium, looked at private investment as a necessary stimulus for spreading educational opportunities (NKC, 2006). It also aimed at 1,500 universities. The very fact that the Prime Minister himself was directly heading the NKC highlights the importance given by the political administration to HE.

The *XI Five-Year Plan* (2007–12) allotted Rs. 849.82 billion. Rs. 306.82 billion was apportioned for starting and helping the new institutions of higher learning. Of this funding, 85 per cent was spent on salaries (Agarwal, 2009). Though some of the autonomous colleges performed very well, they were not allowed to collect more tuition fees. In other words, there was no appreciation or incentive for such performing institutions of HE. In order that funds could be profitably used, the Eleventh Plan also urged the necessity of revisiting the numerous heads to review spending, evaluation and allocation. At the end of this Plan period, India housed 611 universities and 31,324 colleges. Access, equity and excellence were the three key words of this planning period. Booming expansion in university education, including the creation of 30 central universities, eight Indian Institutes of Technology (IITs), eight Indian Institutes of Management (IIMs), ten National Institutes of management (NITs), 20 Indian Institutes of Information Technology (IIITs), 374 model colleges and 1,000 polytechnics, besides three new Indian Institutes of Science Education and Research and two new Schools of Planning and Architecture, expansion of research fellowships, interest-free education loans, provision of hostels for girls, reservation for socially backward classes, ensuring greater participation of minorities and girls, National Mission in Education through ICT (Information and Communication Technology) providing high-speed broadband connectivity to colleges and universities and development of e-content in various disciplines are some of the highlights of the Eleventh Plan (Human Development, 2013).

Public-Private Partnership (PPP) Model

In June 2008, the Union Government proposed a Public-Private Partnership (PPP) model to raise funds for HE. The government's responsibility for maintaining the quality and cost effectiveness remained as before, whereas the private service became accountable for the provision of infrastructure, maintenance and operation. The risk and reward were equally distributed by the public and the private sectors.

Education for Social Change

HE in India is seen as an instrument (i) of social change; (ii) to weed out corruption; (iii) to bring in more transparency in public life and governance; and (iv) to usher in ideals of secular, social, democratic and cosmopolitan attitudes. In essence, a needs-based higher education is the need of the hour. HE should motivate the teachers to teach and the students to learn, for which it should not be specific and specialized. It needs to be more general and less specialized. To make the teaching-learning experience more interesting and a happening one, academics in India need to rededicate themselves like their western counterparts. They need to prod their students to acquaint themselves with blended learning, Socratic Method, inductive and deductive learning, flipped classroom techniques, quizzes, mental gyms, play-way learning methods, etc. The students need to be more inquisitive, creative, productive, positive, energetic, research-oriented and updated in using the latest and safest technologies. This will enable them to be better-equipped catalysts of social change. To achieve this, better, positive and transparent tools of load despatch in management of HE institutions are needed. Research in the centres of advanced learning should cut across the various disciplines. Each centre of advanced learning should have an ideating think-tank, which should be called in at times of emergencies to dwell upon the issues and find solutions. Thus the money spent on HE will create enlightened intellectuals who will become the catalysts of National Development.

Education for Spiritual Change

To create an upright India without graft and corruption, the country needs morally honest teachers. Only spiritually upright and honest teachers and students can create a strong, transparent and democratic India. To achieve this end, value education needs to be incorporated into the curriculum. Mentoring, if pursued honestly, both by the teacher and the learner, especially at the time of depression, stress or crisis, will go a long way in the life of the student.

Democratization of HE in India

The two changes discussed in the two immediately preceding paragraphs will pave the way for a genial democratization process of Indian HE. The real democratization in HE institutions could happen only when the decisions are made, taking into confidence the fresh minds of the junior teaching professionals, students and the parents who face the day-to-day problems. In all probability, semi-literate politicians or administrators make the actual decisions. Hence, paving the way for autonomy, democratization in HE is in greater demand than ever before.

Autonomy, embedded in democratization, brings both pain and pleasure to teaching professionals in HE. Teachers have to design their own syllabi and get them accepted first in the BoS, and then by the Academic Council. This makes the teachers conversant with more texts, books, URLs, websites, libraries, etc. This would also encourage them to enrol in professional organizations, read more and publish in professional journals.

Democratization in HE leading to autonomy also brought in a 'cafeteria' model with a Choice-Based Credit System to students to choose courses of their own. This freedom sought to beat the boredom and monotony in their studies and injected a new blood of enthusiasm. A marked difference could be found between a student coming out of an autonomous curriculum and of a non-autonomous one. An autonomous education makes the student confident, vibrant and ready to face the world. To give a precise example, in the entire pan-Indian situation, Loyola (Autonomous) College, Chennai achieved a 100 per cent placement record during 2012–13 and 2013–14.

What Makes the Autonomous College Effective?

Autonomous colleges, in order to establish a high standard of quality education, rightfully tap the funds from the following bases: (i) the UGC, (ii) Department of Science and Technology, (iii) scholarships and fellowships available outside the purview of the UGC and the government, (iv) government scholarships, grants, loans, etc., (v) fees collection, (vi) alumni, (vii) Parent-Teachers' Association, (viii) endowments, donations, etc., (ix) other earnings from consultancy, research, contracts, twinning programmes, commercial activities, etc., and (x) finance and banking institutions. They show utmost accountability and responsibility in the utilization of grants. They reach out to the immediate neighbourhood effecting social, educational and economic reforms through their Outreach Programmes. They also train and produce student entrepreneurs. Of late, this is seen more as a corporate social responsibility of the HE institutions.

Those who argue against autonomy are the ones who have not experienced autonomy in the right perspective. Either they fear more work and responsibility, or the consequences of failure if they do not perform well. Many think, 'why sweat and slog when you can get a curriculum design and syllabus on a platter from the affiliating university?' It is a sheer slavish or colonial mentality, if it is rightly considered. Autonomy in a HE institution percolates in these three strands: (i) institutional autonomy, (ii) teachers' autonomy and (iii) students' autonomy.

An institution's autonomy lies in: (i) administration, (ii) collection of funds and profitable utilization of such funds, (iii) starting new courses and closing out-dated ones, (iv) admitting economically and socially marginalized students, (v) selecting the teaching and non-teaching staff and (vi) the upkeep of the infrastructure.

Teachers' autonomy, when realized in totality, makes the institution an enlightened one. 'The term "autonomy" means "control over one's own affairs" or "independence". Being autonomous implies *freedom, commitment, flexibility, functionality, quality, responsibility and accountability*' (Devaraj, 2004).

Freedom

Autonomy means freedom to act on one's own. As a teacher of autonomy, an academic incubates the idea of curriculum design, course module and syllabus.

The freedom to design a new course entails certain duties and responsibilities on the part of the teacher. In order to train the new entrants in designing the syllabus, course and curriculum, they can be paired with experienced and mature teachers who can act as their mentors. The needs of society demand that the academic constantly revises the curriculum. The curriculum taught at an autonomous institution should prepare a student to face life. Before outdating a syllabus, one has to check the results of their teaching on that syllabus, the evaluation they have collected from their peers and students, and the feedback from the teaching fraternity outside their own college. After updating the syllabus, the first crucible test is the BoS. After incorporating the ideas and suggestions given at the BoS, the updated syllabus has to face the ratification of the Academic Council. This two-layer system of passing a syllabus for approval and ratification in an autonomous set-up keeps a check on the misuse of freedom of the teacher. Freedom does not imply licentiousness. Hence, the freedom of choice in selecting a new theme, text or book has to face the litmus test of ethical, relevant or conscious checks. The freedom-conscious teacher gives these three checks to the material he chooses to teach:

(1) Is it ethically good to the student?
(2) Is it relevant to the needs of society?
(3) Does it disturb my conscience as I teach this?

Commitment

Autonomy can be successful only when the academics are committed. Commitment means readiness to give a lot of consideration, time, work and energy to realize the goal. 'No pain, no gain' encapsulates the idea of commitment. It calls for sacrifice, running an extra mile, and above all a generous mentality. Committing oneself to an idea of social change through classroom revolution is expending extra energy through hard work. The formula for excellence is: *Unremitting Hard Work* + *Dynamism* = *Excellence.*

Flexibility

The success of autonomy lies in the flexibility of the teacher's attitude. Flexibility lies in several variables, viz., presence of mind, creativity, association of ideas, relevant teaching methods, innovative ability, enlivened spirit, creative problem-solving methods, experiential learning, simulation exercises, variety teaching, PPT, use of chalk/marker board when necessary, student-centred approach, and above all, the teacher's dynamism. The teacher becomes an induction coil in the motor of the classroom-generated electricity called wisdom, which sparks, induces and generates creativity among the students. The formula of success for a creative, dynamic teacher is: *Presence of Mind* + *Dynamism* = *Creativity.*

Functionality

Autonomy owes its success to the functionality of the teacher, which is embedded in the teacher's practical approach and independent work ability. The teacher must be useful to the students, department and institution, as well as to society. The workable formula for functionality is: *Practicality + Independence = Functionality.*

Quality

The culminating aspect of academic autonomy is quality. What informs the quality of education is the calibre of the students who go from the classroom to face the world. Quality assurance denotes maintaining a very high standard in everything on the campus. The forces that challenge the quality are of two types: dormant and dynamic. The dormant forces that operate in a teacher while teaching are the teacher's emotionality, health, preparedness, expertise, ability and the time factor. The dynamic forces include the teaching capability, willingness of the students, the subject, classroom management dynamism, interactive ability and the immediate environment. Precisely speaking, *Expertise + Dynamism = Quality.*

Responsibility

Autonomy translates into targeted reality, when a duty is performed with responsibility. Teaching, the noblest of all the professions, comes from the duty-conscious and conscientious mind-set. To put it otherwise, *Duty + Conscience = Responsibility.*

Accountability

The most notable point of appreciation in autonomy is accountability. A dedicated feeling of responsibility that drives an academic to perform makes the resultant work accountable. Succinctly stating, *Duty + Responsibility = Accountability.*

This democratic autonomy can be granted in concert, to any college, by the following four bodies: (i) the college concerned; (ii) the affiliating university; (iii) the state government; and (iv) the UGC. Autonomy has been fruitfully yielding results in terms of greater success in the teaching-learning process. It has given elbowroom to the academics in academic freedom. It has improved the employability quotient of the products of autonomous colleges, as they are free to choose job-oriented courses. It is interesting to note that the colleges, which steal the national glory in terms of the first top ten colleges in India, are autonomous colleges. It is still more interesting to note that the colleges of excellence as announced by the UGC in April 2014 are all autonomous colleges. Hence there is a need to educate the stakeholders of Indian HE on autonomy.

Challenges to Democratization in HE in India

The forces and factors that work against the success of the democratization process in Indian HE are: (i) LPG, primarily profit-making and capital-creation in practice; (ii) LPG bringing in a kind of consumerism, which compromises the real aim of HE; (iii) commercialization and cosmopolitanism[2] in HE institutions ushering in several cultural, ethical, familial and societal issues which thwart the further spread of HE in India; (iv) a profit-making motive of the self-financed institutions blocking equity and accessibility in HE; (v) a developing economy and the proliferation of self-financing institutions; (vi) the supreme court judgment declaring the degrees obtained through correspondence, continuing education and the open university system are ineligible to access government jobs.

On the other hand, technology aids accelerate the speedy spread of democratization of HE in terms of Virtual Universities, Countrywide Classrooms, Massive Open Online Courses (MOOCs), YouTube Educational Videos, Mobile and Tablet applications, etc. Despite all the challenges enumerated in the preceding paragraph, there continues to be mass acquisition of HE degrees and diplomas through correspondence and open-university education. To avoid the unfortunate results of an unplanned growth of HE in India, the most urgent need is mass orientation and training of HE teachers, upgrading and updating the syllabi and courses. In order to weed out nepotism and corruption in HE, the appointment of Vice Chancellors should be made apolitical.

Another recent concept that scaffolds the democratization process in HE is the quick and easy spread of community colleges through the breadth and length of India. The idea of the community college was ushered in India by Dr. Xavier Alphonse. The first one, Madras Community College, was established in 1996. Slowly it evolved into a movement and spread to other states. Now more than 325 community colleges serve the secondary school dropouts.

> By incorporating the vocational education and training in the middle level of the higher-secondary and tertiary education, they sow the seeds of this silent revolution: 1. they change the negativism of the stigma attached to the label, "school drop-outs"; 2. the so called misfits of the regular stream in the higher education are given a golden chance of starting a new lease of life, thanks to the vocational inputs given in the community college system; 3. they also change the destructive and unwanted behaviour among the so called "misfits" and channelize their energy towards positive economic growth of the society; and 4. they also bridge the gap between the "educationalization"[3] and "vocationalization" at the tertiary level of education.
>
> *Devaraj, 2012, p. 3*

The process of democratization came to a full cycle when a greater number of privately owned polytechnics, engineering, medical and paramedical HE institutions were granted permission to start and admit students. The most striking feature of these private institutions is the reservation of payment seats and the government-allotted seats. The student who gets into this payment seat studies with a money-minded heavy heart which looks at the profession with a sense of making money and not with any commitment. This really is an ugly face of democratization of HE in India. Any democratic move should be backed by a sense of sincerity, commitment and transparency. Absence of it will lead to social inequality and injustice. Hence an immediate ethical and moral check is needed to navigate the democratization process of HE in India.

Notes

1 Like a continent, India is bounded by the Himalayan Range in the north; the east, the south and the west are surrounded by seas and ocean, having people of different ethnicities, cultures and religions. Its history stands very much on its own, not forming part of the history of Asia, the major continent of the world. Its narrative as a nation differs from time to time, because of the politics played by the Arabs, Persians, Moguls and Europeans, to name a few.
2 'Cosmopolitanism' is a feel of representation from different countries, whereas 'globalization' refers to the development of something which is operated worldwide.
3 'Educationalization' was an immediate transitional process of mass literacy in HE institutions in post-independence India towards general education. 'Vocationalization' was intended to create job-ready individuals with a comprehensive knowledge of a trade or vocation.

References

Agarwal, P. (2009). *Indian Higher Education: Envisioning the Future.* New Delhi: SAGE Publications, 133.
Azad, J.L. (1975). *Financing of Higher Education in India.* New Delhi: Sterling.
Dahiya, B.S. (1996). *Higher Education in India: Some Reflections.* New Delhi: Kanishka Publishers, 143.
Devaraj, A. (2004). 'Dynamism of an Autonomous Teacher'. *Autonomy for Colleges: New Dimensions.* Mysore: S.B.R.R. Mahajana First Grade College, 54.
Devaraj, A. (2012). 'Serving the Community: A Look at the Community Colleges'. *Thee Change.* Chennai: Vol.1. Issue 22, 1–15 Jan. 2012, 3.
Human Development. (2013). *Economic Survey 2011–12*, New Delhi, 323.
Ministry of Education. (1948). 'The Report of the University Education Commission', Ministry of Education, Government of India.
Naik, J.P. and Nurulla, S. (1974). *A Student's History of Education in India.* New Delhi: Macmillan, 100.
NKC (National Knowledge Commission). (2006). 'Report to the Nation 2006'. New Delhi, 28 Sept. 2006.
Raza, M., Ed. (1991). *Higher Education in India: Retrospect and Prospect.* New Delhi: AIU, 23.
Reddy, G.R. (1995). *Higher Education in India.* New Delhi: Sterling, 12.
Reddy, M.G. (1997). *Higher Education in India.* New Delhi: A.P.H. Publishing Corp., 8.
Swamy, V.C.K. (2003). *Higher Education in India: Crisis in Management.* New Delhi: Viva Books, 18.

13

MALAYSIAN HIGHER EDUCATION

A Case Study

Enakshi Sengupta

Introduction

Malaysia's progress towards being a developed nation is fraught with many challenges. With a view to realize the dream of nation building, the Malaysian government has crafted its higher education policies towards increasing the nation's competitiveness, productivity and innovativeness. Policy stalwarts drafting the higher education policy of Malaysia realized that knowledge along with innovative thinking, creativity and competitiveness plays a crucial role in shaping the future of the nation. In this age of globalization, the success of a nation depends fundamentally on the knowledge, skills and competencies of its people. Education becomes an essential component towards nation building and unity.

Individuals interacting with people from diverse socio-economic, religious and ethnic backgrounds learn to understand, accept and embrace such differences. The education system of Malaysia strives to inculcate moral values with a focus towards progressiveness and performance-based cultures for nurturing an all-round success of the country. Special emphasis is placed by the government on the development of educational infrastructure, student character, curriculum, research, innovation and development, as well as on the enhancement of the use of technology in the teaching and learning process, including online and distance learning (The National Higher Education Strategic Plan Beyond 2020). With a focus towards the progress of the nation, the Malaysian government drafted the National Mission and Ninth Malaysia Plan which stipulated the development of first-class human capital as one of the five national development thrusts towards crafting a progressive and developed Malaysia (National Higher Education Action Plan 2007–2010). During the tabling of the Ninth Malaysia Plan in March 2006, the then Prime Minister Badawi asserted that the development of quality human capital will be intensified by the government which would be holistic in nature and emphasis shall be given to the 'development of knowledge, skills, intellectual capital in fields such as science, technology and entrepreneurship' (The Star Online, 2006).

The Malaysian government aims to spearhead an effort to transform the national education system at all levels, from pre-school through higher education (Malaysia Education Blueprint 2013–2025). The model human capital as envisioned by the leaders of the country is expected to be well-rounded individuals with an appreciation for humanistic pursuits such as the arts, culture, sports and volunteerism towards social well-being (National Higher Education Action Plan 2007–2010). The Ministry of Education defines the national education philosophy (GETIS, 2000) by stating that education in Malaysia is an on-going effort aimed at developing the potential of individuals in a holistic and integrated manner, which shall result in producing individuals who are 'intellectually, spiritually, emotionally and physically balanced and harmonious'.

The Ministry of Higher Education in Malaysia (MOHE) has set as its mission the creation of a higher education environment that will help foster the development of academic and institutional excellence. Malaysia has been distinctly successful in the democratization and massification of higher education which ensures equitable access to higher education. In order to meet the demands of new global challenges, however, the Malaysian government has realized that it must ensure that the quality remains an integral focus of higher education. (National Higher Education Action Plan 2007–2010).

In the higher education agenda of Malaysia, technical education has been given an emphasis to meet the demands for skilled workers, especially in the engineering field, and all 69 vocational schools are being upgraded to technical schools. In addition to the polytechnics, certificate level courses in mechanical engineering, electronic engineering, machining and welding can also be studied at Industrial Training Institutes (ITIs), Institut Kemahiran Mara (IKM) or at Youth Training Centres.

Since gaining its independence, the Malaysian government has shown signs of sustained high levels of investment in education. As early as 1980, the Malaysian federal government's spending on primary and secondary education, as a percentage of Gross Domestic Product (GDP), was the highest in East Asia. In 2011, the amount spent, at 3.8 per cent of GDP or 16 per cent of total government spending, was not only higher than the OECD average of 3.4 per cent of GDP and 8.7 per cent of total public spending, respectively, it was equal if not more than top-performing higher education systems like Singapore, Japan and South Korea (Malaysia Education Blueprint 2013–2025). In 2012, with an education budget of RM (Ringgit Malaysia) 37 billion, the government has continued to devote the largest proportion of its budget, 16 per cent, to the Ministry. The large amount of spending earmarked for education shows the commitment of the Malaysian government to treat education as a national priority (Malaysia Education Blueprint 2013–2025).

Background of the Malaysian Education System

The large proportion of spending in the education system gained momentum after independence. At the time of independence, over half the population had no formal schooling; the figure shows that only 6 per cent of Malaysian children had been educated to secondary level, and a paltry 1 per cent to post-secondary level (Malaysia Education Blueprint 2013–2025).

Since independence, education has acquired a centre stage in the policy formulations in Malaysia. The Malaysian government has been highly interventionist in its effort to utilize education as a means of achieving economic and social development under the direction of the National Council on Higher Education (Lee, 2002). Education regularly receives over 16 per cent of the annual budget and all Malaysian Prime Ministers have served a term as Minister of Education (GETIS, 2000). The national budget allocation has increased annually since 1996 and in 2003 the allocation reached US$2.4bn (Middlehurst and Woodfield, 2004). In 2002 this allocation represented 26 per cent of the total budget (Suleiman, 2002) which is the second highest level of public expenditure on education amongst World Economic Indicators' (WEI) countries (World Bank, 2003). Five-and-a-half decades since independence and the country boasts a current literacy rate of 97 per cent (Studymalaysia.com, 2002).

The majority of Malaysia's educational system at the time of independence owed its existence to British rule, which was based on ethnic lines. However, the Education Act of 1961 marked the beginning of a process of "Malaysianiza-tion" of the education system, which gathered momentum in the 1970s. The concept of "Malaysianization" began soon after independence, as early as 1961; the government became highly interventionist in using education to fulfil key economic and social objectives. Primary education (7–12 years) was made "free to all" and the enrolment rate was 97 per cent in national schools, religious schools, Chinese and Tamil schools based on ethnicity of the country. Secondary education (from 12–18 years were organized in three levels) was also made free (Middlehurst and Woodfield, 2004).

Since the establishment of private schools in the 1950s, private providers have gradually secured their role in the Malaysian education system. The 1969 Essential (Higher Education Institution) Regulation had barred private sector institutions from conferring degrees, and foreign universities from setting up branch campuses in Malaysia. However, in the early 1970s, with a change in the policy, private institutions began to offer pre-university courses, and in the early1980s private providers became involved with innovative twinning and franchise arrangements in collaboration with foreign universities at bachelor degree level and other qualifications leading to the award of Certificate, Diploma and Professional quali-fications to Malaysian citizens (Middlehurst and Woodfield, 2004).

The Private Higher Education Act 1996, enlisting both the public and private education systems, marked the beginning of a major democratization and liberalization in the education system (Middlehurst and Woodfield, 2004). This Regulation and Act resulted in growth in the number, type, size and scope of private educational institutions at all levels. The Private Higher Education Act 1996 was further amended in 2003 in view of new challenges in the provision of private higher education. The amended Act provides for the establishment and upgrade of private universities, university colleges and branch campuses of foreign universities in Malaysia (Arokiasamy 2010).

The higher education capacity in Malaysia has grown from the formation of the country's first university, Universiti Malaya, in 1961, to the 2007 enrol-ment of 942,2002 students in 20 public universities, 32 private universities and university colleges, four branch campuses of international universities, 21 polyte-chnics, 37 public community colleges and 485 private colleges (National Higher Education Action Plan 2007–2010).

Reason for Growth of Higher Education Institutions in Malaysia

The growth of higher education and the role of the university in the knowledge-based economy are mainly influenced by the presence of four factors as outlined by Inayatullah (1996). One of the main contributing factors according to him is the spread of globalism, which involves the freeing of capital and opening up of the entire world to conduct business. The second factor is that of multiculturalism, which advocates the creation of a culture through practice and civilizations, giving a diverse perspective of the world and that a good society is expected to reflect this diversity in a healthy manner.

The presence of the Internet is also a significant factor with the potential to create virtual universities and decentralized publishing; as is the politicization of higher education institutions (HEIs) where the university is treated as being part of the economic rationalization of society and its post-industrial problems.

Inayatullah and Gidley (2000) explain that these four general factors may not be applicable equally for the growth of higher education in every nation. Globalism and politicization have a long-term impact and can be categorized as historical trends while multiculturalism and the Internet are more emergent trends. While Malaysia is focused towards creating a knowledge-based economy, its trans-formational impact can be felt on the role of the university in Malaysia. Such transformation carries the implication that the future philosophical and functional framework of the university and other HEIs in Malaysia would have to undergo a metamorphosis to ensure their role as incubators of innovation and drivers of social change (Nasruddin and Inayatullah, 2007). Other noted scholars writing on Malaysian education argued that the growth of higher education in this country is 'influenced by global forces and global trends' (Lee, 2004, p. 31) such as econo-mic globalization. Along with the forces of globalization, one cannot deny the influence of internal factors such as the need for an appropriate workforce or human capital to support the Malaysian economy at every transformation stage

(Sato, 2005). The combination of economic globalization and the internal factors of the country are responsible in reshaping the higher education in Malaysia from its economic transition from an agrarian economy to a knowledge-based economy (Singh et al., 2010).

Accessibility of Education

Although Malaysia has seen a rapid growth in higher education, it also faces the harsh reality like many other developing countries, that the government alone can no longer afford to meet the increasing demand for higher education, hence it urges the private higher education institutions (PrHEIs) to partly shoulder their responsibility (Tham, 2011). The PrHEIs are playing a crucial role in the arena of higher education, which becomes evident from the fact that in a large number of countries more than 50 per cent of students are enrolled in such institutions (Devesh, 2008). These figures hold true for both developing countries, such as Indonesia and the Philippines, and developed countries, such as Japan, the Republic of Korea and the United Kingdom (Tham, 2011).

Opportunities for higher education in Malaysia were limited during the time of the country's independence in 1957, with no public universities established in the country. Private institutions, however, were already present as tutorial centres for offering transnational programmes that were geared towards selected skills development and professional qualifications. Post-independence saw a rapid growth of private institutions in the country responding to market forces from within and outside the country (Tham, 2010). The change in government policies accorded a greater role to the private sector to facilitate the growth of a knowledge-based economy, which became prominent after the first economic recession in the year 1985–86. Such changes led to a more utilitarian stand on educational policy, where partnership and growth in the private sector were sought to meet the increasing demand for more qualified human capital towards fostering the growth of the country. The New Economic Policy (NEP) and Vision 2020 plan introduced by Mahathir Mohamad, a former Prime Minister of Malaysia during the tabling of the Sixth Malaysia Plan in 1991, also envisaged Malaysia's vision to achieve a developed economy by the year 2020, which led to the growth of higher education in Malaysia.

Since 1969, the education policy in Malaysia had undertaken affirmative action for Bumiputera's ('son of the soil') enrolment in public universities. The Malay were considered as "Bumiputera" (people of the soil), the majority of whom were Muslim and spoke a dialect of Malay; the Indians, the majority of whom were Hindu Tamils, and the Chinese, the majority of whom practiced a mix of Confucian, Buddhist and Taoist spiritual traditions, and who spoke one of several Chinese dialects as well as Mandarin, were not considered as "Bumiputera" but only Malaysians (Gudeman, 2002). This deprived the non-Bumiputeras from securing their position in such institutions, resulting in the rise of great discontentment with the government (Tan and Santhiram, 2009). The grievances of the non-Bumiputeras could be answered only through the growth of private institutions where they were given equal opportunity to access higher education (Tham, 2011). If one were to measure access and equity in Malaysia, one has to rely on scant sources of data as most of the statistics and data are not recorded. For example, there are no published data on the socio-economic profile of students in HEIs. Nor are there any data on the access provided for physically impaired students (Tham, 2011).

Research findings in the past have found that higher education in Malaysia is skewed towards female enrolment, as female students tend to perform better in schools than their male counterparts and the dropout rate for male students is higher at the secondary school level (Tham, 2011). The better academic performance of female students at the pre-university level has led to higher enrolments of female candidates in public HEIs. However, the male–female ratio is found to be higher in PrHEIs.

The access to higher education in Malaysia also depends upon the affordability of tuition fees. The affordability ranges from 34 per cent to 77 per cent of the annual mean household income for an undergraduate programme in business and engineering in branch campuses, to as low as 6 per cent for an undergraduate programme in business that is conducted in university colleges (Tham, 2011). Study in the past has shown that there exists a broad range in affordability in higher education. At the same time, data have shown that there is substantial government support to facilitate education for students of different economic backgrounds accessing higher education in the country with the help of private institutions in both university and non-university institutions, compared to that of public institutions (Tham, 2011). Malaysia offers two main student support mechanisms in the country, namely student loans and scholarships funded by the government. With the purpose of offering student loans, the government in 1997 created the National Higher Education Fund Corporation (NHEFC) as a semi-autonomous body under the authority of the MOHE, which offers subsidized loans to help students finance their private higher education (World Bank, 2006).

The NHEFC was established to provide low-cost educational loans to needy students in diploma and first-degree level programmes at public and private HEIs. Since its inception in 1997 to 2006, NHEFC has been responsible for 896,500 students to pursue their studies in approved HEIs (National Higher Education Action Plan 2007–2010). All qualified students in Malaysia have access to tertiary education although the challenge lies in providing them with a "world-class" education. The main subsidy offered to students lies in the subsidized annual interest rate of 3 per cent for the repayment of study loans, which is calculated on the balance to be repaid. Moreover, students who achieve first-class honours are exempted from their loan repayment. During the period 2000–2009, the government agency approved more than 1 million student loans. Prior to 2010, students with parental net income of less than RM3,000 were eligible for the full loan, which covers both tuition as well as subsidy; students with parental net income of between RM3,001 and RM5,000 were eligible for partial loans, covering fees and partial subsidy; and students with parental net income of more than RM5,000 were eligible for loans covering only their fees (The Star, 2010). These loans are restricted only for Malaysian citizens who have been accepted into full-time accredited programmes in either public or private HEIs; such loan facilities are not available for international students studying in Malaysia. The loan applicants are expected to achieve a certain minimum standard at their year 11 examinations (equivalent to GCSEs in England, Wales and Northern Ireland, and Standard Grades in Scotland) in Malaysia to qualify for achieving such loans. Foong (2008) noted that apart from the government loan facility, students hailing from low-income groups can also avail themselves of loans or scholarships from various charity organizations and foundations funded by corporate houses in Malaysia.

The government in Malaysia is committed towards providing higher education, which is evident from the share of education in total government development expenditure of around 20–25 per cent from 1996 to 2010 (Foong, 2008). Nelson (2008) noted that Malaysia has spent considerably more public funds, relative to total expenditure, on education than most other Southeast Asian nations, with the exception of Thailand. In terms of access to higher education, the government has made its provision in the National Higher Education Fund Corporation, which remains the biggest funding body for Malaysian tertiary students. To date, the government has approved RM36 billion as loans to fund the studies of 1.6 million students (Nordin, 2011).

The main aims of the Education Development Plan for Malaysia (2001–2010) are to increase access to education, increase equity in education, increase quality of education and improve the efficiency and effectiveness of education management. In term of access, the government is trying to attract premier universities from overseas to set up foreign branch campuses as part of the MOHE's agenda to make Malaysia a regional hub of higher education. Distance education in particular has become a very important and popular dimension in imparting higher education and has also become an integral part in delivering education to its international students. Accessibility in education, and higher education in particular, has been earmarked as one of the thrust areas by the government for Malaysia's new economic transformation programme.

Malaysia as a Regional Hub in Higher Education

The MOHE in Malaysia has drafted the internationalization policy aiming at transforming Malaysia into the hub of excellence in higher education in Southeast Asia, which would involve activities such as student exchange programmes, staff exchange programmes and collaboration with international institutes of higher education.

This policy involving the stakeholders has chalked out the expected outcomes and initial steps that need to be undertaken in the internationalization of higher education in Malaysia. Internationalization of higher education institutions in Malaysia is a complex process and has profound implications towards its various stakeholders (Morshidi Sirat, 2009). With Malaysia aiming to become an emerging force in global higher education, the process of internationalization is seen as an inevitable force to accelerate the country's growth in the field of higher education.

Malaysia has the advantage of low tuition fees and living costs and the usage of English as a language of instruction, which has enabled students, particularly from South Asia and African countries, to come to Malaysia to pursue their higher education.

The policy of internationalization in Malaysia is the fifth thrust area under the National Higher Education Strategic Plan (Pelan Strategik Pengajian Tinggi Negara, PSPTN). Under this thrust, Malaysia aims to become the hub of excellence for higher education internationally by 2020 with 200,000, or 10 per cent, international students enrolled in the institutions of higher education. In keeping with the increasing number of international students, the number of international staff is also expected to increase to 15 per cent by 2020. Malaysia is also expected to draw an annual income of RM60 billion or US\$20 billion by 2020 with the total number of international students targeted at 200,000. The income is expected to be larger when other expenditures like holidaying, graduation, family expenditures and parent visits are taken into consideration.

In order to achieve their targets by 2020 most Malaysian HEIs have focused their international activities towards targeted recruitment of international students, signing treaties with international universities and entering into international collaboration with foreign universities along with the establishment of regional research centres which are incubators of creative and innovative ideas within the HEIs.

To achieve the targets set for the year 2020 it is imperative that Malaysia's internationalization activities are continuous and effective with promotional activities, resulting in creating a conducive environment for international students, staff and researchers, which involves simplifying the immigration procedures and increasing the quality of social amenities and safety for international candidates. The internationalization policy of the higher education sector also has the capacity to contribute towards revenue generation for the country. It was estimated that each international student is spending RM30,000 per year as their tuition fees in the country throughout the course of their study, which translates to approximately RM2 billion for about 70,000 international students residing in the country, along with the money spent by these international students towards their living costs resulting in earnings of foreign exchange for the country. The Internationalization Policy for Higher Education in Malaysia was formulated by stalwarts in the field of education based on national aspirations, which include, among others, Vision 2020, National Higher Education Strategic Plan and New Economic Model. The policy is aimed at providing a framework that encompasses the basic aspects of internationalization within a time frame of ten years (2010–2020) which would enable Malaysia to be recognized as a renowned education hub globally.

The developments in information technology also stimulated and supplemented international contacts which have furthered the growth of the international faculty in Malaysia. HEIs in Malaysia are concentrating on critical areas in science and technology to encourage inbound and outbound mobility of academic staff which would promote not only the expertise of the local staff internationally, but at the same time would also form international linkages that would increase the capacity of Malaysian HEIs in areas related to teaching and research. The non-academic staff working in the areas of international mobility are also encouraged by helping them participate in training and development programmes with regard to effective management and customer care to support international students, visitors and their families to create a positive experience of higher education (Taylor, 2004).

The popularity of Malaysia in becoming an educational hub rests on its offering one of the most competitively priced academic programmes with assured quality in the region (PEMANDU, 2010). The assurance of quality along with competitive pricing has been made possible due to the government's continuous efforts in strengthening the capacity of Malaysian HEIs such as corporatizing public institutions to be more entrepreneurial as well as allowing privatization of higher education through the establishment of more private educational institutions (Mok, 2008).

Striving towards a knowledge-based global economy, the need of the hour will always be for Malaysia to open its doors to the world (NEAC, 2009), and in terms of higher education, this means a necessary, steady inflow of international students into its shores (OECD, 2009). The presence of international students due to the internationalization policy of Malaysia's higher education will not only have an impact on the campus but also have its influence on the surrounding community, given a situation of total and comprehensive internationalization (Olson, 2005).

With the advent of international students come the problems associated with integration of local versus international students. In order to foster optimal integration there is a need for a structured process of interaction between the different groups or individuals (Maleevic, 2002). HEIs should offer an ambience that is open towards foreign cultures and values in order to better understand and accept each other as an important part of the community through social and community engagement. The current status quo envisages a situation where the Malaysian community and international students need to be integrated and the community be made aware of the importance of internationalization to society and the nation as a whole (UNRISD, 1994). HEIs are the bridge that brings together the international students and the local community (Vally, 2009).

Quality Control in Higher Education

The establishment of quality mechanisms in Malaysia was mainly motivated to monitor the diversification of funds through the corporatization policy. The growth of privatization of higher education led to identification of the need to maintain some control over the quality of education offered by private educational institutions in Malaysia (Singh et al., 2010). The country's decision to create an educational hub and attract and retain foreign students was also a driver towards quality mechanisms which needed to be established and improve the standard of education offered by all higher learning institutions (Sohail et al., 2003). The 1990s and early 2000s saw a range of mechanisms introduced by the Malaysian government to ensure the quality of higher education in Malaysia was commensurate with its global competitors. The Quality Assurance Framework for Universities was established (Lee and Gopinathan, 2007) to control, monitor and maintain quality in higher education towards the country's efforts to become the centre of learning and educational excellence by the year 2020 (Jie and Idris, 2009; Kanji and Tambi, 1999).

Total Quality Management and International Standards ISO for quality assurance was established in the year 1992 (Pang, 2008; Sohail et al., 2003), which was authorized by the Malaysian Public Service Department (PSD) (Kanji and Tambi, 1998). Further, in 1996, the Ministry of Education initiated the customer charter concept and established a 'policy and quality section to monitor the implementation of the country's education policy at all levels based on the TQM principles' (Sohail et al., 2003, p. 141). In addition, the National Higher Education Council was established in 1996 to control the standards of public HEIs (Kanji and Tambi, 1998; Sohail et al., 2003).

The National Accreditation Board Act in 1996 was established to oversee the 'quality of courses delivered, reviewing the curriculum, examination scripts, assignments, students' learning outcomes, student support, academic faculty and interviewing staff and students' (Marimuthu, 2008, p. 278). For the first time in Malaysian higher learning institutions, review visits were made by the Board to assure minimum standards of quality in higher education (Lim, 2008).

To strengthen the quality of education in Malaysia in 2001, the Quality Assurance Division (QAD) was further established by the Ministry of Education to govern state-owned HEIs through a set of prescribed standards focused on teaching and learning, programme evaluation, leadership and governance, student assessment and student selection (Tambi et al., 2008).

The goal of creating Malaysia as an educational hub for international students gave the government further impetus to set up even more elaborate quality control measures. In 2007, the Malaysian Qualification Agency (MQA) was established under the Malaysian Qualification Framework (MQF) which aimed at providing quality assurance for both public and private higher learning institutions (Marimuthu, 2008; Pang, 2008).

The main purpose of these elaborate and stricter quality control measures was to establish and maintain internationally recognized standards of quality in the Malaysian higher education system and to strengthen the nation's position in relation to its international competitors and that of its neighbouring countries engaged in similar pursuits of creating educational hubs. The introduction of a Quality Standard assurance regulation by the MOHE has prompted universities to engage themselves in providing high-quality education to their students. The policy makers formulated nine areas of standards to be covered by the institutions comprising: (1) vision, mission and objectives; (2) design of the education programme and teaching learning methodology; (3) student assessment; (4) student selection and support system; (5) academic staff/faculty; (6) education resources; (7) programme evaluation; (8) leadership and governance; and (9) continuous quality improvement (Singh et al., 2010).

These initiatives of quality assurance in higher education were part of a broader programme introduced in the 1990s within the Malaysian public sector referred to as the New Public Management (NPM) values. The NPM project relied on the methods, values and practices that included efficiency, effectiveness, productivity, flexibility, delivery and excellence with the purpose of improving performance (Singh et al., 2010). Educational institutions showed visible signs of improved performance which they owed to the implementation of the NPM. The assurances of quality by providers of higher education and healthy competition between private and public HEIs in Malaysia, coupled with the development witnessed in the educational sector in the early 2000s aimed at consolidating Malaysia's competitiveness in the global education market.

Shuib et al. (2007) argued that an external quality assurance mechanism implemented through accreditation, validation and audited by peer review is an effective way to ascertain continuous improvement in the quality of higher education provided in a country. The implementation of such strict quality control measures has led education practitioners of higher education institutions in Malaysia to comply with the quality and standards set forth in the Quality Assurance guidelines.

The main purpose of these strategies towards quality assurance was to establish and maintain internationally recognized standards in the Malaysian higher education system and to strengthen the nation's position in relation to its international competitors (Singh et al., 2010).

Future of Malaysian Higher Education

Malaysia's Vision 2020 has chalked out a plan towards the overall progress of the nation in achieving the status of a fully developed and industrialized country. Malaysia's five-year Development Plans have continuously emphasized the importance of education as a means of unifying the nation as well as developing a knowledge-based economy for the country. Questions have been raised as to whether lecturers will remain mired in bureaucratic forms or will they be able to focus on teaching and learning methods? The future of the blended learning platforms has been often discussed along with the current need for new digital technologies, an ageing society, changing paradigms in learning and heightened globalization. On September 2012, several academic leaders – deans, deputy deans and deputy vice-chancellors – met in a common forum to discuss the current scenario of higher education in Malaysia. The forum had representation from 13 different universities. The stalwarts in this forum decided that the Malaysian higher education system needs to move from a regimented system to a flexible, adaptive one. The discussion challenged the factory model of education where rote learning and surveillance are considered more important than quality and critical reflection. It was decided that the regimented factory model should give way to an 'à la carte' model wherein students had a more central role in co-designing their education. The forum also looked into the Malaysian university system which had a yawning digital gap between older professors and younger digital natives (both lecturers and students).

The higher education scenario in Malaysia now lays emphasis on new learning platforms that place the student as the central focus of education; it also realized that higher education needs to be far more decentralized, as education needs to become personalized and tailor-made. With the proliferation of digital technology, curriculum contents are being constantly modified to meet the targets laid down as national goals. The current emphasis on curriculum reforms is directed towards science and technology related subjects rather than an emphasis on the arts and humanities.

The Malaysian government is on its way to making Malaysia a regional centre of excellence in education. The growth of higher education in Malaysia is focused on an increase in students' enrolment, increase in the number of HEIs, increase in government spending, additional government policies in promoting education and the country's continuous need for human resources (G8 National priority statement – Malaysia, 2012). Certain foreign universities, such as Monash University, Nottingham University and Curtin University of Technology, have set up their branch campuses in Malaysia giving opportunity to the students to obtain foreign tertiary qualifications locally. The students are studying at 49 universities, 23 university colleges and 411 colleges; out of the 49 universities, six are foreign branches from the United Kingdom, Australia and India (G8 National priority statement – Malaysia , 2012). It is not only that foreign universities have set up their branch campuses in Malaysia, there are also six Malaysian universities that are setting up branches abroad such as University College of Technology and Innovation in Sri Lanka, Management and Science University (MSU) in India, Limkokwing University in Bostwana and Al-Madinah International University (MEDIU) in Indonesia.

Malaysia has begun to explore the feasibility of new collaborative models with high-ranking institutions in the world. The Johns Hopkins University and MIT in the United States, and Manipal University in India, are some of the few institutions that have established collaborations with local companies and institutions and have set up higher academic institutions in Malaysia. In order to support the target, the Economic Transformation Program (ETP) has formulated strategies to develop dedicated education cities of Iskandar, Pagoh, Enstek and Nilai to allow the establishment and operations of branch and offshore campuses. Malaysia has also begun to sketch new geographical areas for Education Malaysia offices to be set up with the intention of attracting a larger number of international students apart from securing collaborative arrangements in student and lecturer mobility programmes. Through new collaborations and models of teaching, Malaysia is offering a range of programmes from full-time programme delivery at an offshore campus, along with face-to-face and flexible delivery options with e-learning (Goodfellow et al., 2001).

The liberalization policy and growth of globalization have led to attract and establish foreign branch campuses in Malaysia. These branch campuses are established as either purpose-built campuses or within designated campuses that consist of several faculties from different universities sharing common facilities, such as Iskandar Education City in Johor, Malaysia. The advancement in higher education in Malaysia lies in a partnership which includes the government, the investment and finance community, the corporate world and public and private educational providers. Malaysia has progressed with its unique appeal of being a forward and modern Muslim country that now holds about 2.5 per cent of the global international student market and ranks at no 11 (G8, National priority statement – Malaysia, 2012).

References

Arokiasamy, A. R. A. (2010). The impact of globalization on higher education in Malaysia. Genting Inti International College, Pahang, Malaysia.

Devesh, K. (2008). Higher education in developing countries. Paper presented at the Second Annual GDI Forum, 10 April 2008.

Foong, K. K. (2008). Funding higher education in Malaysia. East Asia Bureau of Economic Research (EABER) Working Paper Series Paper 44. Jakarta: EABER.

G8, National priority statement – Malaysia (2012). International education summit. Washington DC.

GETIS (2000). Global education and training information service – Malaysia profile. March 2000. British Council.

Goodfellow, R., Lea, M., Gonzales, F. and Mason, R. (2001). Opportunity and e-quality: intercultural and linguistic issues in global online learning. *Distance Education*, 22(1), 65–84.

Gudeman, R. H. (2002). Multiculturalism in Malaysia. Individual harmony, group tension. *Macalester international*. Vol. 12.

Inayatullah, S. (1996). The multi-cultural challenege to the future of education. *Periodica Islamica*, 6(1), 35–40; as Multiculturarlism and education. *New Renaissance*, 6(3) (Autumn), 12–15; in *Prout India* (16–31 July, 1996), 9–13.

Inayatullah, S. and Gidley, J. (2000). Introduction: forces shaping university futures, in *The university in transformation: global perspectives on the futures of university* (pp. 1–16). Westport, CT: Bergin & Garvey.

Jie, F. and Idris, A. (2009). *Education management: perception of TQM and its effect on attractiveness of place of study*. Kuala Lumpur: E-Leader.

Kanji, G. K. and Tambi, A. M. A. (1998). Total quality management and higher education in Malaysia. *Total Quality Management*, 9(4–5), 130–132.

Kanji, G. K. and Tambi, A. M. A. (1999). Total quality management in UK higher education institutions. *Total Quality Management*, 10(1), 129–153.

Lee, M. (2002). Global trends, national policies and institutional responses: restructuring higher education. Paper presented at the CESE Conference 2002 in Institute of Education, London, on 15–19 July 2002.

Lee, M. H. and Gopinathan, S. (2007). Internationalizing university education in Singapore: future directions. *Higher Education Forum*, 4(February), 87–112.

Lee, M. N. N. (2004). Global trends, national policies and institutional responses: restructuring higher education in Malaysia. *Educational Research for Policy and Practice*, 3(1), 31–46.

Lim, F. C. B. (2008). Understanding quality assurance: a cross country case study. *Quality Assurance in Education*, 16(2), 126–140.

Malaysia education blueprint 2013–2025 (2012). Preliminary report – executive summary. Putrajaya: Ministry of Higher Education (MOHE), Malaysia. Retrieved from www. moe.gov.my/userfiles/file/PPP/Preliminary-Blueprint-ExecSummary-Eng.pdf.

Maleevic, S. (2002). Rational choice theory and the sociology of ethnic relations: a critique. *Ethnic and Racial Studies*, 25(2), 193–212.

Marimuthu, T. (2008). The role of the private sector in higher education in Malaysia. In D. Johnson and R. Maclean (Eds.), *Teaching: professionalization, development and leadership* (pp. 271–282). Doredrecht, The Netherlands: Springer.

Middlehurst, R. and Woodfield S. (2004). The role of transnational, private, and for-profits provision in meeting global demand for tertiary education: mapping, regulation and impact: case of Malaysia. Summary report commissioned by the Commonwealth of Learning and United Nations Educational, Scientific and Cultural Organisation (UNESCO). Vancouver, Canada: Commonwealth of Learning and UNESCO.

Mok, K. H. (2008). Varieties of regulatory regimes in Asia: the liberalization of the higher education market and changing governance in Hong Kong, Singapore and Malaysia. *The Pacific Review*, 21(2), 147–170.

Morshidi Sirat, S. K. (2009). *Contemporary issues in the global higher education marketplace.* Pulau Pinang: IPPT.

Nasruddin E. and Inayatullah S. (2007). Constructing future higher education scenarios. *Insights from Universiti Sains Malaysia.* USM special publication series. Pulau Pinang, Malaysia: Universiti Sains Malaysia.

National Higher Education Action Plan 2007–2010, Ministry of Higher Education. Putrajaua, Malaysia: MOHE.

NEAC (2009). New economic model for Malaysia: Part 1. Putrajaya, Kuala Lumpur: NEAC.

Nelson, J. (2008). Malaysia's education policies: balancing multiple goals and global pressures. In K. Nelson, J. Meerman and A. R. Embong (Eds.), *Globalization and national autonomy: the experience of Malaysia* (Chapter 7). Singapore: Institute of Southeast Asian Studies (ISEAS) and Institute of Malaysian and International Studies.

Nordin, K. M. (2011). Higher education in Malaysia. Increasing access and quality. Perdana discourse series. No. 12/2011. Universiti Teknologi Mara. University Publication Centre.

OECD (2009). OECD: Education at a Glance. Paris: OECD Publisher.

Olson, C. (2005). Comprehensive internationalization: from principles to practice. *The Journal of Public Affairs*, 81, 51–73.

Pang, V. (2008). Quality assurance of higher education in Malaysia in the context of globalisation and internationalisation. In S. Kaur, M. Sirat and N. Azman (Eds.), *Globalisation and internationalisation of higher education in Malaysia* (pp. 128–139). Malaysia: Penerbit Universiti Sains Malaysia.

PEMANDU (2010). Education NKEA Lab. Putrajaya: performance management Unit, Prime Minister's Department.

Sato, M. (2005). Education, ethnicity and economics: higher education reforms in Malaysia 1957–2003. *NUCB Journal of Language, Culture and Communication*, 7(1), 73–88.

Shuib, M. K., Syed, Z., Sharifah, N. A., Abdullah, R., Said, F. and Yusof, R. (2007). Implementation of quality assurance in public higher education institutions: University of Malaya experience. Paper presented at Regional Conference on Quality in Higher Education, Petaling Jaya, Malaysia. Retrieved 2 January 2010 from http://eprints.um.edu.my/1019.

Singh, J. K. N., Schapper, J. and Mayson, S. (2010). The impact of economic policy on reshaping higher education in Malaysia. In M. Devlin, J. Nagy and A. Lichtenberg (Eds.), *Research and development in higher education: reshaping higher education*, 33 (pp. 585–595). Melbourne, 6–9 July, 2010.

Sohail, M. S., Rajadurai, J. and Rahman, N. A. A. (2003). Managing quality in higher education: a Malaysian case study. *International Journal of Educational Management*, 17(4), 141–146.

Studymalaysia.com. (2002). Information sourced from Study in Malaysia Handbook (International) 3rd Edition, Malaysian Ministry of Education.

Suleiman, M. (2002). Case study of Malaysia: new providers of higher education in Malaysia. UNESCO report on globalisation and higher education, October 2002.

Tambi, A. M. A., Ghazali, M. C. and Yahya, N. (2008). The ranking of higher education institutions: a deduction or delusion? *Total Quality Management*, 19(10), 997–1011.

Tan, Y. S. and Santhiram, R. R. (2009). The transformation from elitist to mass higher education in Malaysia: problems and challenges. Centre for Policy Research (CenPris) Working Paper 101/09. Universiti Sains Malaysia.

Taylor, J. (2004). Toward a strategy for internationalisation: lessons and practice from four universities. *Journal of Studies in International Education*, 8(2), 149–173.

Tham, S. Y. (2010). Trade in higher education services in Malaysia: key policy challenges. *Higher Education Policy*, 23, 99–122.

Tham, S. Y. (2011). Exploring access and equity in Malaysia's private higher education. ADBI Working Paper 280. Tokyo: Asian Development Bank Institute. Retrieved from www.adbi.org/working- paper/2011/04/19/4513.access.equity.malaysia.higher.educ/.

The Star (2010). PTPTN [Malay acronym for NHEFC] loans to cover students from families with RM4,000 incomes. 24 June 2010.

The Star Online (2006). Full text of the PM's 9th Malaysian Plan speech to Parliament. The Star Online Edition. 31 March 2006. Retrieved from www.thestar.com.my/story/?file=%2f2006%2f3%2f31%2fnation%2f20060331170915&sec=nation.

UNRISD (1994). Social integration: approaches and issues. Switzerland: United Nations Research Institute for Social Development.

Vally, J. S. (2009, June). Unequal 'cultures'? Racial integration at a South African University. *Anthropology Today*, 25(3), 3–8.

World Bank (2003). EDI seminar series. Washington, DC: World Bank.

World Bank (2006). Malaysia and the knowledge economy: building a world class higher education system. Report submitted to the Economic Planning Unit of Malaysia. Washington DC: World Bank.

14

THE FUTURE OF HIGHER EDUCATION

Towards a Democratic Theory of Higher Education

Patrick Blessinger

Introduction

Nearly a century has passed since John Dewey (1916) published his seminal work, *Democracy and Education*. Although it was written mainly within a context of primary/secondary education, the democratic principles and concepts are also relevant to tertiary education. In 1916, tertiary education was hardly a visible blip on the educational radar screen but now, nearly a hundred years later, the tertiary system has drastically changed and expanded and that little blip has grown into a large, bright beacon on the educational landscape. Thus, as we approach the centennial of Dewey's seminal work and given the enormous changes and policy debates occurring now in education at all levels, it is altogether fitting that we revisit some of Dewey's groundbreaking ideas about democracy and education as a starting point for discussing the future of higher education.

Dewey views the development of learning as a continual process and as a communal process. In this view, learning is only meaningful when the individual learner is viewed and treated as an integral part of her/his social community and, conversely, the social community is only meaningful when viewed and treated as an integral part of the individuals that comprise it. In other words, individuals do not and cannot function outside of the social community in which they live and participate. Because people are born into a highly dependent state of being, they must rely on the adult members of the family and the community for their survival and they must rely on them to learn the requisite knowledge, skills, customs, and values needed to become functioning members of society.

According to Dewey, this is especially true for modern democratic societies where there exists an essential need to develop children into socially responsible citizens who possess the requisite knowledge, customs, and values that allow them to participate more fully in the democratic socio-political and economic system in which they live. In addition to the political, social, and economic purposes of education, there is a humanistic purpose to education in that students, as highly complex human beings and lifelong learners, should be allowed to become actively involved in their own learning in order to make learning more meaningful, more effective, and more self-regulating. Education, regardless of level, inherently serves multiple purposes (political, economic, social, and humanistic) for multiple constituencies. Education, regardless of level or institutional type, is by definition a complex learning community. Thus, the ultimate purpose of education (that cuts across all other purposes or aims) is to promote freedom and responsibility—the two sides of the same coin called human agency. Education is designed to accomplish this through the production of learning.

Education as a Social Institution

Today's generation must ask itself several important questions: What does it mean to teach and learn in today's fast-changing globalized world? What is the relevance of a higher education system increasingly flattened by technological and economic interconnectedness and interdependence? What is the meaning of education and learning within modern social and political systems? These questions are important because today's learners are part of a generation beset with rapid change and complex challenges on a scale perhaps not seen in previous generations (Burke, 2012; Carr, 2012; DeMillo, 2011; Kezar, 2014; Kovbasyuk & Blessinger, 2013).

Dewey argued that in an increasingly interconnected and interdependent social system, the socialization process becomes increasingly complex and, as a result, it necessitates the need for more formal and more prolonged systems of learning. He argued that the more complex a social system becomes, the wider the potential gap becomes between what people lack (e.g. knowledge, skills, customs, values, habits) and what they are expected to possess in order to function properly within that system. Dewey believed that, in the modern era, a system of education was most capable of bridging this gap. The logical consequence of this argument naturally leads to a call for all citizens to receive formal learning (i.e. universal education). However, a hundred and fifty years ago the notion of universal education for all youth was a radical idea to most people, but today the idea of universal primary/secondary education for all citizens is viewed as a fundamental human right. One could argue that today's formal system of education is so pervasive and so important to human development that it has now become the primary agent of socialization for citizens. Noddings (2013) asserts that:

> Education is a multi-aim enterprise, and it is time that we recognize that fact and build on it. Schools must address the needs of students for satisfying

lives in all three great dimensions of contemporary life: home and family, occupational, and civic, both domestic and global.

p. viii

Although we now take for granted the notion of universal primary/secondary education, there is a growing view that this basic right should be extended to post-secondary education also, in the form of lifelong and lifewide *learning opportunities*. In light of the growing importance of lifelong and lifewide learning, this view is gaining more traction. Kovbasyuk and Blessinger (2013) elaborated on this core idea and applied it to contemporary higher education by proposing a higher education system oriented around meaningful lifelong learning and open meaning-making educational processes. They note that higher education has undergone major changes as a result of a rapidly changing world, which has radically altered the approach we must take in addressing the need for people to learn throughout the course of their lives. Within this context, a multiplicity of new trends, paradigms, and philosophies have emerged to address the changes occurring in higher education (Altbach, Gumport, & Berdahl, 201; Ayalon & Yogev, 2006; Barnett, 2012; Bloom & Krathwohl, 1956; Chomsky & Otero, 2003; Deardorff, de Wit, Heyl, & Adams, 2012; DeMillo, 2011; Dewey, 1916, 1933, 1938; Freire, 1970; Gagne, 1965; Gredler, 2009; Kezar, 2014; Knapper & Cropley, 2000; Kovbasyuk & Blessinger, 2013; Mezirow, 1991; Noddings, 2013; OECD, 2008, 2009; Polyzoi, Fullan, & Anchan, 2003; Shavit, Arum, & Gamoran, 2007; Vygotsky, 1989; Zepke & Leach, 2002).

These new trends, paradigms, and philosophies suggest that educators and scholars around the world are concerned about the direction(s) in which education at all levels is going in the twenty-first century. With the ubiquity of globally interconnected systems (e.g. communication, information, financial), educators are now taking a more global view and a more interdisciplinary approach to education by viewing students as global citizens and viewing educational institutions as global learning communities (Blessinger & Kovbasyuk, 2012; Kovbasyuk & Blessinger, 2013). Modern globalized societies are highly complex and require higher education institutions to provide more meaningful forms of formal learning opportunities to their constituents. The basic components of the formal learning process that serves as the foundation of higher education can be viewed as illustrated in Figure 14.1.

The Changing Higher Education Landscape

Anchan (this volume) provides a good overview of the history and nature of higher education over the past centuries and the other authors in this volume also provide good overviews of higher education systems within particular national and regional contexts. These chapters illustrate how higher educational systems around the world are undergoing many political, social, economic, and technological changes brought about by the growing demand for a diverse set of higher education services at all levels. New market-based educational business

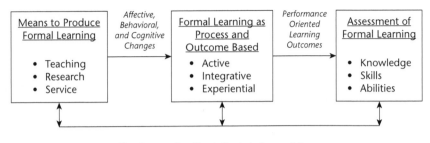

Continuous Feedback Cycle between Means,
Process, Outcomes, and Assessment

FIGURE 14.1   Formal Learning Cycle in Higher Education

models and new access methods brought about by an explosion of new internet-based information and communication technologies have helped to fuel this demand. DeMillo (2011) contends that change in higher education is driven mainly by political and economic factors but is fueled by enabling technologies, especially internet-based technologies. Within this context, traditional higher education models are under increasing pressure from international competition, increased constituency expectations, and spiraling costs, requiring major changes at all levels. These conditions have led to dramatic growth in the diversity and diversification of higher education (e.g. international education, adult education, distance education) over the last several decades. The relationships between the different constituents (e.g. government entities, accreditation organizations, higher education institutions, faculty, students, and society at large) are also changing.

Educational scholars (e.g. Altbach, Gumport, & Berdahl, 2011; Barnett, 2012; Blessinger & Kovbasyuk, 2012; Burke, 2012; Chomsky & Otero, 2003; Dewey, 1916, 1933, 1938; Freire, 1970; Kovbasyuk & Blessinger, 2013; Noddings, 2013; OECD, 2008, 2009; Palfreyman & Tapper, 2009; Vygotsky, 1989; Wankel & Blessinger, 2012) have pointed out that social environments and conditions are the result of a complex interaction between political, economic, socio-cultural, and technological contexts. Although this phenomenon has always been present, to varying degrees, throughout the history of higher education, the rate of change and the types of change have intensified during the last few hundred years. Between the industrial revolution of the late eighteenth century and the digital revolution of the late twentieth century, both of which stand out as two of the major watershed events that have catalyzed many of these changes, numerous wars and political and social revolutions have occurred to bring about change at all levels within and between nations.

Schofer and Meyer (2005) show that expansion of higher education systems tends to be more pronounced in nations where government control over higher education is lower and in nations where democratization and the protection of human rights is more prevalent. Yu and Delaney (2014) show that internal factors (secondary education enrollment rates and the political climate) as well as diffusion factors (technology and innovation) affect how nations develop their tertiary enrollment policies. With respect to the rapid expansion of higher educational systems around the world, these studies together with the data presented in this volume illustrate several trends that are occurring internationally:

1) increased demand for higher education across all demographic sectors of society,
2) growing diversity in the make-up of student populations,
3) growing diversification in the types and number of higher education institutions,
4) increasing funding options with a shift towards reduced public financing and a shift towards increased student and private financing, resulting in more pressure on institutions to raise tuition fees and develop alternate revenue streams,
5) increasing pressure on higher education institutions to respond to the needs of society (e.g. to solve a wide array of social and political problems) and the needs of the economy (e.g. to respond to the workplace needs of employers).

The notion of higher education as a right has gained more traction in recent years because of the growing importance of higher education and lifelong learning in people's lives (Burke, 2012). This growing importance of and demand for higher education has been precipitated by a host of new higher education laws and policies, by new means of access (e.g. internet, online platforms), by new means of funding (e.g. guaranteed student loans, student grants, endowments), and by new business models (e.g. proprietary universities). The rapid expansion of the last few decades is a continuation of the expansion of higher education that has been occurring for the last 150 years.

For instance, higher education in the USA has been marked by three major tidal waves that have fundamentally reshaped and expanded access to higher education in the USA: the Morrill Act of 1862 that created a national system of land-grant universities (the first wave of democratization of higher education in the USA), the GI Bill of 1944 and the development of the community and technical college system throughout the twentieth century (the second wave of democratization of higher education in the USA), and the anytime, anywhere distance education brought about by the internet-based digital revolution in the last several decades (the third wave of democratization of higher education more internationally). We now seem to be entering a fourth wave brought about by expanding the democratic social contract to all segments of society and by the expanding adoption of a democratic ethos that believes that higher education should work for all people and the opportunity for lifelong learning is a basic human right that should be equally available to all people.

Lifelong Learning as a Human Right

Higher education has grown enormously important to society because higher education is often the gateway to a professional career or other job opportunities. In fact, most professions (e.g. medicine, law, education, science, engineering, accounting) can only be accessed through several years of advanced higher education. Thus, the academic profession (e.g. professors, instructors, lecturers) can be thought of as the key profession or gateway profession because it educates (i.e. serves as the gateway) to professional careers. Without higher education, entry into these and other professions is not possible. This configuration puts tremendous power and fiduciary responsibility in the hands of the gateway profession. This arrangement has huge implications therefore for how higher education institutions are structured and how educators are educated and developed (e.g. screening and graduation requirements, on-going professional development). Thus, not only has higher education as a social institution grown much more important but the teaching profession has also grown in importance.

This phenomenon not only applies to university programs but also to community college programs, vocational and technical college programs, and other types of higher education institutions. For instance, more employers are now requiring certification or post-secondary education and training, as well as apprenticeships and internships, for entry into many vocational fields (e.g. cosmetology, culinary, horticulture) because there is a growing recognition of the value of post-secondary formal learning (whether it be academic learning or higher skills training). This increased demand for and access to higher education has, in turn, created a growing diversity of institutional types, course and degree offerings, and new forms of higher education that serve a wide variety of learner interests and needs.

Governments and societies have tended to look favorably towards the potential benefits that higher education of all types can produce, seeing research universities as engines for economic growth, innovation, and social development and seeing non-research colleges (e.g. community colleges, vocational colleges) as a gateway for anyone in society to access higher education regardless of socio-economic status or demographic background, helping society move closer to the democratic ideals of equal educational access opportunities for all and equitable educational outcomes for all. However, different institutions may emphasize different aims, depending on their institutional mission. So, vocational colleges focus on occupational training, preparation, and development for the trades and community colleges may also serve this purpose but also serve as foundation programs to prepare students for transfer to four-year colleges or universities. Thus, different institutional missions help to serve the needs of different segments of society and, in turn, create a highly diversified and differentiated higher education ecosystem. One institutional type is therefore not inherently better than another institutional type—they simply serve different roles.

Knapper and Cropley (2000) contend that lifelong learning and lifelong education are, in part, a response to, 1) certain facets of traditional educational practices as perceived by some (e.g. elitist, exclusionist), 2) a growing displeasure with the view that all required learning and qualifications can be attained through a fixed period time in formal education, and 3) a growing anxiety about the decreasing shelf-life of knowledge and academic qualifications. Traditionally, formal education was seen as an activity that preceded the start of living in the "real world" but current views hold that learning occurs not just formally but also informally and non-formally and throughout one's life. These reactions have influenced the growing democratization of education globally. To better adapt to the fast changing demands of contemporary life, Knapper and Cropley (2000) argue that individuals must learn how to learn and continue to learn throughout every stage of life. Therefore, it follows that lifelong and lifewide learning should be treated as a right of every person. The freedom of every person to learn freely and continually throughout the entire course of her/his life and the opportunity and freedom to pursue whatever education that may be required to fulfill those needs should not be infringed. In a highly differentiated system of post-secondary education, there are presumably many ways to meet the needs of lifelong learning. Thus, lifelong learning is the cornerstone to continual self-development, self-determination, and creative self-expression.

Noddings (2013), Burke (2012), and Dall'Alba (2012), among others, argue that since education is fundamentally a social institution, it therefore has social responsibilities that are wider and of greater importance than solely intellectual development. Consistent with Nodding's idea that the traditional focus of privileging the intellect has come at the expense of developing our capacity to care, Dall'Alba argues that,

> Conceiving education in terms of care for others and things turns attention differently towards education. Not only does it feature what students are expected to know and be able to do (an epistemological dimension), but also who students are becoming or, in other words, how they are learning to be (an ontological dimension).
>
> *2012, p. 115*

This approach addresses both the epistemological and the ontological aspects of education and learning and does not privilege one over the other. Of course, the attitude and act of caring is a value so conceiving education in terms of caring implies that we must adopt a value system that values the contributions of all people and all institutions. Within this context, Barnett (2012) argues for a higher education system that supports and fosters ". . . values connected with democracy, pluralism, dialogue, the public realm, and openness" (p. 203).

Kovbasyuk and Blessinger (2012) elaborate on the need for adopting an educational value system based on human rights and social justice claims and not on unquestioned power and privilege claims, which often manifests itself in terms of domination and oppression. Burke (2012) argues that policies of widening participation should be focused on addressing historical exclusions and long-standing inequalities that have tended to reinforce power and privilege claims. Although we have, by and large, moved from an elite to a mass higher education system in many countries, the resulting stratification (e.g. by gender, race, socio-economic class) of higher education may actually serve to widen relative inequalities, especially when selection processes are embedded in practices rooted solely on merit claims or driven purely by economic concerns rather than the redress of underrepresentation and exclusion. Lamont and Moraes da Silva (2009) argue that, "Tensions between meritocracy and democracy remain at the centre of academic selection process in the United States" (p. 4). These and other tensions (e.g. education as a private investment/good vs. education as a public investment/good, occupational development vs. academic development) will continue to play out as higher education systems become increasingly more diverse and diversified.

Rothblatt (2012) comments on these growing dichotomies in higher education by observing that,

> The university of today is part of a national system of 'higher education' composed of many types of institutions subject to contradictory tendencies. One promotes greater cooperation between colleges and universities, a fuller sharing of resources and commitments in the interests of the greater good. The other encourages competition, rankings, hyperbola and the exploitations of multifarious markets.
>
> *p. 25*

There is tremendous value in difference and inclusivity, not only from political, economic, and social perspectives but also from a humanistic and human rights perspective. Given the scale and complexity of the political, economic, and social problems that all societies are faced with, such as environmental issues, widespread poverty, terrorism, and social injustices of all types, it is a moral imperative that the way forward to a better society for all is to engage everyone in a dialogue concerning the issues impacting us all.

Challenges to Universal Higher Education

The growing importance of higher education in society has also created major challenges as well. In some countries like the USA, the rapidly skyrocketing cost of higher education has contributed to skyrocketing student debt. Total student debt in the USA is now in excess of one trillion USD and the average total cost (e.g. tuition, books, room and board, living expenses) for a bachelor's degree in the USA is roughly 100,000 USD (U.S. Department of Education, 2013). Although new platforms for delivering higher education programs or courses to all are now available for free or at low fees, it is still uncertain whether or not their initial promise will have a significant and sustainable impact on the higher education landscape (Pappano, 2012). With the growing inability of some students in some countries to pay the total cost of their education, many policy makers and educational leaders are now publically expressing their doubts about the fairness and the sustainability of a higher education system that leaves students with huge mountains of debt.

Within this context we see an expansion of traditional institutional missions where institutional boundaries have become increasing fluid as they adapt to these changing environments. Ironically, however, we are also seeing the stratification of higher education in some countries, while at the same time seeing the emergence of a more diverse higher education system. Stratification is based on the notion that students should be accepted based mainly or solely on academic ability criteria. When this notion is enacted at a statewide or national level, or by a significant number of institutions as a matter of policy, it typically results in a tiered system of higher education institutions. Diversification, on the other hand, is based on the notion that students should be accepted based on social and other criteria together with academic ability (Ayalon & Yogev, 2006; Shavit, Arum, & Gamoran, 2007). Today, many institutions are using a wide variety of criteria to determine who gets accepted into a particular institution or program in an attempt to balance the benefits of both meritocracy and democracy and to help mitigate the impact of stratification.

Theories and Models of Higher Education Change

A variety of change models and theories have been developed to explain change in higher education. Burke (2012) and Kezar (2014) provide good overviews of the many theories and models developed to explain change from different disciplinary lenses and from different perspectives. As this research reveals, higher education institutions are shaped mainly by social, political, and economic forces, together with globalization and technological forces. Higher education institutions are also increasingly challenged to harmonize these aims. This implies that higher education institutions must develop new practices that integrate different goals such as educating for high academic standards, educating for employability skills, educating for global citizenry, and educating for humanistic development.

In addition, the public financing model of the so-called welfare state was viewed by some as a reasonably good way to allocate higher education resources and benefits. However, since there is always a limited amount of tax dollars available to fund higher education relative to all the other services demanded by citizens, public financing alone would not only be a difficult way to fund higher education for all, but public financing is not always the most effective way to encourage innovation and creativity in higher education. On the other end of the spectrum are the private financing models of the free market, which tend to be better at encouraging innovation but these private market models are typically not concerned with issues such as fairness and the public interest.

The inherent differences and tradeoffs involved in these different models are driving some nations to develop mixed models. The USA, for instance, is a mixed-model system where institutions of all types are now encouraged to diversify financially by developing multiple income streams and take on increasing responsibility for generating revenues through more forms of privatization that are not at the mercy of state/federal budgets. Given the increasing overall demand for affordable, high-quality higher education by different segments of society, it is plausible to suggest it will take a patchwork of diverse ways (e.g. competency-based degrees, open learning) and a diverse set of new higher education providers using a diversity of educational and learning models to meet the diverse needs of societies. So, the key question then becomes, how do educators and policy makers help shape this emerging higher education ecosystem so that it works for all in a fair way. In other words, this analysis boils down to a fundamental question: how do we help shape a higher education ecosystem that works for all so that our democracy also works for all?

Thus, institutions of all types should focus on the development of both epistemic knowledge and epistemic skills in students (i.e. what they are expected to both know and do—competence), together with the ontological development of students (i.e. what they are passionate about and want to become—self-determination). Educators have also created a variety of new learning activities to meet these epistemic and ontological goals such as service learning, study abroad, internships, peer teaching, research projects, and many other learning activities that combine classroom and field experiences to develop proficiencies such as intercultural competencies, global citizenship, leadership, and community engagement. It seems plausible, therefore, to postulate that the basic democratic ideals of self-determination and inclusion serve as the underlying fundamental mechanisms driving a growing demand for higher education of all types. This basic idea is summarized and illustrated in Figure 14.2.

As we move further into the twenty-first century, higher education institutions must learn how to cultivate a passion for learning in students and cultivate a wide

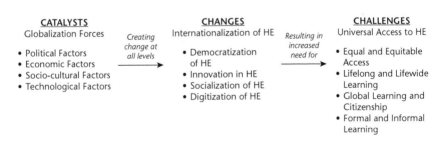

FIGURE 14.2   Change Model of Global Higher Education

variety of different but related types of knowledge (e.g. factual, conceptual, procedural, meta-cognitive) and different forms of learning deemed important in the modern era. This change model (Figure 14.2) supports the democratic principles of 1) institutional diversification, 2) pedagogical pluralism, 3) learning diversity, and 4) freedom of inquiry. This change model also supports a *democratic theory of higher education* that maintains that the ultimate purpose of higher education is to promote personal agency through the development of freedom and responsibility.

This notion of personal agency implies the adoption of equal and equitable access to learning opportunities throughout life to all those who desire to avail themselves of such opportunities. In a democratic society, access to learning opportunities requires both equality and equity, but the principles of equality and equity frame the notion of fairness differently. Equitable access is based on the fairness principle that every person deserves *just* opportunities (i.e. *just* in terms of what is the morally right action to take) to access and participation in higher education. Equal access is based on the fairness principle that every person deserves *uniform* opportunities (i.e. *uniform* in terms of the same treatment without discrimination based on sex, gender, sexual orientation, race, ethnicity, nationality, religion, age, disability, ideology, etc.) to access and participate in higher education. Thus, equality frames the concept of *fairness as uniform access opportunities* whereas equity frames the concept of *fairness as just access opportunities* (Schement, 2001).

When a society, and the higher education systems that function within that society, is highly stratified between the advantaged and disadvantaged (e.g. along sex, race, and socio-economic class lines) as a result of longstanding practices of exclusion and privilege and thus does not have a level and fair playing field, then the notion of fairness as justice (equity) requires that appropriate remedies be enacted in order to redress such practices. Smith (2014, p. 10) notes that, "The existence of stratification requires that power, equity, and discrimination be addressed in any discussion of diversity and identity."

Furthermore, equality and equity should not be viewed as competing principles or as mutually exclusive concepts. The principles of equality and equity can and should work together since they share that same aim. Each society and each educational institution must figure out, through the democratic process unique to each society and within the historical and cultural context of their society, how best to allocate available resources to achieve the twin goals of equality and equity. Achieving these goals also requires a change in mindset. It means intentionally moving from a mindset of exclusivity, which is oriented around power and privilege claims, and towards a mindset of inclusivity, which is oriented around fairness and self-determination claims.

Adopting an Inclusive Mindset

One could argue that this goal is even more important for higher education given its long history of exclusion and privilege (Burke, 2012). For instance, although women have made great gains in accessing higher education over the last few decades in some countries, and they now represent the majority of students in many programs at many universities, historically, women and minorities were barred at many institutions from even accessing higher education. Today, the idea of barring any group from higher education for any reason is unconscionable and would violate basic human rights, but we should not forget that such practices were rationalized by some as acceptable just a few generations ago.

A pecking order mindset is not conducive to a democratic ethos. Every institutional type, whether a vocational college or a research university, has a role to play in a modern democratic society. A diversity of institutional types allows society to meet a variety of different political, economic, social, and humanistic needs, and they all provide different segments of society with a wide array of opportunities for self-determination and social mobility. Higher education should be a means to help narrow persistent and destructive patterns of discrimination, prejudice, and oppression, in all its forms. The highest quality teaching and learning must and should be a top priority for every type of higher education institution, from vocational colleges to community colleges to liberal arts colleges to research universities. No one institutional type has a monopoly on excellence, on quality teaching and learning, or on contributions made to society, and no one discipline or profession has a monopoly on knowledge building or truth seeking. Knowledge building and truth seeking are natural parts of human growth and curiosity that everyone should be engaged in at every life stage. So, we need to remind ourselves that outstanding students and tomorrow's leaders now come from every type of educational institution.

Institutional envy and prestige jealousy should not be motivational factors that drives institutional priorities. Rather, an institution's own unique mission, vision, and core values should drive policies and priorities. Focusing on meeting the needs of one's own constituencies is a more prudent way to lead an organization. The old mindset of privilege and exclusivity needs to be replaced with a mindset of participation and inclusivity. This shift in mindset, however, will require forward-thinking leadership and the adoption of a shared value system that rests on fairness and human rights claims and not on unquestioned power and privilege claims. Systems based on domination and oppression must be replaced with systems based on freedom and responsibility.

Changing the mindset starts with defining the mission and core values of the institution and a shared educational ethos that defines the core identity of higher education. Without a clear set of aims and shared values, one lacks clarity and conviction about what direction to lead. The old paradigm subscribed to the notion that only the privileged in society should be allowed to access higher education. However, a system based on excluding rather than including is not consistent with basic democratic principles. Those who benefit least from the status quo are typically the most inclined to want to change the status quo, for obvious reasons. Thus, the changes occurring in higher education are, to a large extent, reflective of the changes occurring in the broader democratic society in which it operates.

The growing expansion of higher education systems around the world reflects the notion that we are slowly shifting from an attitude of exclusivity and towards an attitude of inclusivity, which should provide us with hope that perhaps we are, by and large, moving in the right direction. Exclusive systems tend to reinforce closed systems, whereas inclusivity is characterized by the needs of society, by democratic ideals, by human and moral rights, by diversity in all its forms, and by removing unnecessary and arbitrary barriers to entry. An inclusive mindset and inclusive systems tend to foster the development of open systems.

Conclusion

The nature and the type of questions we need to be asking, in order to help frame this dialogue, will partly depend on the value system one believes in (e.g. does she/he believe in an exclusive system or an inclusive system), and the assumptions she/he holds, and her/his vision of where higher education should be going. In light of that context, the following core questions may help better focus the core issues at hand:

- How can we make higher education available to all who want to participate in it?
- How can higher education provide meaningful opportunities for lifelong learning?
- How can higher education help prepare students to live and work in a globalized world?

Of course, democracy takes many forms depending on the type of democracy that emerges over time from within a particular socio-political context. But regardless of the particular structures and practices that make up the different types and variations of democracy, all democracies must be able to respond to public demands as well as the wider global forces. The analysis in this chapter provided support for a *democratic theory of higher education* that maintains that the ultimate purpose of higher education is to promote personal agency through the development of freedom and responsibility. This notion implies that opportunities to learn should be equal and equitable. The most fundamental opportunities are access to and participation in learning opportunities. This outcome is more likely to be achieved by moving from a mindset of exclusivity, which tends to be oriented around power and privilege claims, and towards a mindset of inclusivity, which is oriented around fairness and self-determination claims.

In addition, although differentiation implies that institutions tend naturally to set themselves apart, institutions should differentiate themselves based on their unique mission and the needs of their constituencies. In this type of diverse ecosystem, higher education serves multiple purposes (e.g. political/democratic, social/community, economic/professional, humanistic/personal) for multiple constituencies. As we move further into the twenty-first century, higher education institutions must learn how to cultivate a passion for learning in students and foster a wide variety of different but related types of knowledge and learning deemed important in the modern era. In short, democratizing higher education involves a higher education system based on a vision of higher education that is inclusive, participatory, representative, transformative, meaningful, and rooted in practices of shared ethical values and an ethos of political, social, and economic justice.

References

Altbach, P.G., Gumport, P.J., & Berdahl, R.O. (2011). *American higher education in the twenty-first century: Social, political, and economic challenges*. Baltimore, MD: The Johns Hopkins University Press.

Ayalon, H. & Yogev, A. (2006). Stratification and diversity in the expanded system of higher education in Israel. *Higher Education Policy*, 19: 187–203.

Barnett, R. (2012). *The future university: Ideas and possibilities*. London: Routledge.

Blessinger, P. & Kovbasyuk, O. (2012). Higher education needs to build global learning communities. *The Guardian*. Retrieved from www.theguardian.com/higher-education-network/blog/2012/may/23/global-virtual-learning-environments.

Bloom, B. & Krathwohl, D. (1956). *Taxonomy of educational objectives: The classification of educational goals, by a committee of college and university examiners. Handbook 1: Cognitive domain*. New York, Longmans.

Burke, P.J. (2012). *The right to higher education: Beyond widening participation*. Abingdon: Routledge.

Carr, N. (2012). The crisis in higher education. *MIT Technology Review*. See www.technologyreview.com/featuredstory/429376/the-crisis-in-higher-education/.

Chomsky, N. & Otero, C.P. (2003). *Chomsky on democracy & education*. New York: Routledge Falmer.

Dall'Alba, G. (2012). Re-imaging the university: Developing a capacity to care. In Ronald Barnett (Ed.) *The future university: Ideas and possibilities*, (pp. 112–122). New York: Routledge.

Deardorff, D.K., de Wit, H., Heyl, J.D., & Adams, T. (2012). *The SAGE handbook of international higher education*. Los Angeles, CA: SAGE Publications.

DeMillo, R.A. (2011). *Abelard to Apple: The fate of American college and universities*. Cambridge, MA: The MIT Press.

Dewey, J. (1916). *Democracy and education: An introduction to the philosophy of education*. New York: Macmillan

Dewey, J. (1933). *How we think*. New York: Heath Books.

Dewey, J. (1938). *Experience and education*. New York: Touchstone.

Freire, P. (1970). *Pedagogy of the oppressed*. New York: Continuum.

Gagne, R.M. (1965). *The conditions of learning*. New York: Holt, Rinehart & Winston.

Gredler, M. (2009). *Learning and instruction: Theory into practice*. New Jersey: Pearson.

Kezar, A. (2014). *How colleges change: Understanding, leading, and enacting change*. New York: Routledge.

Knapper, C.K. & Cropley, A.J. (2000). *Lifelong learning in higher education*. Sterling, VA: Stylus Publishing.

Kovbasyuk, O. & Blessinger, P. (2013). *Meaning-centered education: International perspectives and explorations in higher education*. New York: Routledge.

Lamont, M. & Moraes da Silva, G. (2009). Complementarity rather than contradictory diversity and excellence in peer review admissions in American higher education. *21st Century Society*, 4(1): 1–15.

Mezirow, J. (1991). *Transformative dimensions of adult learning*. San Francisco, CA: Jossey-Bass.

Noddings, N. (2013). *Education and democracy in the 21st Century*. New York: Teachers College Press.

OECD (2008). Higher Education to 2030 (Vol. 1): Demography.

OECD (2009). Higher Education to 2030 (Vol. 2): Globalization.

Palfreyman, D. & Tapper, T. (2009). *Structuring mass higher education: The role of elite institutions*. New York: Routledge.

Pappano, L. (2012). The year of the MOOC. *New York Times*. Retrieved from www.nytimes.com/2012/11/04/education/edlife/massive-open-online-courses-are-multiplying-at-a-rapid-pace.html?_r=1&.

Polyzoi, E., Fullan, M., & Anchan, J.P. (2003). *Change forces in post-communist Eastern Europe: Education in transition*. New York: RoutledgeFalmer.

Rothblatt, S. (2012). The future isn't waiting. In Ronald Barnett (Ed.) *The future university: Ideas and possibilities*, (pp. 15–25). New York: Routledge.

Schement, J.R. (2001). Imaging fairness: Equality and equity of access in search of democracy. In N. Kranich (Ed.) *Libraries & democracy: The cornerstones of liberty*, (pp. 15–27). Chicago, IL: American Library Association.

Schofer, E. & Meyer, J.W. (2005). The worldwide expansion of higher education in the twentieth century. *American Sociological Review*, 70(6): 898–920.

Shavit, Y., Arum, R., & Gamoran, A. (2007). *Stratification in higher education: A comparative study*. Stanford: Stanford University Press.

Smith, D.G. (2014). Identity and diversity. In D. Smith (Ed.) *Diversity and inclusion in higher education: Emerging perspectives on institutional transformation*, (p. 10). New York: Routledge.

U.S. Department of Education, National Center for Education Statistics. (2013). *Digest of education statistics*, 2012 (NCES 2014–015). Retrieved from http://nces.ed.gov/fastfacts/display.asp?id=76.

Vygotsky, L.S. (1989). *Pedagogical psychology*. Moscow: Nauka.

Wankel, C. & Blessinger, P. (2012). *Increasing student engagement and retention using online learning activities: Wikis, blogs and webquests*. Bingley, UK: Emerald Group Publishing.

Yu, P. & Delaney, J.A. (2014). The spread of higher education around the globe: A cross-country analysis of gross tertiary education enrollment, 1999–2005. *Educational Policy*, 28(5). DOI: 10.1177/0895904814531648.

Zepke, N. & Leach, L. (2002). Contextualised meaning making: One way of rethinking experiential learning and self-directed learning? *Studies in Continuing Education*, 24(2): 205–217.

15

DEMOCRATIZING HIGHER EDUCATION

Concluding Thoughts

Patrick Blessinger

Introduction

The origins for the idea of this book can be traced back to the formation of the International Higher Education Teaching and Learning Association (HETL) in 2010 as well as the editors' interest in this topic as both a scholarly research activity (theory) and a matter of governance (policy) and professional educational praxis (practice). Of course, the general topic of democratizing education is a topic that has a long history and much has been written about this general topic area. The idea of democratizing *higher* education has more recent origins and the need for a collection of international perspectives and case studies on this topic was the impetus for this edited volume.

Given the growing importance of lifelong and lifewide learning in all societies today, the democratization of higher education is an important (and needed) development in the modern era. In many ways we are, by and large, moving in that direction. Trow (1974, 2005) described a higher education system where at least 50 percent of the relevant age group in the population participates (to one degree or another) as a universal system and where 16 percent to 49 percent of the relevant age group in the population participates as a mass system. The empirical data presented in this volume shows that many societies now have mass systems (and some of those moving closer to universal status) and several societies have already reached universal status. In fact, most developing and industrialized countries have been steadily moving towards mass and universal systems of higher education over the last 50 years as a response to political, social, economic, and technological changes occurring both locally and globally.

To explain the why and the how of change in higher education systems, one must also engage in a political and social analysis that integrates an understanding of the cultural, organizational, and professional values, beliefs, and practices embedded within those higher education systems because different higher education systems operate within a milieu of different historical and developmental contexts, as described by the case studies in this volume and as discussed by contemporary educational change scholars (e.g. Altbach, Gumport, & Berdahl, 2011; Burke, 2012; Chomsky & Otero, 2003; Deardorff, de Wit, Heyl, & Adams, 2012; DeMillo, 2011; Kezar, 2014; Knapper & Crople, 2000; Kovbasyuk & Blessinger, 2013; Noddings, 2013; Palfreyman & Tapper, 2009; Polyzoi, Fullan & Anchan, 2003; Trow & Burrage, 2010).

From one perspective, these contexts illustrate the on-going power struggles and competing self-interests playing out at many levels (e.g. international, national, institutional, personal). From another perspective, these contexts illustrate the on-going evolution of human history and the on-going development of socio-political systems. The case studies in this volume help to illustrate that higher education systems in different countries use varying different models that, to a large degree, are reflective of the broad cultural values and socio-political ideals of the country or region. For instance, one could describe the USA higher education system as a mixed model reflective of its pluralistic socio-cultural structure, its increasingly inclusive political structure, and its innovative economic structure. It is no surprise therefore that the US higher education system has increasingly moved towards a mixed public/private funding mechanism and a diverse array of institutional types to address a wide variety of different needs and interests. One of the goals with this book project was to try, within the constraints imposed on any book project, to provide a very broad yet concise overview and analysis of the global changes occurring within higher education internationally and then to provide a plausible argument that the phenomenon of democratizing higher education can yield many benefits in spite of the challenges it brings with it.

Emerging Themes

At one level, every higher education system around the world must be understood on its own terms with respect to each country's own political, social, economic, and historical milieu. Yet, at another level, national systems of higher education must not be viewed solely in isolation but must also be understood as a global system of higher education with macro characteristics. The emerging themes identified in this book represent those common macro characteristics. Notwithstanding the risk involved in making generalizations around higher education trends, gaining a better understanding of these trends allows us to make better *theoretical* sense of the changing landscape, which in turn allows us to make more informed *policy* decisions, which in turn puts us in a better position to improve and adapt professional *practices* relative to the changes occurring. This condition is important because it is at the nexus of theory, policy, and practice that meaningful and positive outcomes can be realized. The following trends are being driven by the increased demand for higher education services:

- Increasing student mobility and internationalization of higher education.
- Increasing use of mixed economic and funding models in higher education.
- Increasing diversity and differentiation of higher education.
- Increasing involvement by institutions, faculty, and students in activities outside the traditional boundaries of the classroom and educational institution.
- Increasing expansion of institutional missions and greater fluidity of boundaries between educational, government, business, and non-profit organizations.
- Increasing importance of professional development of higher education professionals as their roles and professional identities expand and evolve relative to changes in higher education.

The increasing pressures to remove access barriers and to eliminate the monopolization of higher education by historically privileged groups as well as the increasing pressures to mitigate practices that restrict free flow of higher education across borders have created a growing global space for higher education of all types. The increasing pressure for higher education institutions to respond to a wider array of social and economic needs has created a larger number of institutional types, which provides a more effective means to meet the diverse labor demands of an increasingly differentiated economy. Thus, traditional boundaries for all types of educational institutions have become increasingly fluid as they try to adapt to the changing conditions of an increasingly interdependent and interconnected global community.

Conclusion

This book discusses the on-going changes in higher education and proposes a *democratic theory of higher education* that maintains that the ultimate purpose of higher education is to promote personal agency through the development of freedom and responsibility. This implies that opportunities to learn should be equal and equitable. The most fundamental opportunities are access to and participation in lifelong learning. This can only be achieved by moving from a mindset of exclusivity, which is oriented around power and privilege claims, towards a mindset of inclusivity, which is oriented around fairness and self-determination claims.

System-wide and institutional changes need to be proactively implemented to better suit the learning needs of an increasingly diverse society, with a recognition that there is no one-size-fits-all approach or model that will work for all institutions in all contexts. To a large extent, higher education has become the primary means by which disadvantaged and underrepresented groups are able to exercise social mobility, economic self-sufficiency, and personal empowerment. Higher education can serve as a powerful catalyst and vehicle to help achieve these goals. Democratizing higher education ultimately involves a higher education system based on a shared vision of higher education that is inclusive, participatory, representative, transformative, meaningful, and rooted in practices of shared ethical values and an ethos of political, social, and economic justice.

References

Altbach, P.G., Gumport, P.J., & Berdahl, R.O. (2011). *American higher education in the twenty-first century: Social, political, and economic challenges.* Baltimore, MD: The Johns Hopkins University Press.

Burke, P.J. (2012). *The right to higher education: Beyond widening participation.* Abingdon: Routledge.

Chomsky, N. & Otero, C.P. (2003). *Chomsky on democracy & education.* New York: RoutledgeFalmer.

Deardorff, D.K., de Wit, H., Heyl, J.D., & Adams, T. (2012). *The SAGE handbook of international higher education.* Los Angeles, CA: SAGE Publications.

DeMillo, R.A. (2011). *Abelard to Apple: The fate of American college and universities.* Cambridge, MA: The MIT Press.

Kezar, A. (2014). *How colleges change: Understanding, leading, and enacting change.* New York: Routledge.

Knapper, C. & Cropley, A.J. (2000). *Lifelong learning in higher education.* Sterling, VA: Stylus Publishing.

Kovbasyuk, O. & Blessinger, P. (2013). *Meaning-centered education: International perspectives and explorations in higher education.* New York: Routledge.

Noddings, N. (2013). *Education and democracy in the 21st Century.* New York: Teachers College Press.

Palfreyman, D. & Tapper, T. (2009). *Structuring mass higher education: The role of elite institutions.* New York: Routledge.

Polyzoi, E., Fullan, M., & Anchan, J.P. (2003). *Change forces in post-communist Eastern Europe: Education in transition.* New York: RoutledgeFalmer.

Trow, M. (1974). Problems in the transition from elite to mass higher education. *Policies for Higher Education.* Paris: OECD.

Trow, M. (2005). *Reflections on the transition from elite to mass to universal access: Forms and phases of higher education in modern societies since WWII.* Berkley, CA: Institute of Governmental Studies, University of California.

Trow, M. & Burrage, M. (2010). *Twentieth-century higher education: Elite to mass to universal.* Baltimore, MD: The Johns Hopkins University Press.

ABOUT THE CONTRIBUTORS

The Editors

Patrick Blessinger is the founder, executive director, publisher, and chief scientist at the International Higher Education Teaching and Learning Association and he is co-director of the Institute for Meaning-Centered Education. Patrick has managed academic programs in the USA and Europe. Patrick is an internationally recognized scholar on the topics of leadership, innovation, learning, student engagement, faculty development, and international education.

John P. Anchan is Professor of Education and Associate Dean of the Faculty of Education, University of Winnipeg, Canada. He has taught at the University of Alberta, Canada, and also worked as the Executive Director of a non-profit organization in Edmonton. John has 34 years of teaching experience and he has taught in India, United Arab Emirates, and Canada. John is the current President of the International Higher Education Teaching and Learning Association.

The Contributing Authors

Arshad Ahmad is the Associate Vice President at McMaster University in Hamilton, Ontario, Canada. He is also the Director of McMaster's Institute for Innovation and Excellence in Teaching and Learning. Arshad is the President of The Society for Teaching and Learning in Higher Education and Vice-President of The International Consortium for Educational Development.

Lars Birch Andreasen is Associate Professor of Interaction in Virtual Learning Environments at the Department of Learning and Philosophy, Aalborg University,

Copenhagen, Denmark. He is a member of the Research Lab: ICT and Designs for Learning; and education director of the Danish Master's program in ICT and Learning.

Jeanette C. Botha is the Director in the Office of the Principal at the University of South Africa. She is responsible for research, national and international higher education trend analyses, writing, and providing an advisory and liaison service. She is also involved in institutional strategy and planning, and institutional governance initiatives.

María Luisa Pérez Cañado is Associate Professor at the Department of English Philology of the University of Jáen, Spain, where she is also Vicedean of the Faculty of Humanities and Education. Her research interests are in applied linguistics, bilingual education, and the EHEA. María Luisa has been granted the Ben Massey Award for the quality of her scholarly contributions regarding issues that make a difference in higher education.

Arputharaj Devaraj has served as the Resource Person in English & Adult Education, Sub Editor in A. I. R, and Social Welfare Organizer (all at Pondicherry: 1979–82); Overseas Education Officer, Govt. Teachers' Training College, Damaturu, Nigeria (1982–86); Associate Professor in English at Garyounis University, Libya (2009–2011); then Director, Training & Placement (2012–14) and now Professor, Graduate Program, English, Loyola College, Chennai, India (1987 to date).

Catarina Faria is an educational psychologist at the psychological counseling service at University of Madeira, Portugal. She is very interested in the research topic of special needs in higher education, in particular of non-speaker students. She won a national award with her Master's thesis entitled, "The perception of higher education teachers about special need students".

Lori Goff is the Manager of Program Enhancement at McMaster University, Ontario, Canada, and the outgoing co-chair for the Council of Ontario Educational Developers. At McMaster, she supports departments in the development of new programs and in preparing for academic program reviews.

Olga Kovbasyuk has taught for 30 years in various educational institutions and has managed many international academic programs and intercultural projects. Olga is the founder of the Linguistic School and Global Learning Center in Russia, and co-founder of the Institute for Meaning-Centered Education. Olga is a Fulbright Scholar and DAAD Fellow.

Helena Lim is Assistant Director, Partnerships, Wales and Northern Ireland at the Higher Education Academy (HEA), UK. Prior to joining the HEA, Helena was

Senior Research Fellow at Southampton Solent University where she had responsibility for research and information pertaining to the student experience.

Craig Mahoney is Principal and Vice-Chancellor of the University of the West of Scotland. He was formerly Chief Executive of the Higher Education Academy (HEA), UK. Previous roles have included Deputy Vice-Chancellor at Northumbria University and founding Dean of the School of Sport, Performing Arts and Leisure at Wolverhampton University.

Mandla S. Makhanya is the Principal and Vice-Chancellor of the University of South Africa (Unisa). He was previously Unisa's Pro Vice-Chancellor. Recently, the University of Athabasca in Canada conferred an honorary doctorate on Mandla in recognition of his outstanding leadership at Unisa and his contribution as a distinguished scholar in distance education.

Natalia Moscvina is Professor at the Far East University of Humanities, Khabarovsk, Russia. She is Head of the Innovative Development and Maintenance Grants' department. She holds a Doctor of Sciences in Education, Pedagogy, and Psychology. Natalia has been teaching in the Far Eastern State University of Humanities for around 20 years.

Jørgen Lerche Nielsen is Associate Professor of ICT and Learning at Roskilde University, Denmark. His research areas include designing networked problem-based learning processes, on learning processes in communities of practice, blended learning, collaborative learning, students' activities in group work, and the roles of the professor as supervisor, and change processes within higher education.

Enakshi Sengupta is Assistant Professor in Business Administration at the American University of Central Asia, Kyrgyz Republic. She teaches at both Master's and undergraduate levels. Her research interests include integration of racially diverse student communities, curricular changes to incorporate integration in a class room situation, strategizing and creating scorecards to measure levels of integration, in group and out group integration in higher education, and aftermath of racial hatred and genocide.

Luísa Soares is Professor of Psychology at University of Madeira, Center of Arts and Humanities, Portugal. She is also a Researcher at Larsys (Lab Robotic Systems in Science and Engineering) in Madeira Interactive Technologies Institute and Researcher at University of Porto, Psychology Research Center, Portugal. Luisa is also the Director of Post graduation studies on human aspects of technology at University of Madeira.

Lorraine Stefani is Professor of Higher Education Strategic Engagement in the Faculty of Education at the University of Auckland, New Zealand. She was recently seconded to Princess Nora University (PNU) in Riyadh, Saudi Arabia, where she was working in the Deanship of Development and Skills Enhancement to support the development of a Centre for Excellence in Learning and Teaching.

Hei-hang Hayes Tang is College Lecturer in Asian Studies at The University of Hong Kong's School of Professional and Continuing Education. A sociologist, Hayes is interested in the fields of academic profession, global migration, and China studies. Hayes received the Outstanding Teacher Award by his School in 2012.

Linda S. Watts is Professor of American Studies in the School of Interdisciplinary Arts and Sciences at the University of Washington, Bothell, USA. Her interests include American social history; USA literature and culture; visual art practice, production, and exhibition; women's studies; multicultural education and curriculum revision; critical and alternative pedagogy; institutional change and educational leadership.

INDEX